ROLAND H. BAINTON

AN EXAMINATION OF HIS REFORMATION HISTORIOGRAPHY

ROLAND H. BAINTON

AN EXAMINATION OF HIS
REFORMATION HISTORIOGRAPHY

Steven H. Simpler

Texts and Studies in Religion
Volume 24

The Edwin Mellen Press
Lewiston/Queenston

Library of Congress Cataloging in Publication Data

Simpler, Steven H.
   Roland H. Bainton : an examination of his Reformation
historiography.

   (Texts and studies in religion ; v. 24)
   Bibliography: p.
   1. Bainton, Roland Herbert, 1894-   --Contributions in
Reformation historiography. 2. Reformation--Historiography--History
--20th century. 3. Renaissance--Historiography--History--20th century.
I. Title. II. Series: Texts and studies in religion ; 24.
BR307.B26S56 1985   270'.092'4   85-21567
ISBN 0-88946-812-5 (alk. paper)

This is volume 24 in the continuing series
Texts and Studies in Religion
Volume 24 ISBN 0-88946-812-5
TSR Series ISBN 0-88946-976-8

The Edwin Mellen Press   The Edwin Mellen Press
Box 450   Box 67
Lewiston, New York   Queenston, Ontario
USA 14092   CANADA L0S 1L0

Printed in the United States of America

For
Joel, John and Anne

TABLE OF CONTENTS

PREFACE

This book is a study of methodology. As a
teacher of the history of Christianity, I have often
been drawn to the issue of historical methodologies.
I recognize that methodology serves as a tool to
facilitate the historian's task of interpreting historical data. It is with this interest in methodology
that I have approached the study of Roland H. Bainton's
historical writings.

This book is not a paean to a great person.
Academicians recognize Bainton as a gifted teacher,
prodigious scholar, and winsome personality. A
volume could be written simply on his colorful life.
This present study however is a critical analysis of
his historical writings with special attention given
to his method of handling the historical materials of
the Renaissance and Reformation.

Bainton would note that any individual effort
is shaped by a composite of factors. Indeed my own
effort in studying his works has been strengthened by
a number of significant persons. Professors William
Pitts and Glenn Hilburn of Baylor University provided
the initial guidance and critical assessment of the
writing of this manuscript. Likewise Professor Ronnie
Littlejohn of Belmont College contributed much needed
encouragement in the process of completing this book.
Ms. Kim Peterson with remarkable patience typed and
proofread the manuscript and demonstrated a scrupulous
attention to detail which I think would have been
admired by Roland Bainton himself.

CHAPTER 1

INTRODUCTION

Roland Herbert Bainton (1894-1984) ranks as one
of the leading Reformation scholars of the twentieth
century. For forty-two years he taught Church history
at Yale Divinity School where he held the Titus Street
Professorship of Church history from 1936 until his
retirement in 1962. During his years as an active
Church historian Bainton spoke frequently in the capacity of distinguished lecturer. From the research for
these lectures came many of his monographs and journal
articles. His prolific writings cover a broad spectrum
of the history of the Church and made him a popular
author among both scholars and laymen. His chief
literary contributions lie in the field of Reformation
research. Paul A. Crow contends that the interest in
the continental Reformation and related movements which
has been on the increase for the past four decades is
"in no small measure related to the research, teaching,
and dramatic presentations of this great scholar."[1]

Bainton's fecundity as a writer explains his
significance in the field of Church history. In a
career spanning fifty-six years he produced thirty-two
books as well as a great number of journal articles.[2]

-----

[1]Paul A. Crow, "Recent Reformation Studies,"
Encounter 26 (Winter 1965): 80.

[2]A complete list of the Bainton corpus is found
in the bibliography which illustrates graphically his
literary productivity.

Likewise his scholarly expertise evidenced itself in
his work as a translator and as an editor of primary
source materials.

Throughout this voluminous literary production
one can detect an underlying sensitivity to the "non-
specialist" in Church history, thus giving Bainton's
works a distinct readability. This is not without ex-
ception however, since several of his works demand an
esoteric knowledge on the part of the reader.[1] Bainton
states, "Unfortunately scholars frequently lack the
capacity to make their work understandable and appealing to the non-specialist, and the popularizers do not
have a mastery of the facts."[2] Consequently his writings communicate serious scholarship marked by clarity
of style and an attentiveness to precision. Commenting
on Bainton's ability as a writer of Church history,
W.E. Garrison contends, "No professional student of
history can put down a book by Bainton without sincere
admiration for the thoroughness of the research underlying it and the clarity with which the findings are
expressed."[3] Such an opinion on a widespread basis

---

[1]For an example see Roland H. Bainton, "Basilidian Chronology and New Testament Interpretation,"
Journal of Biblical Literature 42 (1923): 81-134. This
essay was based on Bainton's doctoral dissertation at
Yale and entails a meticulously written, copiously
footnoted examination of the gospel chronology of
Basilides, the second century Alexandrian theologian.

[2]"Bainton, Roland H(erbert)," Current Biography
Yearbook (New York: H.W. Wilson Company, 1962), pp. 21-22.

[3]W.E. Garrison, review of Hunted Heretic: The
Life and Death of Michael Servetus, 1511-1553, by Roland
H. Bainton, in Christian Century, 18 November 1953,
p. 1327.

has created a large reading audience for Bainton. His
books have sold in the millions of copies and are
available in eleven different languages. Appreciation
for his writings perhaps will continue due to his "rare
combination of diligent research and graceful literary
expression."[1]

Bainton's scholarship is discernible not only
in the quality and number of his writings on Church history but also in his involvement in numerous professional societies. He held memberships in the American
Historical Society, the Medieval Academy, and the
American Society for Reformation Research. Moreover,
he was an honorary member of the American Academy of
Arts and Sciences, the International Academy of Arts
and Letters, and the Heidelberger Akademie der Wissens-
chaften.[2] He served as president of the American
Society of Church History in 1940, as a council member
for the Renaissance Society of America, and as a
trustee for the Foundation for Reformation Research.[3]
In the latter years of his life Bainton served as
president of the Erasmus of Rotterdam Society.

Such activities as these magnified the stature
of Bainton within the academic community and distinguished him as a renowned and respected American
scholar. The honor given to him by his colleagues
confirms the academic and professional achievements
of Bainton. Reformation Studies: Essays in Honor of
Roland H. Bainton, a festschrift published in his honor

---

[1]Bernhard Erling, review of Studies on the Reformation, by Roland H. Bainton, in The Lutheran
Quarterly 16 (Fall 1964): 84.

[2]"Bainton," Current Biography Yearbook, p. 22.

[3]Archiv für Reformationsgeschichte 64 (1973): 5.

in 1962, contains sixteen studies by prominent Reformation scholars who were at one time students of Bainton at Yale. Likewise the 1973 issue of Archiv für
Reformationsgeschichte was dedicated to Bainton, calling him "the Nestor of Reformation studies in America"
and recognizing him as "the man who has contributed
such wisdom and spirit to the field of Reformation
history."[1]

In light of the significance of Bainton to the
field of Reformation research, this book will examine
thoroughly his Reformation history writings. The
study of Bainton's Reformation writings is a worthy
topic due to his pervasive influence in twentieth century Reformation historiography. Although "influence"
is a difficult category to measure, Harold J. Grimm
states that "[f]ew American scholars have exerted as
great an influence on the development of Church history
as Roland H. Bainton."[2]

Biographical Sketch of Roland H. Bainton
Born on 30 March 1894 in Ilkeston, England, Roland Herbert Bainton was the only son of Congregationalist minister James Herbert Bainton.[3] As a young
minister James Bainton grew restless in his first
pastorate in England, and in 1898 he moved from Ikleston

---

[1] Ibid.

[2] Harold J. Grimm, review of Early and Medieval
Christianity, by Roland H. Bainton, in The American
Historical Review 68 (October 1962): 180.

[3] The major source of information in this biographical section comes from Bainton's biography of
his father, Pilgrim Parson: The Life of James Herbert
Bainton (New York: Thomas Nelson and Sons, 1958).

to a struggling Congregationalist church in Vancouver,
British Columbia. In Pilgrim Parson: The Life of James
Herbert Bainton, Bainton tells of his own early experiences of observing his father's struggles with this
Canadian pastorate. His father's opposition to England's involvement in the Boer War caused such controversey among his church members that the small
church suffered a schism. The expedient move for the
Baintons was to leave Canada, a decision which they
made in 1902.

In this year Bainton moved with his family to
Colfax, Washington, where his father assumed what was
to be an eighteen-year pastorate.[1] Colfax was a pros-
perous town, the center of a fertile farming district.
Moreover the town provided a peaceful, agricultural
environment in which Bainton matured. Although the
pastorate of a thriving Congregationalist church in
Colfax brought some financial security to James Bainton, he continued to raise his family in an austere
atmosphere. Recalling the parsimony of his father in
these years, Bainton writes, "If in the evening, Father
was helping Hilda [Bainton's only sister] with her
lessons and I withdrew to another room, I would be
recalled lest I use another light."[2]

This overt attentiveness to the family's
economic well-being did not detract from the instill-
ing of a strong religious piety in the Bainton children.
Bainton's youth reflected the pious recognition of the
Providence of God, and from his earliest years his life

---

[1]Roland H. Bainton, Pilgrim Parson: The Life of
James Herbert Bainton (New York: Thomas Nelson and Sons,
1958), p. 71.

[2]Ibid., p. 99.

embodied the religious training of his parents. For
example, in discussing an incident of his youth Bainton writes, "I weeded the lawn, often sulkily, until I
recalled that Grandma in heaven had her eye on me."[1]

The religious quality of Bainton's youth made
a lasting impact on his life. He recalled in Pilgrim
Parson the deep impression his father's sermons had
on his youthful thinking and of the reverence for life
that the simplicity of his childhood brought. Of his
father's churches, Bainton writes:

> But if Father had called his church at Ilkeston
> a barn by metaphor, this time [in Colfax] there
> was no need for any figure of speech. It was a
> plain rectangle capped with a belfry, and that
> bell was hardly as melodious as the cowbells in
> Switzerland. For four years as church janitor
> I rang it; and if now I ever chance to hear one
> like it, the clang is more truly a call to prayer
> than any carillon.[2]

This strong piety developed in his childhood and youth
later influenced not only Bainton's attitude as a
professor at Yale but also his historical perspective
as a writer of Church history. This point finds
graphic illustration in the conclusion of Yesterday,
Today, and What Next? as Bainton discusses the role
of the historian of Christianity. He states, "Of this
I am convinced that one can never understand the religion of the past who has not been brushed by the winged
seraph, nor said with St. Augustine, 'My soul is restless
until it find its rest in Thee.'"[3]

---

[1]Ibid., p. 56.

[2]Ibid., p. 83.

[3]Roland H. Bainton, Yesterday, Today, and What
Next? (Minneapolis: Augsburg Publishing House, 1978),
p. 128.

Much of the religiosity of Bainton's youth resulted from the intimate relationship which he had with
his father, a relationship described by Bainton as "a
singular delight."[1] Although a pastor, his father
exerted no pressure upon Bainton except that as a
boy he was expected at Sunday dinner to repeat the
sermon. "I relished the exercise, and soon began to
discuss and correct."[2] Thus developed between father
and son a relationship of mutual respect characterized
by lengthy theological discussions. When Bainton went
to college and seminary, these discussions continued
orally during vacations and during the term by correspondence.[3]

The influence of his father extended far beyond the pious environment of youth; James Bainton in-
stilled in his son a love for education. Bainton recalled of his father that "his library was my library
and one of the privileges of being sick was to have my
bed placed beside the shelves."[4] Such a respect for
learning consequently led to the development in Bainton of a keen, inquiring mind. He writes, "Father
was responsible . . . in that he had bequeathed to
his children, not beliefs, but an inquiring mind."[5]
This intellectual inquisitiveness coupled with an interest in religious studies led him to Yale Divinity
School after his graduation in 1914 from Whitman College in Walla Walla, Washington.

---

[1]Bainton, Pilgrim Parson, p. 105.

[2]Ibid., p. 105.

[3]Bainton wrote his father a letter a day while
in college, a letter a week and a postcard a day while
in seminary.

[4]Bainton, Pilgrim Parson, p. 105.

[5]Ibid., p. 104.

At Yale he completed his Bachelor of Divinity
degree in 1917 and his Doctor of Philosophy degree in
1921. He took his undergraduate degree in classics
and his Ph.D. in Semitics and New Testament Greek.
Yale exposed Bainton to fields of studies and methodologies of study which he had never experienced.
This period proved to be one of theological realign-
ment as well as one of academic achievement. For example, he writes of his first encounter with Biblical
criticism, saying that the shock of critical studies
first came at Yale where he "encountered Biblical
criticism with the breastplate of erudition and the
helmet of piety . . . . I pursued the new interest with
fervor, and espoused the method and the teaching of my
professors with zeal."[1]

His studies at Yale were interrupted by the
American entry into World War I. It was at this point
that Bainton confronted a crisis of conviction. His
father was mildly pacifistic, and likewise Bainton
struggled earnestly with pacifistic thinking. He
oscillated for a time between qualified endorsement
of the war and total nonresistance. His decision was
for pacifism, and he served with the American Friends
Service Committee under the Red Cross in France. This
commitment to pacifism developed throughout his career
and strongly influenced several of his Church history
writings.

After World War I he received an appointment
from Yale in 1920 as instructor of Church history and
New Testament. In 1923 he became assistant professor
of Church history. The appointment as associate professor came in 1932 and the honor of Titus Street

---

[1]Ibid., p. 106.

Professor of Church history came in 1936. As Titus
Street Professor at Yale, he followed the professor-
ships of George P. Fisher and Williston Walker, both
of whom were instrumental in establishing Church history studies at Yale. Other honors came to Bainton
during his distinguished career. He received honorary
Doctor of Divinity degrees from Meadville Theological
Seminary (1949), Oberlin College (1953), and from his
alma mater, Whitman College (1954). He also received
the honorary Doctor of Letters from Gettysburg College
(1958), and in 1948 received the prestigious Doctor of
Theology from the University of Marburg, the oldest
Protestant Seminary in Germany.

Ordained as a Congregationalist minister in
1927, Bainton also held an affiliate membership in the
Society of Friends. Many of his writings depict a
social involvement through the church in such causes
as religious toleration, pacifism, and ecumenics. His
commitment to social activism brought him some notoriety
during the 1950s. During this time he was investigated
by the House Committee on Un-American activities because of his outspoken pacifism and because of his
conscientious objector status during World War I. "I've
always been a rebel," he said in a 1983 interview. "I
was a radical conservative before I was four."[1] Bainton's distinguished career was terminated when he died
on 13 February 1984 in New Haven, Connecticutt.

Bainton's significance as an influential Church
historian must include a consideration of his role as
a teacher. Georgia Harkness, one of his former students, points out that Bainton's gift for teaching

---

[1]Interview reported in the Associated Press
Obituary of Bainton, 13 February 1984.

provided strong motivation for a student's own scholarly pursuits. Recalling a class taken under Bainton
Harkness writes,

> I do not remember all that I heard in that small,
> darkish, booklined room. Yet I recall vividly
> the scholarly information, marvelously detailed
> and enlivened with humor and the touch of down-
> to-earthiness, that poured forth from the teach-
> er's lips. It came faster than I could write
> it down, but enough "stuck" for Calvin, Farel,
> Beza, Castellio, Servetus, and other figures of
> those dramatic days to come alive for me. From
> then on, the long hours and many weeks spent
> with the dusty folios of the *Calvini Opera* in
> the semidarkness of the dungeon-like stacks of
> the old library had a purpose. I cannot say
> there was no drugery about it, but the drugery
> was redeemed by an interest that made it worth-
> ful.[1]

The rich quality of Bainton's teaching was enlivened
by his unusual skill in phrasing. He possessed the
ability to call forth the right word or image in a
lecture so that even the most technical material would
be presented with clarity and animation.[2] This same
characteristic of skillful presentation evidences itself throughout his historical writings.

Non-Reformation Writings

    Bainton was a specialist in Reformation stu-
dies, yet the corpus of his writings depicts broad
ranging interests in subjects as diverse as "Piety
and Art" and "Basilidian Chronology and New Testament
Interpretation." Frederich A. Norwood states, "Bainton, for all his specialized competence in Lutheran

---

[1] Georgia Harkness, "Roland H. Bainton: A biographical Appreciation," in Reformation Studies: Essays
in Honor of Roland H. Bainton, ed. Franklin H. Littell
(Richmond, Va.: John Knox Press, 1963), p. 14.

[2] Ibid., p. 15.

Reformation, was never one to be limited to special-
ties."[1] An assessment of the total work of Bainton
provides a useful perspective in analyzing his fifteenth and sixteenth century studies.

General History

Bainton produced a survey of the history of
Christianity, the text of which appeared in a variety
of formats. Originally published as The Horizon History of Christianity (1964) this text provided a
general Church history illustrated by hundreds of
photographs, reproductions, and woodcuts. The text
appeared in 1966 in a revised and expanded form as
the two-volume illustrated Christendom: A Short History
of Christianity and Its Impact on Western Civilization.
A compressed form of this same text was the two volume
Penguin History of the Church (1967).

Beginning with the background of Christianity
in the Old Testament, this study surveys the ebb and
flow of Christianity up to contemporary efforts of
ecumenism. Reviewing this general history of the
Church, Virgil Foster concludes that it "is comprehensive in scope and brings together the pieces of knowledge and experience that form the complex drama of
the Christian church."[2] Brevity is a strength and
weakness of this writing. Bainton's popular writing
style makes this history readable and understandable
to the non-specialist.

---

[1]Frederich A. Norwood, review of Early and
Medieval Christianity, by Roland H. Bainton, in Church
History 31 (December 1962): 458.

[2]Virgil E. Foster, review of The Horizon History of Christianity, by Roland H. Bainton, in International Journal of Religious Education 41 (April 1965): 4.

Also in the category of general history are
Bainton's three volumes in the Anvil series. Early
Christianity (1960), The Medieval Church (1962), and
The Age of Reformation (1956) are very brief and popularly written. Following a common format, each has
a brief overview of the particular period followed
by selected source readings corresponding to the era
under consideration. In each book Bainton blends
political history, the history of doctrine, and the
history of the Church while also giving attention to
developments in art and missionary activity.

One of Bainton's most widely read books is
The Church of Our Fathers (1941) written specifically
for children and young adults. This work is distinctive as a scholarly treatment of Church history written for youth. Ross Snyder criticizes the work because of its lack of a dominant theme which he contends "leaves a feeling of endless and perhaps point-
less see-sawing through history."[1] Nonetheless, Church
of Our Fathers ranks as a standard work in the curric-
ulum of youth educational materials.

The Collected Papers in Church History comprise another three-volume work. Early and Medieval
Christianity (1962), contains several germinal articles,
among which are "Ideas of History in Patristic Christianity" and "Religious Liberty and the Parable of the
Tares."[2] Studies on the Reformation (1963) appeared
as series two of the collected papers. In this selection the most notable works are his collection of essays

---

[1]Ross Snyder, review of The Church of Our
Fathers, by Roland H. Bainton, in Church History 10
(December 1941): 378.

[2]Grimm, review of Early and Medieval, p. 180.

on Luther and on the left wing of the Reformation.
The final volume in this series, Christian Unity and
Religion in New England (1964) contains the widest
diversity of topics in the collection. Articles on
ethical issues, American Church history, and ecumenism
demonstrate Bainton's breadth of interests as a Church
historian. In an evaluation of these three volumes,
Harold Grimm states that this collection provides not
only a well-rounded discussion of various aspects of
the periods but also a "fascinating index of the development of an influential scholar."[1]

A standard research tool published by Bainton
is his Bibliography of the Continental Reformation:
Materials Available in English (1935, 1972). As the
title indicates, the bibliography proposes to meet
the needs of the student limited to research in the
English language. Wilhelm Pauck surveyed the original edition (1935) and pronounced it "astonishingly
complete."[2] The second edition, expanded and revised
by Erich W. Gritsch, shows the increasing amount of
Reformation research published in English since 1935.
The method of compilation remained the same, with
several new topics added, e.g., "Roman Catholic Reform," "Erasmus," and "Reformation in Baltic Lands."
The Bibliography represents an English language supple-
ment to the well-known European Reformation biblio-
graphies.

---

[1] Ibid.

[2] Wilhelm Pauck, review of Bibliography of
the Continental Reformation: Materials Available in
English, by Roland H. Bainton, in Church History 4
(September 1935): 243.

Social History

War and Peace

Perhaps the most distinct social issue on which
Bainton consistently wrote was that of war and peace.
As a committed pacifist his writings reveal more than
merely an academic interest in the subject. The articles which he published on war and peace generally
approached the issue from an historical perspective.[1]
His work in this area culminated in the publication of
Christian Attitudes Toward War and Peace: An Historical
Survey and Critical Re-evaluation (1960). His interpretation of the historic Christian attitude discerns
three major positions: pacifism, the just war, and the
crusade. In his final two chapters Bainton concludes
that the development of technology and the dehumaniza-
tion of war are unique historical situations. He contends that the lone alternative for a Christian on the
issue of war is pacifism. Such a stance for Bainton
assumes no "blind martyr complex, but . . . the stand
to which one must come in sheer prudence and in thorough
obedience to Christ, come what may."[2]

Sex, Love, and Marriage

A theme which appears in several of Bainton's
general works is the Christian concepts of sex and

---

[1]See Roland H. Bainton, "War and the Christian
Ethic," in The Church and Social Responsibility, ed.
J. Richard Spann (New York: Abingdon-Cokesbury Press,
1953), pp. 201-19; Bainton, "The Churches Shift on
War," Religion in Life 12 (Summer 1943): 323-35; and
Bainton, "The Early Church and War," Harvard Theolo-
gical Review 39 (July 1946): 189-212.

[2]Edward Krusen Ziegler, review of Christian
Attitudes Toward War and Peace, by Roland H. Bainton,
in Brethren Life and Though 6 (Autumn 1961): 60.

marriage. What Christianity Says About Sex, Love, and
Marriage (1957) developes ideas which Bainton had introduced in earlier journal articles.[1] Approaching
marriage from an historical perspective, he posits
three different views which held precedence among
Christians in the past, i.e., marriage as sacramental,
as romantic, and as companionship. He contends that
the Renaissance and Reformation introduced romance to
marriage by rejecting the sacramental idea of marriage. This theme emerges also in the three-volume
Women of the Reformation (1971, 1973, 1977).

Toleration

        A major emphasis in Bainton's writings is the
theme of religious toleration, and much of his research deals with the development of toleration in
the Reformation era. A germinal article on toleration, "The Struggle for Religious Liberty," constituted Bainton's presidential address to the American
Society of Church History.[2] In this article Bainton
traces the ebb and flow of toleration from the Reformation to the twentieth century. He asserts that the
only ground for toleration is expediency, which may
take ecclesiastical, political, or religious forms.
A discussion of the perennial problems of toleration
concludes the article which represents a concise
statement of Bainton's own position on the issue of
religious liberty.

---

        [1]See Roland H. Bainton, "Marriage and Love in
Christian History," Religion in Life 17 (Summer 1948):
391-403.

        [2]Roland H. Bainton, "The Struggle for Religious
Liberty," Church History 10 (June 1941): 95-124.

Art

          Although Bainton's writings clearly show an in-
terest in Christian art, he published very little specifically on this subject. Behold the Christ (1974) is
Bainton's most thorough statement on Christian art.[1]
He addresses himself not to art historians but to those
persons "religiously experienced" in order to show how
art "can lead to a deeper faith understanding of key
events in Christ's life."[2] Explaining why some events
in the life of Christ have been more popular than
others in Christian iconography, Bainton informs the
reader that some cultures have merely accommodated
Christ to their own romantic imaginations. Elizabeth
Douglas criticizes Bainton for the cursory way in which
he considered the works represented in the book, yet
contends that his work represents an effort to overcome the Evangelical Christians' bias against the validity of religious expression in the visual arts.[3]

Ecumenics and Ecclesiology

          Several of Bainton's writings reflect his in-
terest in the area of ecumenics and ecclesiology. Although he produced no book on the subject, three seminal

---

          [1]See Roland H. Bainton, "Piety and Art," in
Traditio, Krisis, Renovatio, aus Theologischer Sicht,
ed. Bernard Jaspert and Rudolf Mohr (Marburg: Elwert,
1976), pp. 609-12.

          [2]Virginia McNally, review of Behold the Christ,
by Roland H. Bainton, in America 131 (2 November 1974):
263.

          [3]Elizabeth A. Douglas, review of Behold the
Christ, by Roland H. Bainton, in Christian Scholar's
Review 7 (November 1977): 262.

articles depict his main lines of interest. "Friends
in Relation to the Churches" displays Bainton's personal affinity with the Quaker spirit. In this article
he discusses Quaker origins, distinctives, and relationship with the broad spectrum of Christianity.[1] A
similar interest emerges in "Congregationalism: The
Middle Way" in which Bainton approaches Congregationalism as an ecumenical concept.[2] He expresses hope
that Congregationalism may be the unifying medium of
the Church. The historical development of the ecumenical ideal receives appropriate attention in "The Unity
of Mankind in the Classical Christian Tradition."[3]
This article provides a history of the idea of "unity"
through Chistian history and offers this tradition as
a hope for present day efforts at unity. Taken together, these three articles demonstrate the thinking
of Bainton on practical and current social issues, and
represent his scholarly approach to twentieth century
ecclesiastical problems.

American Church History Writings

Bainton wrote little on American Church history
proper, yet he did produce a number of articles and

---

[1]Roland H. Bainton, "Friends in Relation to
the Churches," in Christian Unity and Religion in New
England (Boston: Beacon Press, 1964), pp. 57-70.

[2]Roland H. Bainton, "Congregationalism: The
Middle Way," Christendom 5 (Summer, 1940): 345-54.

[3]Roland H. Bainton, "The Unity of Mankind in
the Classical-Christian Tradition," in The Albert
Schweitzer Jubilee Book, ed. A.A. Roback (Cambridge,
Mass.: Sci-Art Publishers, 1945; reprint ed., Westport,
Conn.: Greenwood Press, 1970), pp. 277-96.

monographs on selected topics relating to his personal
interests. His most complete work in the area of
American Christianity is Yale and the Ministry: A History of Education for the Christian Ministry at Yale
from the Founding in 1701 (1957). This book ranks as
an important contribution to American Church historiography since Bainton writes the history of Yale within
the context of religion in New England. Consequently
Yale and the Ministry provides not only a history of
Yale but also a general history of New England Christianity. Bainton makes the point frequently that the
three ingredients of Yale's religious tradition are
the Reformation, the Enlightenment, and pietism.
Albert Outler contends that Bainton treats the theological issues of Yale's history too superficially, but
Outler agrees that Bainton captures the spirit of New
England religion masterfully.[1]

Other selective topics of interest for Bainton
include "The Appeal to Reason and the American Constitution," a careful discussion of the enlightenment
view of reason and the implications of this view for
colonial America.[2] Likewise he produced The Office of
the Minister's Wife in New England as the Dudleian
Lecture at Harvard University for the academic year

---

[1]Albert C. Outler, reivew of Yale and the
Ministry: A History of Education for the Christian
Ministry at Yale from the Founding in 1701, by Roland
H. Bainton, in Christian Century 74 (6 November 1957):
1319.

[2]Roland H. Bainton, "The Appeal to Reason and
the American Constitution," in The Constitution Reconsidered, ed. Conyers Read, rev. ed. (New York:
Harper and Row, 1968), pp. 121-30.

1954-1955.[1] This tediously researched work examines
the various tasks of the New England minister's wife
in the eighteenth and nineteenth centuries. Two
articles on Alexander Campbell survey the distinctiveness of Campbell as a social thinker and religious
leader of the nineteenth century.[2] In this same genre
"The Making of a Pluralistic Society--A Protestant
View" discusses the contribution of pluralism to inter-
faith dialogue and to the search for truth.[3] Hence
the diversity of Bainton's American Church history
writings reveal his interests in selected issues of
American church life.

Miscellaneous

Bainton published much which has no generic
relationship with the main corpus of his work. A clear
example of this is his publication Yesterday, Today,
and What Next? Reflections in History and Hope (1978).
He states, "Having devoted my life to the study of
history, I am prompted in my latter days to ask whether

---

[1]Roland H. Bainton, The Office of the Minister's
Wife in New England (Cambridge: Harvard University,
1955).

[2]Roland H. Bainton, "Alexander Campbell and
Church Unity," in The Sage of Bethany: A Pioneer in
Broadcloth ed. Perry E. Gresham (St. Louis: Bethany
Press, 1960), pp. 81-94; and Bainton, "Alexander Camp-
bell and the Social Order," in Sage of Bethany, pp.
117-29.

[3]Roland H. Bainton, "The Making of a Pluralis-
tic Society--A Protestant View," in Religion and the
State University, ed. Erich A. Walter (Ann Arbor, Mich.:
University of Michigan Press, 1958), pp. 42-57.

one can make sense of it all."[1] The thrust of the book
entails Bainton's reflections on the meaning and purpose of history. Yesterday is popularly written and
appears to be more devotional than any of Bainton's
other works.

Bainton produced a short biography of his father
entitled Pilgrim Parson: The Life of James Herbert
Bainton (1958). The value of this work lies in its
detailed description of Bainton's own childhood and
family environment, yet he wrote the book because he
contends that his father's life has an appeal beyond
his family's circle.

---

[1]Bainton, Yesterday, p. 9.

CHAPTER II

RENAISSANCE WRITINGS

The writings of Bainton on the Renaissance
comprise a limited portion of his entire corpus. The
first section of this chapter examines his methodology
of interpreting the Renaissance era. The second treats
his interpretation of Erasmus. Both sections center
on the salient elements which characterize his historiographical treatment of the subject matter.

A distinct motif stands out in Bainton's Renaissance writings, namely, his emphasis on the particular
weltanschauung of the Renaissance era. Bainton maintains that the emergence of the Hellenic spirit marks
the Renaissance attitude toward life and characterizes
the endeavors of this period.

Renaissance Interpretation

The assessment of Bainton's interpretation of
the Renaissance begins with an inquiry into his methodological approach to the period. Wallace K. Ferguson
contends that such an inquiry leads to the heart of
the methodological problem of Renaissance historiography. Ferguson states:

> [H]ow are we to establish an adequate basis for
> the interpretation of the age? In any work of
> synthesis, the first task is to decide what are
> the characteristic traits of the civilization of
> an age and to arrange them in hierarchical order
> of importance.[1]

---

[1]Wallace K. Ferguson, The Renaissance in Historical Thought: Five Centuries of Interpretation (New
York: Houghton Mifflin Company, 1948), p. 394.

From this perspective the task remains to discern the
"characteristic traits" which Bainton finds in the
Renaissance through which he develops a synthesis of
the period.

Twentieth century scholars differ as to the
distinctive elements of the Renaissance era. Two examples will suffice. For Ferguson the characteristic
traits of the age are threefold: 1) the vitality of
culture, 2) the spirit of individualism, and 3) the
revival of antiquity.[1] Hanna Holborn Gray understands
the "pursuit of eloquence" as the characteristic trait
of the Renaissance. Gray proposes that the pursuit of
eloquence "reveals the identifying characteristic of
Renaissance humanism. The bond which united humanists
. . . . was a conception of eloquence and its uses."[2]

Bainton interprets the characteristic trait of
the Renaissance era to be the resurgence of Hellenic
thought in Western culture. He discerns a tension in
Western thought between the Greek and Hebrew world
views. In the medieval era the Hebrew *weltanschauung*
dominated whereas in the Renaissance era the Hellenic
weltanschauung gained acceptance. Bainton tends to
equate humanism with the Renaissance and detects in
the humanists' approach to life a distinctive Hellenic
motif. He states:

---

[1]Wallace K. Ferguson, "The Interpretation of
the Renaissance: Suggestions for a Synthesis," Journal
of the History of Ideas 12 (October 1951): 492-93.

[2]Hanna H. Gray, "Renaissance Humanism: The
Pursuit of Eloquence," Journal of the History of Ideas
24 (October-December 1963): 498.

> Humanism meant on the one hand the cultivation of
> *litterae humaniores*, a concern for form and poetry,
> nurtured by a revival of the literature of classi-
> cal antiquity, including that of the fathers of
> the Church. At the same time humanism was a way
> of life, *Humanitas*, the ideal of the cultivated
> man, rich in interests, urbane and magnanimous in
> spirit.[1]

Bainton summarizes this interpretation by stating that
Renaissance humanism emerged "mainly by an exaggeration of the Hellenic elements in the Christian synthesis, with an ever-present tendency to destroy the distinctiveness of the Christian revelation."[2] This concept of a resurging Hellenism appears to be the alembic
through which Bainton interprets the historical materials of the period.

In delineating this Hellenic element in Renaissance thought, Bainton often contrasts it with the
traditional Hebraic element in Western thought. For
example, Judaic theology interpreted God as the trans-
cendent Lord who delivered His commandments to Moses
from Mount Sinai. However, Bainton argues, if this God
is removed from the Mount and made to dwell in every
stream and meadow, then the necessity for a unique
and divine revelation is less acutely felt. Immanentism

---

[1]Roland H. Bainton, "Religion of the Renaissance,"
in Early and Medieval Christianity, The Collected Papers
in Church History, series 1 (Boston: Beacon Press, 1962),
pp. 204-5; this article originally appeared as "Renaissance
and Religion," in Die Religion in Geschichte und Gegenwart,
6 vols. (Tubingen: J. C. B. Mohr, 1961), 5: 159-63.

[2]Roland H. Bainton, "Man, God, and the Church in
the Age of the Renaissance," in Early and Medieval Christianity, The Collected Papers in Church History, series
1 (Boston: Beacon Press, 1962), p. 203.

was the kernel of the Hellenic concept of God; Renaissance thinkers muted the idea of transcendence.[1] The
Renaissance thus "may be viewed as another of the
perennial upsurges of the Hellenic against the Hebraic
spirit."[2]

Bainton discusses several manifestations of
this Hellenic spirit in his writings. A "this worldly"
spirit pervaded the culture thereby diminishing the
power of "other worldliness" in medieval thinking. The
life to come was not necessarily "excluded from the
purview, but obviously the emphasis was comparatively
this-worldly."[3] Bainton speculates that the popular-
ity of proverbs in the Renaissance era indicates that
men were "turning from the art of dying to the art of
living."[4] The *elan* of the age appeared to be a re-
structuring of life toward the pursuit of fulfillment
in an earthly life rather than the hope of blessing in
the life to come.

This spirit took root in the Renaissance understanding of truth. Hebraic thought held truth to be
a divine deposit while Hellenic thought perceived
truth to be a quest. Medieval thinkers assumed God's

----

[1]Ibid., p. 194; see also Roland H. Bainton,
"The Problem of Authority in the Age of the Reformation," in Luther, Erasmus and the Reformation: A Catholic-Protestant Reappraisal, ed. John C. Olin, James D.
Smart, and Robert E. McNally (New York: Fordham University Press, 1969), pp. 14-16.

[2]Bainton, "Man, God, and the Church," p. 194.

[3]Roland H. Bainton, The Reformation of the Sixteenth Century (Boston: Beacon Press, 1952), p. 16.

[4]Roland H. Bainton, Erasmus of Christendom (New
York: Charles Scribner's Sons, 1969), p. 45.

will as given through revelation recorded in sacred
Scripture, but for Renaissance thinkers "truth was
deemed rather to be discovered alike from Scripture
and from nature by observation and the exercise of
critical faculties."[1] The quest for truth in this
light demanded that the researcher be unhindered and
the findings of the search be made accessible.

The spirit which engendered this quest for
the unadulterated truth also changed views of the
nature of man. Man was given dignity, potential, and
creativity. These ideals contributed to a burgeoning
creativity among artists and intellectuals and to a
renewed religious vitality. Bainton is reluctant to
claim a "new" view of man arising in the Renaissance.
The Renaissance did not so much introduce a new view
of man as display a distaste for overly refined distinctions. Consequently the "Renaissance man" (the
homo universale) was the man who excelled in a diversity of endeavors: sports, art, literature, theology,
or war. Ferguson writes that he finds it quite difficult to think of the "spirit" of the Renaissance and
impossible to envisage "the Renaissance man."[2] Yet
Bainton interprets quite freely the idealized man of
the Renaissance by saying, "The ideal was the rounding
out of man's personality, the development of all his

[1]Roland H. Bainton, "Freedom, Truth, and Unity:
Reflections on the Renaissance," in Early and Medieval
Christianity, The Collected Papers in Church History,
series 1 (Boston: Beacon Press, 1962), p. 237. Bainton
contends that from this attitude emerged what was later
called *Freis Foreschung* or "academic freedom."

[2]Ferguson, "Interpretation of the Renaissance,"
p. 493.

capacities, the subjection of all disciplines to his
rational control."[1] The Renaissance man laid stress
in art on perspective, in statecraft on diplomacy, in
business on bookkeeping, and in war on strategy.[2]

A similar motif which Bainton understands to
emanate from the Hellenic *weltanschauung* of the Renaissance was the concept of the organic solidarity of
mankind. Bainton finds two divergent tendencies in
the fourteenth and fifteenth centuries. On one hand
there was a nascent nationalism which threatened to
disrupt the medieval unity of Christendom. On the
other hand there was a revival of the classical understanding of the unity of mankind. The unity of mankind was an outgrowth of Hellenic thought. Bainton
describes it as follows:

> Petrarch resuscitated *humanitas* as an ideal of
> the man both cultivated and humane. Erasmus
> was the spokesman of the state as a moral or-
> ganism within and without. The new nations
> should be components of a single Christendom
> bound with adamantine chains in that harmony
> which holds not only men but also the stars
> and the beasts in the unity of the spirit and
> the bond of peace.[3]

This perspective allowed the humanists to soften the
sharp edge of Christian distinctions and to propagate

---

[1] Bainton, "Man, God, and the Church," p. 188.

[2] Bainton, The Reformation, p. 16. As a proto-
type of the Renaissance view of man Bainton speaks of
Lorenzo de Medici who was equally adept in plotting an
assassination, making merry at a carnival, or in judg-
ing a horse, a sermon, a poem, or a picture.

[3] Roland H. Bainton, "The Unity of Mankind in
the Classical-Christian Tradition," in The Albert
Schweitzer Jubilee Book, ed. A.A. Roback (Cambridge,
Mass.: Sci-Art Publishers, 1945; reprint ed., Westport, Conn.: Greenwood Press, 1970), p. 18.

the belief in the organic unity of mankind. J. W.
O'Malley sees this perspective personified in Erasmus.
Comparing Luther and Erasmus O'Malley states that
Erasmus had a tendency to "blur distinctions," to
emphasize connections, and to bind together whereas
Luther had a tendency to sharpen distinctions and to
emphasize differences.[1] For Bainton the appeal of
the organic unity of man during the Renaissance indeed is consistent with the Hellenic spirit of the
age.

　　　　The motif of the resurgence of the Hellenic
spirit stands out clearly in Bainton's periodization
of the Renaissance. It is the emergence of this idea
which in his view marks the Renaissance as a distinct
era.

　　　　In discussing the period of 1300-1600 Ferguson
proposes that these centuries are neither medieval nor
modern but rather constitute an age of their own.[2]
One might reasonably ask of Bainton: In what way does
he interpret the Renaissance as constituting a distinct age? In the writings of Bainton there emerges
a guarded tendency to periodize the Renaissance on
the basis of intellectual currents appearing in late
medieval years. Some historians, he contends, mark
the Renaissance simply as a chronological period,
e.g., from 1300 to include Dante to 1600 to include
Shakespeare. Likewise a Church historian may chronicle

---

[1]J. W. O'Malley, "Erasmus and Luther: Continuity and Discontinuity as Key to Their Conflict," Sixteenth Century Journal 5 (October 1974): 47.

[2]Wallace K. Ferguson, "The Church in a Changing
World: a Contribution to the Interpretation of the
Renaissance," The American Historical Review 59 (Octo-
ber 1953): 2.

the period from the pontificate of Nicholas V in 1450
to the sack of Rome in 1527.

Bainton's periodization derives from his assessment of an ideological metamorphosis of the late
Middle Ages. For him the "period" of the Renaissance
developed through a changing attitude toward life,

> which valued earth more than heaven; the immor-
> tality of fame more than the immortality of the
> soul; self-cultivation more than self-effacement;
> the delights of the flesh more than asceticism;
> the striving for success more than justice; in-
> dividual and intellectual freedom more than
> authority; and classical Humanism more than
> Christianity.[1]

Bainton maintains this attitude toward life is more
evident in the fourteenth and fifteenth centuries than
in the preceding centuries and that it constitutes a
definitive epoch in European history.

By defining the period of the Renaissance in
terms of new attitudes, Bainton recognizes that the
historian must ask "to what degree such attitudes and
behavior are more clearly discernible in this period
than in the preceding [period] . . . ."[2] Bainton
points out that contemporary scholarship conceives the
Renaissance "to have been at variance with the Middle
Ages and nowhere more so than in the area of religion."[3]
He rejects this contention as a misapprehension of
medieval life and religion. Bainton argues that historians have too often caricatured the Middle Ages as
an era of strong religious devotion and have portrayed
the Renaissance as a time of irreligion.

------

[1]Roland H. Bainton, Christendom: A Short History of Christianity and Its Impact on Western Civilization, 2 vols. (New York: Harper and Row, 1966), 1:242.

[2]Ibid., pp. 242-43.

[3]Bainton, "Man, God, and the Church," p. 185.

Bainton finds in the Middle Ages both religious piety and religious degeneration, the "St. Bernard types" as well as the "Abelard types." His tendency is to interpret the institutional stagnation of the Church quite caustically while interpreting the piety of the common man quite positively. For example, Bainton contrasts the ecclesiastical grandeur of the pontificate of Innocent III with the decadence of the Renaissance papacy. He writes that Renaissance popes "were scarely to be distinguished from the secular princes with their splendid vices and dazzling endowments. Spirituality was not among their distinguishing marks."[1] At the same time, the Middle Ages was an age of spiritual vitality, and in the late Middle Ages Bainton finds several upsurges of religious devotion. From groups like the Brethren of the Common Life and the Friends of God he finds evidence to conclude, "In the hamlets all over Europe there was more of simple faith and godly living than the annalists saw fit to record."[2] Likewise in speaking of St. Francis, Savonarola, Wycliff, and Hus Bainton states that "the Church cannot have been devoid of vitality when she was able to bear such sons. They were at the same time the witness to her residual integrity."[3] Hence Bainton discerns religious strength and religious decay existing within the same context of the medieval era.

---

[1] Bainton, Christendom, 1:248.

[2] Bainton, The Reformation, p. 20.

[3] Roland H. Bainton, "The Ministry in the Middle Ages," in Early and Medieval Christianity, The Collected Papers in Church History, series 1 (Boston: Beacon Press, 1962), p. 80.

Employing religion as an indicative factor,
Bainton illustrates a continuity between the Renaissance and the Middle Ages. Rather than forging a
break with the Middle Ages, the Renaissance produced
the gradual disintegration of the ecclesiastical and
feudal systems of Europe. Bainton contends that
Renaissance humanism was the intellectual force
which precipitated a changing world view, although he
recognizes that the "Humanists did not bespeak the
mind of the entire culture."[1] In the realm of ideas
changes are less tangible but often more significant.
Consequently he states that if there is "any area in
which one may speak of the waning of the middle ages,
it is in the sphere of thought."[2] However, Bainton
interprets the relationship of the Renaissance with
the Reformation as an even more conspicuous intellectual and religious breach than the transition from the
Middle Ages to the Renaissance.

He contends that in the early sixteenth century the younger generation of Renaissance men "aban-
doned nondogmatic syncretism [of Renaissance religion]
for the flaming dogma of Wittenberg and Rome"[3] A
breach did occur. The Luther controversy precipitated
a recognizable change from the preceding centuries.

The Renaissance thinkers had sought a return
to the spirit of classical culture; Bainton piquantly
described this movement by writing: "The glory of

---

[1]Bainton, Christendom, 1:243.

[2]Roland H. Bainton, "Changing Ideas and Ideals
in the Sixteenth Century," in Early and Medieval
Christianity, The Collected Papers in Church History,
series 1 (Boston: Beacon Press, 1962), p. 155.

[3]Bainton, "Religion of the Renaissance," p. 208.

Greece, the grandeur of Rome, the grace of Galilee
should repristinate society and revivify the Church."[1]
According to Bainton's interpretation, the Renaissance and the Reformation were both movements of reform, both seeking to refashion the immediate past
by a return to a more remote past. To Renaissance
thinkers, reform meant a return to classical antiquity
with emphases on classical languages, literature, and
art forms. To Reformation thinkers reform meant a
return to the gospel with emphases on personal salvation, theology, and early Church life. The Renaissance was a reform mediated through education; the
Reformation was a reform mediated through religious
experience. Bainton draws this distinction clearly
in his comparison of Erasmus's and Luther's decisions
to enter the monastery. He writes: "Luther entered
the monastery to save his soul by good works, Erasmus
to enlighten his mind by good books."[2] As Bainton
notes, a passion for personal salvation marked Luther's
own life while a passion for knowledge marked Erasmus's life. In Luther and Erasmus, Bainton sees the
personification of the conflicting views of reforming
the Church.

The Reformers' insistence on a return to a
primitive confessionalism leads Bainton to state that
the Reformation may be regarded as the renewer of
Christendom. The Renaissance had dulled the distinctiveness of Christianity; the Reformation sharpened
Christian distinctives. The Renaissance created an
incipient secularism so that "even the popes did not

[1]Bainton, Erasmus, p. 5.

[2]Ibid., p. 12.

disdain to make alliances with the unbelieving Turks
against the believing monarchs of Europe."[1] Bainton
asks,

>   But if the Reformation was primarily religious,
> what then of its relation to the Renaissance? The
> answer of course depends in part on the interpre-
> tation of the Renaissance . . . .[2]

Scholars such as Harold Grimm, Owen Chadwick, and E.
Harris Harbison interpret the Renaissance as an early
"conception of reform" which came to fruition in the
Reformation.[3] Interpreters of this persuasion find no
cause and effect relationship but they do note a close
connection between the two movements. Ferguson contends that the Renaissance period created "an intellectual and moral atmosphere favorable to the reception
of Luther's doctrine of the freedom of the Christian
man and the priesthood of all believers."[4]

Interpreters have generally stressed the influence of the Renaissance in creating an intellectual
atmosphere which fostered certain Reformation movements
such as the Reformers' interest in linguistic studies
of the Biblical texts. Scholars have conversely
stressed the Reformers' rejection of Renaissance

---

[1]Bainton, The Reformation, p. 4.

[2]Roland H. Bainton, "Interpretations of the
Reformation," in Studies on the Reformation, The
Collected Papers in Church History, series 2 (Boston:
Beacon Press, 1963), pp. 111-12.

[3]Harold J. Grimm, The Reformation Era 1500-
1650, 2d ed. (New York: Macmillan Publishing Company,
1973); Owen Chadwick, The Reformation (Grand Rapids:
Wm. B. Eerdmans Publishing Company, 1964); E. Harris
Harbison, The Age of Reformation (Ithaca, N.Y.: Cornell
University Press, 1955).

[4]Ferguson, "Church in a Changing World," p. 17.

humanism because of its optimistic view of human nature.[1] Robert Kleinhans rejects this traditional
interpretation of Renaissance-Reformation relations
and states that "it should be possible to entertain
the hypothesis that Luther did have some minimal
but important influence on Erasmus. This would mean
that the relationship between Renaissance thought and
Reformation theology was hardly a one-way street."[2]
Paul O. Kristeller likewise rejects this traditional
position, claiming that Renaissance humanism produced
a "steady and irresistible growth of nonreligious intellectual interests."[3] Such interests competed with
religion for public attention but did not suffer rejection at the hands of the Reformers. These scholars
propose some degree of continuity between these two
movements.

　　　　Bainton's interpretation, on the other hand,
finds discontinuity between the two. He is duly careful to point out the cultural and theological preparation by the Renaissance period for the Reformers. Yet
his interpretation centers more on the divergence of
these two efforts of reform. According to Bainton
the Reformation marked a return to the Hebraic elements of Christianity whereas the Renaissance was
marked chiefly by an exaggeration of the Hellenic

---

[1]An excellent discussion of this historio-
graphical theme can be found in Robert Kleinhans,
"Luther and Erasmus; Another Perspective," Church
History 39 (December 1970): 459-69.

[2]Ibid., p. 469.

[3]Paul Oskar Kristeller, "Paganism and Christianity," in The Classics and Renaissance Thought (Cambridge, Mass.: Harvard University Press, 1955), p. 72.

elements in Christianity. It is at this point that
the Renaissance and the Reformation came into irre-
concilable conflict.[1]

The Reformation, he argues, rejected the Renaissance view of immanence. Bainton states that for the
reformers,

> God is not merely the hidden God. He is the
> indignant God, who hideth himself in his anger.
> Man has defiled him and broken his law. Nothing
> that man can do can effect any reconciliation.[2]

The Renaissance spirit enhanced the dignity of man,
the immanence of God and religious syncretism. The
reformers spoke of the depravity of man, the transcendence of God, and the necessity of salvation by grace.

Such was the cleavage between two converging
movements in the early sixteenth century, both of which
ultimately sought reform in the Church. Their relationship bears the mark of conflicting ideologies rather than concomitant reforms.

One notes in Bainton's Renaissance writings
the method of interpreting this era in terms of the
history of ideas. He describes the Renaissance as
an upsurge of Greek ideals which diverged from the
Hebraic thought of both the Middle Ages and the Reformation. Bainton is comfortable with reducing the com-
lexities of such issues as periodization to the concern with two major intellectual currents. Likewise

---

[1]Bainton sees this conflict as a persistent
tension in Christianity. In antiquity it was represented by Hellenism and Hebraism, in the sixteenth
century by the Renaissance and Reformation, and in the
seventeenth and eighteenth centuries by the Enlightenment and Puritanism. See Bainton, "Freedom, Truth,
and Unity," p. 236.

[2]Bainton, "Changing Ideas and Ideals," p. 163.

he considers the ideas which underlie an era to be of
paramount importance in historical analysis. Although Bainton's interpretation is well-grounded in
primary sources, his overall approach to the Renaissance appears simplistic. The Renaissance is far too
complex a phenomenon for the historian to reduce to
one dominant motif, viz., the Hellenic upsurge in
Western culture. Yet in Bainton's approach to the
Renaissance, simplicity of explanation appears to
take precedence over the complexities of detailed analysis.

Erasmus

Several standard biographies augmenting contemporary Erasmus research have appeared in the twentieth century. A now-dated but classic biography is
Preserved Smith's Erasmus: A Study of His Life, Ideals
and Place in History (1923). Smith presents Erasmus
as the champion of "undogmatic Christianity" and as a
proponent of "rational piety." Many scholars rank
Johan Huizinga's Erasmus and the Age of Reformation
(1924) as the most discerning biography of Erasmus.
George Faludy states that this work towers above all
other popular studies mainly because Huizinga's "insight into Erasmus's mind is matched by his knowledge
of the fifteenth century."[1] Huizinga's approach is
often critical and unsympathetic, yet he presents
Erasmus fairly within the vicissitudes of the Renaissance and Reformation era.

---

[1]George Faludy, Erasmus (New York: Stein and
Day, 1970), p. x.

A more popularly written biography is that of
Austrian novelist Stefan Zweig entitled Erasmus of
Rotterdam (1934). Zweig's work does not attempt to
be a scholarly treatment of Erasmus and as a result
it is not always factual. It is, however, fascinating
in its style and quite understandable to the less-in-
formed reader. The book which Bainton terms the "most
satisfactory general biography" is Margaret Mann
Phillips's Erasmus and the Northern Renaissance (1949).[1]
This work, primarily intended for the use of the neo-
phyte in Renaissance studies, attempts to cast Erasmus
as the greatest representative of the Renaissance in
Northern Europe.

A more recent publication (1970) is Erasmus by
George Faludy. Faludy bases his interpretation more
on the works of Erasmus than on his letters. This biography is a reassessment of Erasmus's life in light
of the changing attitudes toward Erasmus and in light
of Faludy's own empathy with Erasmus. Bainton's biography of Erasmus, Erasmus of Christendom (1969), is
an attempt to give Erasmus his due: Erasmus founded
no church to perpetuate his memory, and Catholic and
Protestant Church historians have largely ignored him.
Bainton contends that many scholars have failed to
appreciate the life of Erasmus in its full significance for the Church. As the title suggests, Erasmus
of Christendom is an attempt to give Erasmus appropriate

[1]Bainton makes this judgment as an annotation
in his extensive bibliography included in Erasmus of
Christendom, p. 293.

recognition within the spectrum of the history of
Christianity.[1]

Several prominent motifs stand out in Bainton's treatment of Erasmus. The following pages examine Bainton's interpretive treatment within the context of twentieth century biographical scholarship of
Erasmus.

One distinct interpretive theme employed by
Bainton is his stress on the piety of Erasmus. In a
review of Erasmus of Christendom Clyde Manschreck
notes that Bainton places great emphasis on Erasmus's
inward spirituality, a point also discerned by other
reviewers.[2] Bainton finds in Erasmus's early contact
with the Brethren of the Common Life an influence
which pervaded the spirit and work of his life.

Bainton suggests that Erasmus represented the
blending of two traditions within the *Devotio Moderna*:

> One observes two strands in the tradition of
> the Brethren. The one represented by à Kempis
> was fearful lest any sort of learning might wither
> the spirit. The other, stemming from [Gerard]
> Groote and flowering in [Rudolf] Agricola and
> [Alexander] Hegius, could appropriate the classical

---

[1]Bainton, Erasmus, p. vii; also see Bainton,
"Interpretations of the Reformation," p. 116 where he
writes: "The Lutherans take care of Luther, the
Calvinists of Calvin and Schwenckfeldians of Schwenckfeld . . . Erasmus, however, kept *au-dessus de la melee*
and there he stays."

[2]Clyde L. Manschreck, review of Erasmus of Christendom, by Roland H. Bainton, in Church History 41 (December 1972), p. 525; James D. Tracy, review of Erasmus
of Christendom, by Roland H. Bainton, in The American
Historical Review 77 (February 1972), p. 129; Philip
S. Watson, review of Erasmus of Christendom, by Roland
H. Bainton, in Christian Century 86 (23 July 1969), p.
996.

heritage . . . . Erasmus was to champion the
liberal wing while retaining essentially the
piety of à Kempis.[1]

The cultivation of the inner life was preeminent for
Erasmus.

Ferguson agrees fully with this interpretation of Erasmus. He states, "The kernel of Erasmus'
thought is an abiding faith that piety is a matter of
the spirit, and all else is secondary."[2] George Faludy's biography does not stress this element in Erasmus's life, yet he does concur with Bainton as to the
influence of the *Devotio Moderna*. Erasmus's religious
views were to go beyond those of the Brethren, Faludy
contends, yet the simple piety of Erasmus always resembled the primitive Christianity which the Brethren
preached.

Margaret Mann Phillips discerns in Erasmus's
piety a *via media* between rationalism and mysticism.
She contends that in reading The Praise of Folly one
comes into contact with a man who exemplifies the mind
of a rationalist and the intuition of a mystic.[3]
Phillips stresses the influence of the Brethren of the
Common Life. Discussing the Enchiridion she writes,
"He had a deep distrust of intellectual subtlety, and
here, in the work of his maturity, we can trace the
flowering of those seeds sown long ago in the schools
of the Brethren of the Common Life,"[4] Bainton would
consider this distrust of intellectual subtlety to be

[1]Bainton, Erasmus, p. 11.

[2]Wallace K. Ferguson, "Renaissance Tendencies
in the Religious Thought of Erasmus," Journal of the
History of Ideas 15 (October 1954): 503.

[3]Ibid., p. 83.

[4]Bainton, Erasmus, p. 67.

an outgrowth of that strand of tradition represented
by Thomas à Kempis.

In the piety of Erasmus Bainton finds a key to
the understanding of Erasmus's dislike of religious
ritual. The thrust of the Enchiridion, according to
Bainton, "made for rendering the outward apparatus
of religion superfluous."[1] One of Erasmus's three
great aversions was "Pharisaism" or legalism, i.e.,
the effort to secure salvation through meticulous
observance of rules.[2] The piety of Erasmus easily
transcended such externalism and placed him in conflict with many of the religious practices of his
day. The monks in particular became the focus of
many of Erasmus's attacks against legalism.

Whereas Bainton empathizes with Erasmus's disdain for externals *vis à vis* inner piety, Johan
Huizinga contends that Erasmus seemed unaware that
religious observances may contain valuable sentiments of unexpressed and unformulated piety.[3] Bainton sees Erasmus's piety as a dominant factor in his
life. Huizinga sees Erasmus's piety as but one of
many factors in Erasmus's quest for the ideal life.

The spirit of Erasmus's piety manifested
itself in the well-known characteristics frequently
attributed to him: simplicity, peacefulness, sincerity, and gentleness. He sought mediation in conflict, treasured solitude in study, and cultivated

---

[1] Bainton, Erasmus, p. 67.

[2] Ibid., p. 6.

[3] Johan Huizinga, Erasmus and the Age of Reformation, trans. F. Hopman (New York: Charles Scribner's Sons, 1924; reprint ed., New York: Harper and
Row, 1957), p. 101.

propriety in deportment. For Bainton, Erasmus's
character traits emanate from the piety of his religious commitment. Phillips's understanding of Erasmus
supports Bainton's interpretation on this point, for
she contends that Erasmus's concept of Christianity
revealed itself in his desire for peace, quiet, and
study. "To him the Christian life was . . . above
all a way to a nobler living."[1]

Huizinga likewise interprets Erasmus's most
cherished ideals and his most prominent characteristics as those of gentleness, sincerity, simplicity,
and purity. Personal piety, however, was not the
source of these personal characteristics in Huizinga's
interpretation; rather it was Erasmus's personal "delicacy" which forced him to be as he was. Huizinga
states,

> In the moral sphere Erasmus's delicacy is rep-
> resented by his great need of friendship and con-
> cord, his dislike of contention. With him peace
> and harmony rank above all other considerations,
> and he confesses them to be guiding principles
> in his actions.[2]

Likewise Huizinga sees in Erasmus a "dangerous fusion"
between inclination and conviction. "The correla-
tions between his idiosyncrasies and his precepts are
undeniable."[3] The man who condemned abstaining from
meat could not himself tolerate eating fish. Huizinga
finds in Erasmus not piety but a personal delicacy
which formed the bedrock of his actions. Idiosyncrasies coupled with idealism were the foundation of his
character.

---

[1]Phillips, _Erasmus_, p. 182.

[2]Huizinga, _Erasmus_, p. 119.

[3]Ibid., p. 120.

A clearly delineated distinction emerges in
Bainton's interpretation of Erasmus when compared with
other biographies. He makes inwardness and piety an
interpretive theme. In the conclusion of Erasmus of
Christendom Bainton discusses several of Erasmus's
final writings. Concerning the Catechism Bainton
states, "Once again the whole emphasis of the Catechism is on the inwardness of religion."[1] In the essay "Continuity of Thought of Erasmus" Bainton writes,
"From the monastery at Steyn to the death bed at Basel
Erasmus was preaching a simple interior piety."[2] This
theme is followed throughout his biography of Erasmus
in the interpretation of his character, his writings,
and his faith. One can find in this theme of piety a
key not only to Bainton's interpretation of Erasmus
but also to Bainton's own religious presuppositions.

A second interpretive theme found in Bainton's
work on Erasmus concerns the continuity of Erasmus's
thought. Bainton maintains that there was a consistency of thought which characterized Erasmus from his
earliest years at Steyn to his final days at Freiberg.
Several twentieth century scholars find in the career
of Erasmus sharp turning points through which earlier
attitudes were rejected and replaced by newer ways of
thinking. According to Bainton four such turning
points stand out in the interpretations of Erasmus
scholars: 1) his post-monastery days when he became
critical of monasticism, 2) his first visit to England
and the subsequent influence of John Colet, 3) his

---

[1]Bainton, Erasmus, p. 267.

[2]Roland H. Bainton, "Continuity of Thought of
Erasmus," American Council of Learned Societies News-
letter 19 (May 1968): 7.

first trip to Italy and the writing of The Praise of
Folly and 4) his final days and alleged reactionary
tendency.[1] Bainton discounts any of these developments
as precipitating changes in Erasmus's thinking.

The first turning point marks the years at the
end of the fifteenth century as the time when Erasmus,
having experienced freedom beyond the monastery, engaged in a sharp critique of monasticism. This is the
position entertained by Albert Hyma in The Youth of
Erasmus. Hyma arrives at his position by an examination of two of Erasmus's tracts of this period, especially the tract On Contempt of the World. This
particular tract devotes eleven chapter to the praise
of monastic seclusion; then it offers one final chapter as a criticism of monasticism. Hyma concludes that
this final chapter was a later addition, not part of
the original manuscript. He believes that Erasmus
added it nearly thirty-five years later at the time
of its publication.[2]

Bainton disagrees clearly with Hyma concerning
a radical change in Erasmus's attitude toward monasticism. He interprets the tract On Contempt of the
World as a formal literary exercise. As such the tract
comprised a persuasive essay (suasoria) and a dissua-
sive essay (dissuasoria). Chapters One through Eleven
argued positively for monasticism while Chapter Twelve
briefly argues against monasticism. He delineates his
interpretation as follows:

---

[1]Ibid., p. 1.

[2]Albert Hyma, The Youth of Erasmus, University
of Michigan Publications in History and Political
Science, vol. 10 (Ann Arbor: University of Michigan
Press, 1930), pp. 145-204.

> I would suggest, in the absence of proof, that
> the twelfth chapter of the *De Contemptu Mundi*
> is the outline of the dissuasive with regard
> to monasticism, and although possibly written
> later, may perfectly well have been coincident
> with the initial draft.[1]

In Erasmus, even in the early monastic period, one
finds an attitude toward monasticism which Bainton
terms "discriminating," neither hostile nor uncriti-
cal.[2]

The monastic period provided a vital formative
time in Erasmus's life. During this period Erasmus
formulated his ideas for restoring the Church and
Christendom to the original state of grandeur. "I
would contend that while in the monastery Erasmus
came into the clear with regard to his mission and
message and pursued them with undeviating fidelity."[3]
Hence Bainton can find no sharp turning point in
Erasmus's attitude toward monasticism as proposed by
Hyma.

The second turning point in Erasmus's life
purportedly came during his first trip to England.
John Colet proposed that Erasmus lecture at Oxford on
either Genesis or Isaiah. Erasmus declined the offer,
pleading personal incompetence as the cause. The
position of Huizinga is that this offer by Colet
coupled with Colet's personal influence turned Erasmus from secular studies to sacred studies. Huizinga
comments that it was "Colet's word and example which
first changed Erasmus's desultory occupation with
theological studies into a firm and lasting resolve

---

[1] Bainton, "Continuity of Thought," p. 3.

[2] Bainton, Erasmus, p. 16.

[3] Bainton, "Continuity of Thought," p. 1.

to make their pursuit the object of his life."[1]   Other
biographers also discern a change in Erasmus due to the
influence of his English visit. Phillips claims that
in these six months in England Erasmus caught the first
true glimpse of the meaning and purpose of his life.
In England Erasmus resolved his "inner conflict" and
brought his divergent interests into harmony."[2]   Faludy
stands with Huizinga in finding Erasmus turning from
humanist studies to the "new Biblical theology," and
interpreting him as ready to devote all his energies
to this pursuit.[3]

The traditional interpretation, held by scholars such as Huizinga, Phillips, and Faludy, asserts
that through the influence of Colet Erasmus's focus
shifted from secular studies to theological studies.
Erasmus's refusal to lecture at Oxford supposedly indicates his inadequacy in matters of theological studies. Bainton finds fault with the contention that
Erasmus radically changed in England. Erasmus's refusal to lecture at Oxford reveals no departure from
the consistent course of his life. Bainton argues
that Erasmus arrived in England after having been a
student of theology in Paris, and after leaving England
he was never to give up secular studies. He was there-
ford engaged in both secular and theological studies
before and after his visit to England. If Colet
brought any change in Erasmus it may have been to turn
him from patristic studies to biblical studies. Above
all else, Colet's regret that he knew no Greek firmly

---

[1] Huizinga, Erasmus, p. 33.

[2] Phillips, Erasmus, p. 40.

[3] Faludy, Erasmus, pp. 79-80.

convinced Erasmus of the necessity of mastering the
language.[1]   Bainton finds Erasmus emerging from his
first visit to England with the same ideals, same
program of reform, and same attitudes as those formulated in the monastery at Steyn.

    A third turning point supposedly occurred when
Erasmus visited Italy for the first time. This position, put forth by Werner Kaegi, proposes that in
Italy Erasmus experienced the amenities of gracious
living and consequently revolted against the intense
strivings of northern Europe. Up to this point Erasmus
had engaged in scholarship with indefatigable energies.
Leaving Italy he questioned the value of such devotion to his work and wrote The Praise of Folly.[2] No
biographer develops such a position, and Bainton rejects Kaegi's thesis altogether. Erasmus had already
"sipped the ambrosia of gracious living" at the estate
of Lord Mountjoy in England, and while in Italy he
had "emulated the labors of Hercules" in compiling
thousands of new adages.[3] The Praise of Folly, contends Bainton, was not the signalling of a change in
his thinking, but was a satirical restatement of the
thesis expressed earlier in the Enchiridion. The
visit to Italy had increased Erasmus's collection of
proverbs for the Adagia, had increased his command of
Greek, but had not deterred him from his lifelong
ideals and purpose.

---

[1]Bainton, Erasmus, p. 62; Bainton, "Continuity
of Thought," pp. 4-5.

[2]Werner Kaegi, "Hutten und Erasmus," Historische
Vierteljahrschrift 22 (1924-25): 247.

[3]Bainton, Erasmus, p. 90.

The fourth turning point for Erasmus supposedly arose from the situation of his last years.
Huizinga asserts that Erasmus became a reactionary near
the end of his life. Bainton interprets Huizinga as
maintaining that Erasmus "defended his orthodoxy to such
a degree . . . as to lapse into obscurantism and reactionary orthodoxy."[1] In the final period at Freiburg, claims Huizinga, Erasmus moved away from the
radicals and Lutherans and moved toward conservative
Catholicism.[2] Faludy finds that the elder Erasmus continued to hold ideas of his youth as was especially
evidenced by the writing of On the Sweet Concord of the
Church.[3] Phillips agrees: "But he still spoke as one
who would tolerate the old practices for the sake of
peace, but who did not himself believe in them. He
was still refusing to take sides."[4] Erasmus perceived
the middle way, asserts Phillips, as an ultimate conclusion.

According to Bainton's interpretation Erasmus's
attitude did become more conservative during the Freiburg period yet not to the extent of refuting a lifetime of work. Bainton states that the best way to
respond to the issue raised by Huizinga is to look at
Erasmus's own productions during the Freiburg period.
He wrote commentaries, psalms, a treatise on preaching,
and a meditation on the preparation for death. All
breathe the spirit of the Enchiridion.[5] In a letter to

---

[1]Bainton, "Continuity of Thought," p. 6.

[2]Huizinga, Erasmus, pp. 167-68; 170-78, 190.

[3]Faludy, Erasmus, pp. 247-48.

[4]Phillips, Erasmus, p. 218.

[5]Bainton, Erasmus, p. 257.

Cardinal Sadoleto in which Erasmus discusses the saints
and images, he expressed the same ideas which always
characterized his thought.[1] Consequently, the final
years of Erasmus's life depict not a reactionary return to orthodoxy but the continuation of the ideals
and positions developed through a lifetime of work.

        Bainton contributes a new perspective on the
great humanist by presenting Erasmus as an unyield-
ingly consistent reformer. Bainton perceives incon-
sistency as a weakness, and often in his writings he
attempts to find a consistent theme in an individual's
life which provides a sense of unity in the person's
life. For Erasmus the unifying factor is his ideal
of reform. Bainton shows that Erasmus's ideal of reform, developed in his monastery days at Steyn, continued throughout his life. This thesis is valid
based on Bainton's interpretation of the primary
source materials of Erasmus's life. However, this
thesis is not so convincing as to discount totally
the traditional interpretations of Erasmus's life
which locate several marked changes. Bainton attempts
to provide an appealing portrait of Erasmus and as
such he superimposes a continuity of purpose upon the
life of Erasmus. He thus shows Erasmus not as a
timorous and vacillating scholar but rather as a consistent proponent of piety, simplicity, and truth.

        A third interpretive theme distinguished in
Bainton's treatment casts Erasmus in the role of a
liberal reformer of religion. He presents Erasmus as
one who is immersed in the Renaissance humanism of the

---

[1]Bainton, "Continuity of Thought," p. 6.

fifteenth and early sixteenth centuries, yet he is reluctant to present him as principally a Renaissance
figure. Instead he presents him most often from the
perspective of the religious man intent on reforming
the Church and society.

     Bainton questions whether one can rightly re-
fer to Erasmus as a true Renaissance man. Michelangelo
was adept in painting, sculpture, and poetry; Leonardo
was proficient in art and mechanics; Servetus excelled
in medicine, theology, and geography. Erasmus, in
contrast to these men, was chiefly a literary man. A
man of wide ranging interests, Erasmus was preeminently
the cultivated Christian man. Bainton says, "Erasmus
might be called the cultivated Christian man who would
enlarge his interests insofar as compatible with his
obligations."[1] Bainton appears most comfortable with
the interpretation of Erasmus as the intellectual leader of the Renaissance whose raison d'être was the re-
pristination of Christendom.

     No one so epitomized the spirit of reform in
all of its aspects as did Erasmus. This is the judgment of Bainton.[2] Faludy accents this perspective,
stating that Erasmus was the individual who united
the diverse trends of his day toward reform more ef-
fectively than anyone else.[3] Phillips and Ferguson,
however, see Erasmus as best characterized in the role

---

[1]Bainton, Erasmus, p. 227.

[2]Ibid., p. 6.

[3]Faludy, Erasmus, p. 72.

of the leading proponent of Renaissance humanism rather
than simply the reformer of religion.[1]

Bainton's portrait of Erasmus makes no dichotomy between Erasmus's role as a literary figure and
as a liberal reformer. Instead he casts Erasmus as a
synthesizer of Christian and classical ideals. By
holding these two ideals in conjunction Erasmus hoped
to effect reform within the Church. Commenting on the
task of synthesis which lay before Erasmus Bainton
writes:

> Erasmus essayed the task afresh, not in order
> to systematize theology, but in order to give
> substance to a reform. He would purge the Church
> and refashion the world. At first he was highly
> optimistic as to the possibility of a revival
> through the dissemination of the literature of
> Christian and classical antiquity.[2]

Erasmus adopted the whole humanist program for reforming the mind of Christendom. His method was intel-
ligent persuasion using the art of the rhetorician
and the word of God. At this point Bainton's interpretation shows an affinity with that of Gray who sees
the humanist program as primarily the pursuit of eloquence.[3]

This program of reform was not an outright rejection of medieval scholasticism as Bainton carefully

---

[1]Phillips, Erasmus, p. xi; Ferguson, "Renaissance Tendencies," p. 499.

[2]Bainton, Erasmus, p. 5.

[3]Gray, "Renaissance Humanism," pp. 497-514;
see also Roland H. Bainton, "The Responsibility of
Power According to Erasmus of Rotterdam," in The Re-
sponsibility of Power: Historical Essays in Honor of
Hajo Holborn, ed. Leonard Krieger and Fritz Stern
(Garden City, N.Y.: Doubleday and Company, 1967), p. 62.

points out. Rather it was a movement back to the
sources, a movement concerned with simplifying the
abstractions so prevalent in the medieval Church. As
Faludy states, "Erasmus was determined to reduce the
theological mountain of Christianity to the molehill
he thought it ought to be."[1] Phillips terms Erasmus's
vision of reform as "his work of liberation."[2]
Huizinga, however, frequently pictures Erasmus as out
of touch with the major movements of his time. His
reclusive nature, states Huizinga, "did more than anything else to prevent Erasmus from understanding the
true nature and purport" of the reform movements in
the sixteenth century.[3]

        Often taking a more critical view of Erasmus's
reform efforts, Huizinga questions the causes of
Erasmus's magnetism. What made Erasmus the man from
whom his contemporaries expected their salvation? The
answer, writes Huizinga, is that his contemporaries
saw in Erasmus the bearer of a new liberty of mind and
a new simplicity of knowledge. Bainton perceives
Erasmus as more than the bearer of intellectual liberty, for in Erasmus he sees one holding in balance
the simplicity of the gospel and the traditions of
the Church.

        From Erasmus emanated a spirit which took root
in a broad spectrum of sixteenth century religious
reform movements. Bainton writes:

----

[1]Faludy, Erasmus, p. 93.

[2]Phillips, Erasmus, p. 53.

[3]Huizinga, Erasmus, p. 138. Huizinga does
present Erasmus as working as a reformer, but not
with the prominence and vision attributed to him by
Bainton.

So many statements . . . can be culled from the
works of Erasmus that he can rightly be called
a precursor of the Counter-Reformation. On the
other hand he so spiritualized everything within
the Church and so denuded the hierarchy of all
sanction save utility that the lines run also
from Erasmus to the Sacramentarians; Zwingli,
Oecolampadius, and Pellikan, and even to the
spiritualists and rationalists such as Caspar
Schwenkfeld, Sebastian Franck, and Sebastian
Castellio.[1]

In this passage Bainton points out the complexity of

Erasmus's influence as a reformer. His non-dogmatic

approach to Christianity gave Erasmus an affinity with

the multifarious endeavors of reform. For example,

Erasmus concurred with the early writings of Luther

against the abuses of the Church.[2] Likewise Erasmus

sympathized with the left wing radicals such as the

Anabaptists even though he did not agree with their

methods of effecting reform.[3]

If Erasmus, then, did have an affinity of

thought with the radicals and if he did pour scorn on

the abuses of the Church, why did he remain in the

Church of Rome? Bainton raises this question and of-

fers several possible answers. Perhaps, writes Bain-

ton, Erasmus found in the Church the confluence of

classical and Christian strains. Possibly he remained

in the Church because he acquiesced to political

pluralism and was desirous of ecclesiastical monism.[4]

---

[1]Bainton, _Erasmus_, p. 193.

[2]Ibid., p. 158.

[3]Ibid., p. 220; see also Roland H. Bainton
"Erasmus and the Persecuted," in _Scrinium Erasmianum_,
2 vols., ed. J. Coppens (Leiden: E.J. Brill, 1969),
2:201.

[4]Bainton, _Erasmus_, p. 196.

Another suggestion offered by Bainton is that
Erasmus felt most at home in the Catholic Church.
Erasmus had no strong attachment to any country, and
the Church offered him solidarity. Likewise in the
Church he had many close personal friends to whom he
was extremely loyal.[1] Another possible reason for
his staying in the Church was simply that Erasmus
abhorred *discordia*.[2] Bainton appears to find no answer beyond conjecture as to Erasmus's loyalty to the
Church. Nevertheless, Erasmus is deemed by Bainton
to be "the mouthpiece of the liberal Catholic reform."[3]

Other biographers seem equally at a loss to
explain Erasmus's lifelong Catholic loyalty. Huizinga
claims that while Erasmus always regarded himself as
a Catholic, he was unaware that his attitudes toward
the Church, the sacraments, and the dogmas were not
purely Catholic. To leave the Church and unite with
a faction was beyond the character of Erasmus who "remained far too much the man of spiritual decorum to
identify himself with those irregular believers."[4]
Although Erasmus quarreled with the old, he could not
accept the new. Phillips offers the proposition that
Erasmus's faithfulness to the Church was a lifelong
commitment which he never deserted. She states that

[1] Ibid.

[2] Roland H. Bainton, "Erasmus and the Wesen Des
Christentums," in Glaube Geist Geschichte; Festschrift
für Ernst Benz, ed. Gerhard Muller and Winfried Zeller
(Leiden: E.J. Brill, 1967), p. 205.

[3] Bainton, Erasmus, p. 65.

[4] Huizinga, Erasmus, p. 178.

he had no intention of leaving the Church but adopted
all efforts to bring about its restoration.[1]

Likewise some Roman Catholic scholars interpret
Erasmus as an orthodox Catholic. For example, Louis
Bouyer in Erasmus and the Humanist Experiment states
that he "took considerable pains to establish the sincerity and effectiveness of his [Erasmus's] attachment to the Church in all his dealings."[2] Another
Catholic interpreter of Erasmus, Harry J. McSorley,
writes that in regard to the papacy Erasmus was "more
Catholic than either the papal absolutists or the con-
ciliarists . . . ."[3] Thus Bainton, like other contemporary Erasmus scholars, portrays Erasmus as a loyal
(although misunderstood and controversial) son of the
Church. The reason for such loyalty lies in the realm
of supposition for as Bainton writes, "Loyalties often
defy analysis."[4] The approach to Erasmus as a liberal
Catholic reformer emerges throughout Bainton's biography,
and consequently forms a distinctive viewpoint in the
history of Erasmus scholarship.

A fourth interpretive theme evident in Erasmus
of Christendom is the frequently positive perspective
from which Bainton considers Erasmus. Often Bainton's
positive assessment runs diametrically opposed to the

---

[1]Phillips, Erasmus, p. 108.

[2]Louis Bouyer, Erasmus and the Humanist Experiment, trans. Francis X. Murphy (London: Geoffrey Chap-
man, 1959), p. 215.

[3]Harry J. McSorley, "Erasmus and the Primacy
of the Roman Pontiff: Between Conciliarism and Papal-
ism," Archiv für Reformationsgeschichte 65 (1974): 53-
54.

[4]Bainton, Erasmus, p. 196.

assessment by other biographers. Bainton's treatment
of two of Erasmus's personal traits will suffice to
demonstrate this approach.

Bainton has the tendency to present Erasmus
as an activist. He points to Erasmus's involvement
in the pursuit of scholarship, in the quest for Church
reform, and in the developing of friendships. Likewise he shows Erasmus's intense activity in the mediation of conflicts as well as in the attacking of ideo-
logcial opponents. One does not read Erasmus of Christendom and find Erasmus to be a timid and sheltered
recluse. Instead one finds that "Erasmus was no recluse and no neutral in controversies which lay within
his competence and about which he cared."[1]

As an activist scholar Erasmus served as the
counsellor of popes and as the mentor of Europe. His
life epitomized the spirit of industry in the cause of
reform through learning. Moreover, Bainton describes
Erasmus as earnestly involved in mediation for the persecuted, e.g., for Reuchlin, Luther, the Hussites, and
the Anabaptists. A further evidence of Erasmus's
activism relates to the presentation of him as an attractive personality. Although Bainton points out
Erasmus's preference for quiet and solitude, he nevertheless indicates that Erasmus was the gregarious and
winsome friend. "What was the secret of his appeal?"
asks Bainton. "No doubt in a measure his charm, ur-
banity, and wit which would mollify opponents in personal encounter . . . ."[2]

---

[1] Ibid., p. 112.

[2] Ibid., p. 5.

Such a judgment of Erasmus's activism also appears in the work of Phillips. She finds Erasmus deeply involved in the social, ecclesiastical, and literary currents of his day. Erasmus, contends Phillips, remained always in contact with others through personal and scholarly encounter. His study was the meeting place of all the currents of thought in Europe. This constitutes one of his claims to originality, allowing him to be the man of his era who could best survey the whole European scene.[1]

Far different from the similar views of Bainton and Phillips is the perspective of Huizinga. He caustically criticizes Erasmus as a weak personality who shunned personal contact and avoided social encounter. Erasmus desired to be alone, he was a recluse, and he was hampered by greatness. Huizinga claims that Erasmus was "one of those whom contact with others weakens."[2] Compared to Luther, Calvin, and the statesmen of the age Erasmus confronts the world with reticence. In spite of all his receptiveness and sensitivity, Erasmus was never fully in contact with life. He was out of touch with his own times, and the world of his mind was imaginary. Erasmus remained remote from the great happenings of the fifteenth and sixteenth centuries.

Faludy appears to equivocate between the positions of Bainton and Huizinga on this issue. Erasmus stands very pale indeed before his contemporaries, writes Faludy. Occasionally he sees Erasmus as a "near-recluse," yet he finds in Erasmus an intellectual

---

[1] Faludy, _Erasmus_, p. 152.

[2] Bainton, _Erasmus_, p. 7.

aggressiveness. He states, "If Erasmus was timid to
the point of cowardice in everyday affairs, he was
heroically resolute where his work was concerned."[1]
Thus Faludy presents Erasmus as intellectually bold
and active but socially shy and timorous.

A positive assessment of Erasmus's character
emerges in Bainton's works. He rejects the negative
treatment of Erasmus as a withdrawn and timid recluse.
Rather Erasmus is the involved activist, the charming
personality, and the industrious academic.

Another indication of Bainton's favorable
treatment of Erasmus is seen in his interpretation of
Erasmus' relativity as a mark of integrity. Most
twentieth century biographers discern in Erasmus the
spirit of mediation, and most detect in him a proclivity for vacillation. Bainton depicts Erasmus in
this light, yet his assessment of this Erasmian tendency proves positive. He writes, "Erasmus was a
man of moderation partly because he perceived the am-
biguities of all things human."[2] The relativity which
characterized Erasmus was a strength rather than a
weakness.

To illustrate Bainton's defense of Erasmus's
vacillation, one may consider the treatment of Erasmus's
view of martyrdom. Erasmus was ready to face martyrdom, contends Bainton, but only in his own way. He
would not die for the paradoxes of Luther. Bainton
laments that for four hundred years scholars have ac-
cused Erasmus of an unwillingness to die for anything.
Attempting to vindicate Erasmus's attitude on this

---

[1]Faludy, *Erasmus*, p. 152.

[2]Bainton, *Erasmus*, p. 7.

issue Bainton states, "But in passing judgment one
should recall that he who mistrusts himself may be
more courageous under test than one who like Peter
boasts in advance."[1] The ambiguity of Erasmus's attitudes and the moderation of his endeavors emanated
from a *weltanschauung* tempered with relativity.

Phillips stresses this attitude in Erasmus,
for his gravitation toward the "middle way" forms a
distinct interpretive theme of Erasmus and the Northern
Renaissance. As with Bainton, Phillips sees Erasmus's
relativity as a positive attribute. Speaking of the
spirit of the middle way she states, "It needs on one
hand a liberated intellect, on the other a realisation
of the realms outside the reach of reason . . . ."[2]
Erasmus realized the relativity of the human situation
and perceived the middle way as the most consistently
valued position.

The relativity of Erasmus's thinking leads
Huizinga to develop a negative rather than positive
assessment. Erasmus's conceptualization of the ambiguity of all of life precipitated Erasmus's "fear of
directness." Everywhere Erasmus found shadings and
distinctions. He could not longer perceive the world
with the certainty of a medieval man. Huizinga maintains that this relativity reveals the "one tragic
defect running through his whole personality: his
refusal or inability ever to draw ultimate conclusions."[3]

---

[1] Ibid., p. 167.

[2] Phillips, Erasmus, p. 223.

[3] Huizinga, Erasmus, p. 147.

Erasmus's ambiguity, growing from a conviction
as to the relativity of life, finds a positive assessment with Bainton.   In Erasmus, Bainton finds the in-
ception of a modern mind and the conviction of a scholar
able to see beyond his own time.   For Bainton, a questionable characteristic proves to be a mark of integrity.

Herein lies an interpretive theme of Bainton's
Erasmus of Christendom.   He proceeds to assess Erasmus from a positive perspective.   Bainton differs most
markedly with Huizinga whose critical examination often casts Erasmus in a negative role.   As Bainton expresses in the "Preface" of Erasmus of Christendom,
"I have long been drawn to Erasmus on a number of
counts."[1]   Bainton liked Erasmus, and his biography
is quite sympathetic to Erasmus.   Perhaps no interpretive theme evidences itself as clearly as Bainton's positive assessment of Erasmus.   From the out-
set of Erasmus of Christendom it is clear that Bainton
intends to cast Erasmus in the best possible light.
In view of a previous generation's disdain of many
of Erasmus's personal traits, the interpretation set
forth by Bainton offers a much-needed corrective.

Conclusion

Several critical considerations frame this brief
evaluation of Bainton's Renaissance writings.   First,
a distinct religious *leitmotiv* underlies all of his
Renaissance works.   For example, he interprets the
Renaissance as a movement of religious reform.   He
contends that both the Renaissance and Reformation

---

[1]Bainton, Erasmus, p. vii.

sought to purge and revive the Church. Both sought
a return to an earlier manifestation of grandeur:
the Renaissance to classical antiquity and the Reformation to the gospel. Likewise another example is
Bainton's depiction of Erasmus as a liberal reformer
of religion whose goal was to repristinate the Church
and society. He writes that Erasmus "ended as a
battered liberal" by virtue of a life of attempted
reform.[1] The conclusion of Erasmus of Christendom
compares Luther and Erasmus on their respective methods
and objectives of reform. Such interpretations reveal the religious *leitmotiv* in Bainton's Renaissance
writings.

A second consideration involves the virtual
exclusion of certain themes, ideas, and phenomena in
Bainton's works. Ferguson writes that the historian
"can scarcely avoid the temptation to regard as most
important in the past what seems most important to
him, what he values or what interests him most."[2]
Perhaps Bainton has a tendency to regard as most important in the Renaissance that which interests him
most. For example, Bainton accentuates Renaissance
themes of indivdualism, toleration, pacifism, and
the unity of man. Yet Renaissance endeavors such as
art, music, architecture, and literature receive little treatment. The virtual exclusion of certain topics
offers an insight into Bainton's treatment of the
Renaissance by giving an indication of the themes and
ideas which he deems important.

---

[1] Ibid., p. viii.

[2] Ferguson, The Renaissance in Historical
Thought, p. 395.

A third consideration emanates from Bainton's
inclination to interpret the Renaissance from the perspective of the history of ideas. He writes that
external changes, such as discoveries and inventions,
are easy to chronicle but their impact on the European
outlook is slow and elusive. Often more subtle but
more important, he contends, is the changing of ideas
in a culture.[1] Bainton often interprets the Renaissance
in light of changing ideas. An example of this tendency is his characterization of the Renaissance as
the period of a resurging Hellenic spirit. The exaggeration of the Hellenic elements in the Christian
synthesis as opposed to the Hebraic elements of Christianity is for Bainton a key phenomenon in Renaissance
life. Consequently, Bainton's approach to the Renaissance materials gives paramount importance to the
history of ideas in this period.

A final consideration deals with Bainton's
interpretation of Erasmus. Scholars of the previous
generation tended to cast Erasmus in a poorer light
by condemning him, for example, for his alleged moral
cowardice. This perspective is obvious in Huizinga's
Erasmus and the Age of Reform. Bainton represents a
reversal of this approach by framing Erasmus in a more
appealing interpretation. The biography by Bainton
demonstrates the work of a critical scholar whose works
exalt Erasmus as a man of peace, a man of integrity,
and a man of conviction.

---

[1]Bainton, "Changing Ideas and Ideals," p. 155.

CHAPTER III

THE LUTHER WRITINGS

Bainton's reputation as a Reformation scholar
depends heavily on his extensive writings on Martin
Luther. The centerpeice of his Luther scholarship is
Here I Stand: A Life of Martin Luther. There are also
significant numbers of articles and monographs on various aspects of Luther's life which augment the biography.

Approaching the study of Luther through the
method of biography presents distinct problems for the
historian. The greatest problem, writes Bainton, is
the abundance of materials on Luther. The historian
must omit exceedingly large amounts of material and must
limit his presentation of Luther to the areas which the
historian deems most significant.

> Of all the inevitable omissions none is more
> regrettable than the exclusion of the reasons for
> judgments as to what Luther said or did. There are
> few points in his career devoid of pros or cons.
> The biographer can do no more than weigh the evi-
> dence, make up his mind, and arbitrarily announce
> his conclusions.[1]

---

[1]Roland H. Bainton, "Luther's Life in Review,"
in Studies on the Reformation, Collected Papers in
Church History, series 2 (Boston: Beacon Press, 1963),
p. 92. This article is a composite of several short
writings on Luther's life. The writing entitled "Problems in Luther Biography" is the English translation
of the article "Probleme der Lutherbiographie," in
Lutherforschung Heute, ed. Vilmos Vajta (Berlin:
Lutherisches Verlagshaus, 1958), pp. 24-31.

Secondly, Bainton regrets the inability of the biographer to discuss moot points because so many points in
Luther's life are open to question.

Bainton's analysis of the problems involved
in writing a biography of Luther appears to lack
depth. In his brief essay "Problems in Luther Biography" Bainton notes two problems: the plethora of
sources and the lack of space in a biography to explain reasons for various interpretations. These
two problems are external matters in Luther biography and do not approach the highly complex nature
of attempting to understand Luther. Bainton's inclination is to simplify a very difficult task for
the historian.[1] Issues such as interpreting the
young Luther, assessing Luther in the context of late
medieval Catholicism, and understanding the socio-
political nature of the Luthern movement are problems
more difficult for the historian than the problem
of abundant materials.

Contemporary Luther biographers share Bainton's judgment concerning the difficulties involved
in writing a critically accurate portrait of Luther.
Franz Lau maintains that the four hundred year old
effort to achieve an understanding of Luther has led
to no clear result. Schwiebert argues that a "true
evaluation of Luther's contributions to the world
would require the combined talents and training of
a linguist, political scientist, historian, sociologist,
and theologian, scarcely to be found in a single

---

[1]This position appears somewhat inconsistent
for Bainton. His own biography of Luther reflects
a keen sensitivity to the complexities of interpreting
Luther.

individual."[1] Nevertheless, a spate of biographies
of Luther have appeared in the twentieth century.

Several selected biographies will serve as
a basis for comparative study in order to analyze
the historiographical approach which Bainton employs
in his Luther writings. Critical Luther research in
the first half of the twentieth century was mainly
initiated by Karl Holl. Holl's work concentrated in
part on the inner development of Luther in which
Luther's religious experience was viewed as of paramount significance. The essay by Holl entitled "What
Did Luther Understand By Religion?" is indicative of
his approach to Luther. Holl's work precipitated
the modern "Luther Renaissance." Following Holl's
approach to Luther, biographers concentrated on the
early years of the reformer. Two biographies which
represent this attention to the young Luther are
Heinrich Boehmer's Road to Reformation: Martin Luther
to the Year 1521 (1946) and Gordon Rupp's Luther's
Progress to the Diet of Worms (1951, 1964). A popular
treatment of Luther's early life from the perspective
of psychohistory is Erik Erikson's Young Man Luther:
A Study in Psychoanalysis and History (1958).

Gerhard Ritter's Luther: His Life and Work
(1959) attempts to present Luther immersed in sixteenth century German culture and also attempts to
accent the universal significance of Luther's work.
A very brief portrait of Luther comprises Franz Lau's

---

[1]Franz Lau, Luther, trans. Robert H. Fisher
(Philadelphia: Westminster Press, 1963), p. 13; E.G.
Schwiebert, Luther and His Times (St. Louis: Concordia
Publishing House, 1950), p. 2.

Luther (1963). Lau narrates the events of Luther's
life while emphasizing the necessity of placing him
within the context of Renaissance Europe. The English biographer V. H. H. Green published Luther and
the Reformation in 1964. This work provides a terse
chronicle of Luther's life and offers very little
interpretation of Luther's religious development.
The voluminous biography by E. G. Schwiebert, Luther
and His Times (1950), gives particular emphasis on
the philosophical, theological, and socio-geographi-
cal factors that contributed to Luther's life and
thought.

Catholic historiography of Luther, undergoing
a transition in recent years, has moved generally
from a polemical approach to a more affirmative interpretation.[1] Hartman Grisar's Martin Luther: His
Life and Work (1930, 1971) assumes a polemical view of
Luther. Grisar is scrupulously accurate: he pays
tribute to Luther's courage and piety, but he considers Luther psychopathic. Grisar's work follows the
traditional Catholic approach to Luther led by such
scholars as Heinrich Denifle which presented the reformer in a very negative light. The research of
Joseph Lortz, however, produced a new appreciation
for Luther among some Catholic historians. The first
volume of Lortz's The Reformation in Germany (1939),

---

[1]Joseph Lortz, "The Basic Elements of Luther's
Intellectual Style," in Catholic Scholars Dialogue with
Luther, ed. Jared Wicks (Chicago: Loyola University
Press, 1970), pp. 6-7. On page 7 of this article Lortz
states: "Gradually Catholics have come to recognize
the Christian, and even Catholic, richness of Luther,
and they are impressed."

1968) provides a sensitive and positive view of Luther's work.[1]   John M. Todd follows the direction of
Lortz in Martin Luther: A Biographical Study (1965).
Todd approaches Luther as "justus et peccator" and
views him with mixed emotions.

Bainton's biography of Luther, Here I Stand:
A Life of Martin Luther (1950), comprises an analysis
of the reformer's religious development.   Harold J.
Grimm maintains that the biographies by Bainton and
Schwiebert are perhaps "the most important stimulus
to Luther research in recent times."[2]

Luther as a Man of Religion

Luther's career has elicited strong and widely
varied responses. Bainton points out that even in
Luther's own day diverse judgments arose as to the
proper understanding of the reformer. The Catholics
pictured him as a rebel while the evangelicals saw
him as the "new Paul" restoring Christian purity.
Likewise German nationalists hailed Luther as the German Hercules, the peasants of Germany interpreted him

---

[1]For a general treatment of Catholic historiography of Luther see Richard Stauffer, Luther as Seen
by Catholics, Ecumenical Studies in History, vol. 7
(Richmond: John Knox Press, 1967). Stauffer delineates
the historical development of Luther research among
twentieth century Catholic scholars. He see Heinrich
Denifle and Hartman Grisar as part of "destructive
criticism" while later Catholic scholars look at Luther
with "interest and respect."

[2]The Encyclopedia of the Lutheran Church, s.v.
"Luther Research," by Harold J. Grimm.

as a sycophant of princes, and the radical sectaries
portrayed him as a "lost Moses" who had led the children of Israel out of Egypt and into the wilderness
to die. Before the contemporary biographer casts
Luther in the role of a rebel, a nationalist, or a
prophet, Bainton maintains that he must first attempt
to understand Luther the man. One will not go far
toward understanding Luther unless he initially recognizes that above all else Luther was a man of religion.[1]

        This approach forms the thesis of Bainton's
Luther writings. He states:

        Luther is to be interpreted above all else
        as a man of religion and his break with the Roman
        Church cannot be accounted for either on economic
        or ethical grounds. Luther himself said that he
        was to be distinguished from previous reformers
        in that they attacked the life whereas he attacked
        the doctrine.[2]

Although many other factors entered into Luther's life,
the proper starting point to understand him is his religious quest. Other biographers share Bainton's
approach to Luther from this perspective. For example,
Ritter writes: "Luther is a religious prophet . . . .
Only those who view Luther in this light can hope to
arrive at any understanding of his essential character."[3]

---

        [1]Roland H. Bainton, Here I Stand: A Life of
Martin Luther (New York: Abingdon-Cokesbury Press,
1950), p. 22.

        [2]Roland H. Bainton, "Luther in a Capsule,"
Bulletin of the American Congregational Association
3 (May 1952): 3.

        [3]Gerhard Ritter, Luther: His Life and Work,
trans. John Riches (New York: Harper and Row, 1959),
p. 7.

Todd states that the "basic simplicity of Luther's insight is only fully intelligible in its religious
context."[1]

Luther broke with the Church, contends Bainton, because the problem of his personal salvation
obsessed him. He rebelled only because he declared
the Church's way of salvation was erroneous. Hence
his motivation was primarily religious. This thesis
appears throughout Here I Stand. For example, in
discussing The Babylonian Captivity of the Church
Bainton writes: "Luther did not attack the mass in
order to undermine the priests. His concerns were
always primarily religious and only incidentally
ecclesiastical or sociological."[2] Likewise in delineating Luther's attitude toward the Jews (near the
end of Luther's life) Bainton states, "His position
was entirely religious and in no respect racial."[3]

The nature of Luther's religious quest forms
the structure in which Bainton narrates the reformer's
life. His faith grew out of the Hebraic tradition in
Christian thought. Luther was a man

> entranced by the song of angels, stunned by the
> wrath of God, speechless before the wonder of
> creation, lyrical over the divine mercy, a man
> aflame with God. For such a person there was
> no question which mattered much save this: How
> do I stand before God?[4]

The ultimate problem was always God and man's relationship to Him. This is why Bainton finds it fallacious

---

[1]John M. Todd, Martin Luther: A Biographical
Study (Westminster, Md.: Newman Press, 1965), p. xviii.

[2]Bainton, Here I Stand, p. 138.

[3]Ibid., p. 379.

[4]Ibid., p. 216.

to ask if Luther was a democrat, an aristocrat, or an
autocrat; for Luther the chief end of man was religion
and all else was peripheral. The summation of Luther's
religious principles resides in the proposition that
religion is paramount, that Christianity is the one
true religion, and that man apprehends God by faith
channeled through Scripture, preaching, and sacrament.[1]

The distinctiveness of Luther's religion, asserts Bainton, lies in his recovery of the historical
element in Christianity. Although Luther imbibed
medieval Catholic mysticism, he rejected the mystics'
endeavor to denude history of all temporal significance.
For him, Christianity spoke of God's active participation within history in the experiences of Old Testament patriarchs and prophets as well as in Christ's
suffering on the cross. It was this understanding of
the historicity of Christianity which nurtured the
seeds of the Reformation.[2]

The appropriation of this concept of Christianity in Luther's own life led not to a complex system of theology but rather to a simple, childlike
faith in God. Herein is a notable motif in Bainton's

---

[1]Ibid., pp. 216, 225.

[2]Roland H. Bainton, "The Problem of Authority
in the Age of the Reformation," in Luther, Erasmus and
the Reformation: A Catholic-Protestant Reappraisal, ed.
John C. Olin, James D. Smart, and Robert E. McNally
(New York: Fordham University Press, 1969), p. 23;
Roland H. Bainton, "The Bible and the Reformation," in
Five Essays on the Bible: Papers Read at the 1960 Annual Meeting of the American Council of Learned Societies (New York: American Council of Learned Societies,
1960), p. 22.

treatment of Luther's religion. Bainton writes that

> Luther found himself a child with his children
> and even a pupil of his bairns. Before God he
> was no more than they, and with the same simpli-
> city and trust he must come into the presence
> of the Heavenly Father.[1]

Bainton extracts statements from Luther on birds, dogs,
and babies. These statements depict a perspective of
Luther's faith which Bainton emphasizes, viz., that
birds, dogs, and babies display a simple and unsophis-
ticated faith which Luther applied to his own life.

The simplicity of Luther's faith, the earnest-
ness of his quest, and the profundity of his theology
emerged from another significant characteristic of his
religious endeavor. Bainton terms this significant
characteristic the *Anfechtungen* of Luther's faith, a
term which Luther himself used to describe his spiritual struggles.

In Here I Stand Bainton defines the import of
the term *Anfechtung*. He states:

> Creatureliness and imperfection alike oppressed
> him. Toward God he was at once attracted and
> repelled . . . . Before God the high and God the
> holy Luther was stupified. For such an experi-
> ence he had a word which has as much right to
> be carried over into English as *Blitzkrieg*. The
> word he used was *Anfechtung*, for which there is
> no English equivalent. It may be a trial sent
> by God to test man, or an assault by the Devil
> to destroy man. It is all the doubt, turmoil,
> pang, tremor, panic, despair, desolation, and
> desperation which invade the spirit of man.[2]

---

[1] Roland H. Bainton, "Luther on Birds, Dogs,
and Babies," in Studies on the Reformation, Collected
Papers in Church History, series 2 (Boston: Beacon
Press, 1963), p. 74.

[2] Bainton, Here I Stand, p. 42.

C. Warren Hovland offers a more succinct interpretation of *Anfechtung*, stating that it is "the terror
the individual feels in the moment he is confronted
with some dark aspect of God."[1] Most scholars interpret this term in ways which revolve around inner
conflict. Trials, temptations, assault, perplexity,
and doubt are among the translations generally accepted for *Anfechtungen*.

In the writings of Bainton this distinctive
feature of Luther's religious life forms a central
theme of interpretation. Hovland, a student of Bainton at Yale, states that Bainton first introduced
him to "the centrality of the term [*Anfechtung*] in
Luther's thought . . . ."[2] Bainton states that his
own interest in Luther's struggle for faith is not
merely to determine the historical chronology of his
religious quest. He asks, "How was it that Luther,
despite his travailing of spirit, could be so tremen-
dous in his faith, so incredible in his courage, so
astounding in his output?"[3] The answer to this lies
in Bainton's contention that the results of Luther's
Anfechtungen clearly marked his development as a man,
as a theologian, and as a reformer.

---

[1] C. Warren Hovland, "*Anfechtung* in Luther's
Biblical Exegesis," in Reformation Studies: Essays
in Honor of Roland H. Bainton, ed. Franklin H. Littell (Richmond, Va.: John Knox Press, 1962), p. 48.

[2] Hovland, "Luther's Biblical Exegesis," p. 46.

[3] Roland H. Bainton, "Luther's Struggle for
Faith," in Studies on the Reformation, Collected Papers in Church History, vol. 2 (Boston: Beacon Press,
1963), p. 13.

Bainton is not necessarily unique in the employment of this approach to Luther. Most contemporary Luther scholars give appropriate attention to
Luther's struggles, and several prominent scholars
interpret his *Anfechtungen* as a significant theme in
his religion. Grimm maintains that "Luther was a
man of conflicts. The solution of these conflicts is
the story of his development as a reformer."[1] Likewise Lau asserts the prominence of this aspect of
Luther. He states: "That the spiritual assaults
(*Anfechtungen*) of Luther are extremely important for
the understanding of his whole personality, his will
and his thought, is not only a passing opinion but
an unassailable fact."[2] In the biographies of Todd
and Ritter the theme of Luther's struggles for faith
finds a significant place.[3]

A traditional Catholic interpretation found
in Grisar's work accepts the fact of Luther's inner
conflicts but interprets the phenomenon as a patho-
logical manifestation rather than a religious quest.
In contrast, the Catholic scholar Joseph Lortz interprets Luther's *Anfechtungen* as a basic clue to the
understanding of his faith. The English scholar
Gordon Rupp likewise interprets Luther's theological

---

[1]Harold J. Grimm, "Luther's Inner Conflict:
A Psychological Interpretation," Church History 4
(September 1935): 186.

[2]Lau, Luther, p. 15.

[3]Todd, Luther, p. 22; Ritter, Luther, pp.
40-41.

development along the lines of *Anfechtungen*, calling
this struggle the "good fight of faith."[1]

Bainton maintains that the content of Luther's
Anfechtungen was always the same: the loss of faith
that God is good and that he is good "to me." Luther
so internalized and personalized religion that his
struggle took on the nature of a man wrestling with
God. Luther agonized over his own salvation. His
anguish left him without peace of mind. He questioned
the justice of God as well as the graciousness of God.
Bainton piquantly describes the content of Luther's
travail, stating:

> Despair invaded Luther's spirit. Panic swept
> over him. He trembled at the rustling of a wind-
> blown leaf. Prayer afforded no surcease, for the
> tempter was always at hand insinuating doubts.
> Of what avail is prayer when addressed by man who
> is dust, ashes, and full of sin to a God who is
> holy, majestic, and devastating?[2]

Paul Althaus writes that for Luther theological thinking did not occur apart from doubt and temptation.
Faith rather was grasped within the framework of *Anfechtung*. To believe demanded that Luther live in
constant contradiction. In this same vein, Schwiebert
proposes that the content of Luther's struggles arose

---

[1]Hartmann Grisar, <u>Martin Luther: His Life</u>
and Work, 2d ed.. (New York: AMS Press, 1971), pp.
40-41, 99; Lortz, pp. 10, 20; Gordon Rupp, <u>Luther's</u>
<u>Progress to the Diet of Worms</u> (London: S.C.M. Press,
1951; reprint ed., New York: Harper and Row Publishers, 1964), pp. 73, 44-47.

[2]Roland H. Bainton, <u>The Reformation of the</u>
<u>Sixteenth Century</u> (Boston: Beacon Press, 1952), p.
33.

from his endeavor to render an angry God gracious to
him.[1]

    Bainton extracts from Luther's life three
"storms" which overtook him in his early years: first,
the events surrounding Luther's entering the monastery; second, the saying of his first mass; and third,
the evangelical experience in the tower. Bainton
interprets these three critical events as highly
significant in the religious development of Luther.
Biographers of Luther generally deal in some measure
with these events, but Bainton's treatment of them
appears distinctive. By proposing a continuity to
Luther's struggles through each of these events, Bainton provides a trenchant interpretive approach.

    The opening lines of Here I Stand recount the
episode in Luther's life when he encountered a storm
on the road near Stotternheim. The sudden bolt of
lightning precipitated Luther's vow to become a monk.
Bainton sees this as a vital turning point in Luther's
career. The vow to become a monk was unpremeditated
but not unprepared. For some time as a young man
Luther had struggled with the meaning of existence.
His depression over the prospect of death and his intense fear of God were acute but by no means unusual
for a medieval man. Luther knew the way to heal his
sick soul. He entered the monastery. Bainton thus
interprets the vow to become a monk as arising from
the Anfechtungen of the young Luther.

---

[1]Paul Althaus, The Theology of Martin Luther,
trans. Robert C. Schultz (Philadelphia: Fortress Press,
1963), p. 33; Schwiebert, Luther, p. 152.

[2]Bainton, Here I Stand, p. 21.

The step which Luther took to save his soul
marks the beginning of Luther's quest which ultimately
led to the break with Rome. Bainton writes:

> The man who thus called upon a saint was
> later to repudiate the cult of saints. He who
> vowed to become a monk was later to renounce
> monasticism. A loyal son of the Church, he was
> later to shatter the structure of medieval Catho-
> licism. A devoted servant of the pope he was
> later to identify the popes with Antichrist.[1]

The meaning of Luther's entrance into the monastery
lies in the fact that the great revolt against the
medieval Church emanated from the desperate attempts
of a struggling young man to find salvation through
the means which the Church provided.

Schwiebert agrees with Bainton that Luther
had contemplated entering the monastery for some time.
The storm acted simply as a catalyst to bring about
an emotional decision. He entered the monastery determined to live the life of a pious monk. Two divergent perspectives concerning Luther's vow emerge
in the biographies of Ritter and Grisar. Ritter attributes Luther's decision to "religious fear whose
relationship to primitive folk-religion [in Germany]
. . . has only recently been fully explained."[2] For
Grisar the determinative factor was the shock of the
lightning bolt which dealt a permanent blow to Luther's
physical condition. He says, "When the lightning
struck, he sustained a terrible nervous shock, which

---

[1]Bainton, Here I Stand, p. 21.

[2]Ritter, Luther, p. 35.

must have profoundly affected his future."[1] Todd
questions the assertion that anguish and doubt led
Luther to monasticism. Rather it was an act of
courageous faith emanating from an inner religious
determination. Rupp draws no conclusion; he states
that one can have no certainty as to the "inward state
of his mind" which prompted Luther's decision.[2]

Bainton finds the encounter with the storm
near Stotternheim to be incidental when compared to
the brooding storm in Luther's soul. The *Anfechtungen*
of young Luther led him at that point to find spiritual shelter in the monastic life.

Luther's entrance into the monastery brought
him a period of inner tranquility and composure. He
gave himself to this new life because it promised him
the surest way of salvation. He might have continued
in this life of prayer and meditation, writes Bainton, "had he not been overtaken by another storm, this
time of the spirit. The occasion was the saying of
his first mass."[3]

Not only the presence of his father Hans Luther
but also the unique presence of God at the mass overpowered Luther and left him limp and trembling. Bainton states that the terror of the holy and the horror

---

[1]Grisar, Luther, p. 40. Grisar appears to
stress the results of the storm on Luther's nerves.
This incident, claims Grisar, had much to do with
Luther's psychological problems for the remainder
of his life.

[2]Todd, Luther, pp. 26, 32; Rupp, Luther's
Progress, p. 15.

[3]Bainton, Here I Stand, p. 39.

of infinitude smote him like a new lightning bolt
from heaven. He suffered from the savage's fear of
the malevolent diety. He trembled at the recognition
of his own unworthiness. The *Anfechtung* of his soul
again overtook Luther. Todd and Lau likewise affirm
that the intense struggles which characterized the
young Luther emerged again at his first mass and precipitated an inner breakdown.[1]

This event in Luther's experience inaugurated
a new stage in his struggles. Bainton states:

> The day which began with the ringing of the
> cloister chime and the psalm "O sing unto the
> Lord a new song" ended with the horror of the
> Holy and doubt whether the first thunderstorm
> had been a vision of God or an apparition of
> Satan.[2]

This upheaval of Luther's soul prompted the forthcom-
ing *Anfechtungen* which would end in his abandonment
of the cowl.

The religious conflicts set in motion by the
"second storm" persisted for several years in the
monastery. In Bainton's interpretation, there is no
precise delineation of their course. The culmina-
tion of Luther's struggles in the monastery was his
evangelical experience. Scholars such as Bainton
point out that at a critical point in Luther's monastic years he arrived at a new understanding of salvation. This understanding of salvation initially
came during Luther's study in an upstairs room in
the monastery at Wittenberg. Meditating on the
twenty-second Psalm, Luther "discovered" the salvation of God effected by Christ's sufferings. From

---

[1]Todd, Luther, p. 37; Lau, Luther, p. 54.

[2]Bainton, Here I Stand, p. 44.

this new insight Luther formulated a doctrine of salvation which came into conflict with the teachings
of the Church of Rome. The discovery in the monastery
room is termed by scholars as "the evangelical experience" or as the *Turmerlebnis* (the "tower experience"). Bainton maintains that the *Anfechtungen* in
the monastery did not mount "in unbroken crescendo"
to a single crisis. Instead Luther passed through a
series of crises which culminated in the *Turmerlebnis*.
These crises arose from his probing of every available resource in medieval Catolicism for "assuaging
the anguish of a spirit alienated from God."[1]

Bainton narrates Luther's struggles through
the way of self-help, the merits of the saints, confession, and mysticism. The climax of this quest led
to the final and most devastating doubt: perhaps not
even God himself is just. It was at this point that
Staupitz informed Luther that he should study for
his doctorate and become a preacher. This was a
crucial alteration for Luther, as Bainton states:

> The studies [for his doctorate] proved to be for
> Luther the Damascus road. The third great reli-
> gious crisis which resolved his turmoil was as
> the still small voice compared to the earthquake
> of the first upheaval in the thunderstorm . . .
> and the fire of the second tremor which consumed
> him at the saying of his first mass.[2]

But the third crisis was decisive; Luther had
now turned to the Scriptures. Bainton interprets the
tower experience as being the result of Luther's discovery that Christ himself had *Anfechtungen*. Luther

---

[1] Ibid., pp. 53-4.

[2] Ibid., p. 60.

found that in some inexplicable way God reconciled the
world to Himself in the utter desolation of the for-
saken Christ. For Luther, the judge upon the rainbow
became the derelict on the cross. Luther came to a
new view of God and Christ. As no one before him in
more than a thousand years, Luther "sensed the import
of the miracle of divine judgment."[1]

Biographies of Luther tend to approach the
Turmerlebnis from the perspective of their own historiographical partiality. Perhaps no single event
in Luther's life precipitates more diverse treatments
than the tower experience. For example Bainton, Todd,
Lau, and Ritter interpret the experience from the perspective of Luther's struggle of the soul with medieval religion.[2] Schwiebert places the experience
within a larger context. Whereas Bainton interprets
Luther's *Anfechtungen* in the monastery as the struggles of an individual with God, Schwiebert finds in
these struggles the anguish "of the whole Germanic
mind." The gulf between the Germanic and Latin minds
had not been bridged by medieval religion. Luther
responded to the complexity of medieval Catholicism
with the Germanic proclivity toward personal and individual experience.[3] The experience was no new

---

[1]Bainton, The Reformation, p. 34.

[2]Bainton, Here I Stand, pp. 62-3; Todd, Luther,
p. 78; Lau, Luther, p. 65; Ritter, Luther, p. 50.

[3]Schwiebert, Luther, p. 157. Schwiebert explains
the dilemma by stating (on page 157): "The Roman mechaniza-
tion of the whole sacramental system, making it the sole
source of the means of grace, seemed strange to a people
who felt they could go directly to their God."

discovery in Grisar's explanation, but was rather a
deviation from the Church which resulted in further
self-delusion. Rupp denies that the tower experience
was an evangelical conversion and claims that historians read too much into this experience.[1] Nevertheless,
most historians find, as does Bainton, a significant
landmark in the *Turmerlebnis*.

The *Anfechtungen* which epitomized Luther's
religion in the monastery did not subside with his
discovery of a new view of God and Christ. Bainton
maintains that Luther never fully resolved the crises
of his faith, and that he agonized in his religious
quest throughout his life.[2]

Bainton's interpretation of the three "storms"
of Luther's life reflects the continuity provided by
the phenomena of religious struggles. A unique interpretation of Luther evidences itself in Bainton's
correlating the events of the entrance into the monastery, the first mass, and the tower experience. In
Here I Stand these three events stand out as watershed experiences in Luther's life. Likewise, these
events reflect the recurring nature of Luther's
spiritual trials. Ultimately these events signify
Luther's progressive religious development toward the

---

[1]Grisar, Luther, p. 108; Rupp, Luther's Progress, p. 38.

[2]This point made by Bainton merits further
consideration. Bainton uses the motif of *Anfechtungen*
as an interpretive tool by which he relates the "young"
and the "mature" Luther. He finds a continuity throughout Luther's life in this facet of his religion. A
thorough discussion of this continuity appears in another section of this chapter.

confrontation with the Church of Rome and his subsequent formation of an evangelical faith.

     The persistence of Luther's inner conflicts
leads many interpreters to propose diverse explana-
tions of his *Anfechtungen*. In his various Luther
writings Bainton assesses the various schools of
thought on this significant facet of Luther's life and
defends his thesis that Luther's struggles were theological in origin.

     Bainton concedes that Luther's moods were
highly erratic and evoke scholarly curiosity as to
their explanation. Some interpreters find a correlation between Luther's struggles and his physical ail-
ments, e.g., glandular and gastric deficiencies. This
correlation produces very slight success in understanding Luther, and Bainton holds that physical de-
bilitation was more the effect rather than the cause
of Luther's anguish. Another school of interpretation notes a correlation between the *Anfechtungen* and
external experiences such as the thunderstorm at Stotternheim or the Peasants' War. There is some correlation between the two in Luther's experience yet Bainton claims that the relationship is not sufficient to
understand the *Anfechtungen*. A third major perspective
perceives Luther's struggles as brought on by psychological disorder. Bainton strongly disapproves of
this perspective, yet because of the prevalence of
this interpretation Bainton deals more fully with this
school of thought than with any other.[1]

     The intensity and frequency of Luther's *An-
fechtungen* throughout his life lead Bainton to maintain

---

[1]Bainton, "Luther's Struggle," p. 16.

that one cannot blithely dismiss the possibility of
abnormal psychology. The biography of Luther by Erik
Erikson popularized this interpretation, and Bainton
responds often and vigorously to Erikson's position.

Erikson contends that Luther was an "endan-
gered" young man who displayed a "syndrome of conflicts"
which modern psychiatry has learned to recognize.[1]
In Young Man Luther Erikson develops the position that
Luther suffered from an identity crisis as a youth
which precipitated much of his inner conflict. Erikson
states: "The need for devotion, then, is one aspect
of the identity crisis which we, as psychologists,
make responsible for all these tendencies and sus-
ceptibilities. The need for repudiation is another
aspect."[2] Luther's conversion was necessary so that
he could transfer his devotion from his father to God;
his need for repudiation emerged in his vitriolic de-
fiance of the Pope. Erikson traces Luther's development along the lines of his struggle for personal
identity and relates Luther's *Anfechtungen* to his
constant battle to achieve individual independence.[3]

Erikson summarizes the psychological development of Luther as follows: Young Luther, at the

---

[1]Erik Erikson, Young Man Luther: A Study in
Psychoanalysis and History (New York: W. W. Norton
and Company, 1958), p. 15.

[2]Ibid., p. 42.

[3]Ibid., pp. 47-8. Erikson tersely summarizes
this point on page 148 where he writes: "It seems to
me entirely probable that Martin's life at times approached what today we might call a borderline psychotic
state in a young man with prolonged adolescence and re-
awakened infantile conflicts."

end of a harsh childhood, experienced a severe identity
crisis for which he sought cure in the silence of the
monastery. In the silence of the monastery he became
"possessed" and consequently learned to speak a new
language, viz., *his* language. Able to speak for himself, Luther talked himself out of the monastery and
much of his country out of the Roman Church. He forged
for himself a new psychological awareness. In the end,
however, he still experienced the terrifying anxiety
of the soul.[1]

Bainton's response to psychological interpretations of Luther's struggles is sharply critical.
He agrees that the historian should employ methods of
psychiatry. Bainton writes, "The claim is valid that
whatever casts light upon the present should be thrown
upon the past."[2] Yet although the use of psychiatry
to understand men and movements of the past is a valid
historical approach, it remains replete with difficulties. The historian cannot summon the deceased for
examination. Bainton aptly states his reservations at
this point when he writes, "There are . . . grave
difficulties in psychoanalyzing the dead."[3]

The central problem which Bainton finds in
Erikson's approach to Luther is the presuppositions
which Erikson brings to bear upon the interpretation
of the facts. Erikson portrays Luther's theological

---

[1]Ibid.

[2]Bainton, "Luther's Life," p. 87.

[3]Roland H. Bainton, "Interpretations of the
Reformation," in Studies on the Reformation, Collected
Papers in Church History, series 2 (Boston: Beacon
Press, 1963), p. 112.

development in terms of his struggle to achieve independence from his parents so that he might become a
person in his own right. Erikson's assessment of
Luther's theology, contends Bainton, reflects a pro-
jection of this struggle for identity upon the cosmos.
This explanation Bainton rejects completely.[1] Luther's
youth was normal except that he was extremely sensitive and subject to an oscillation of moods. Bainton
states:

> One cannot dismiss these states [of moodiness] as
> occasioned merely by adolescence since . . . simi-
> lar experiences continued throughout his adult
> years. Neither can one blithely write off the
> case as an example of manic depression, since the
> patient exhibited a prodigious and continuous
> capacity for work of a high order.[2]

Bainton sees no radical difference between the *Anfechtungen* of the young Luther and the struggles of the
mature Luther. Consequently he finds no validity in
the thesis that Luther's struggles were a progression
toward psychological independence.

Most contemporary Luther scholars reject a
narrowly defined psychological interpretation of Luther.
Todd maintains that the pure psychological perspective
appeals only to those of a completely positivist position in which religion plays no part. Todd assumes
that the psychological factor comprises but one element

---

[1]Heinrich Bornkamm agrees with Bainton on this
point. Bornkamm argues that Luther's father image
should not be isolated from other theological concerns.
See Heinrich Bornkamm, "Luther und sein Vater,"
Zeitschrift für Theologie und Kirche 66 (1969): 38-
61.

[2]Bainton, Here I Stand, p. 28.

in the historian's approach to Luther. The severity
and abnormality of Luther's childhood are a misinter-
pretation of the sources, according to Schwiebert and
Green. There is no real historical evidence to sub-
stantiate the psychological interpretation. Likewise
Lau finds in Luther's early development no unusual
experiences which would precipitate an abnormal psychological condition in Luther.[1]

Bainton proposes a further criticism of the
psychological interpretation of Luther's inner conflict. Such a perspective, he contends, necessarily
must misuse the sources of Luther's early life. The
material for Luther's later life is overwhelmingly
abundant yet for the young Luther sources are "dis-
concertingly slight." The difficulty of psychoanalyzing the young Luther is almost insurmountable because of the dearth of evidence. What little material
there is comes from the mature Luther after an interval
of thirty years, and this material is often second-hand
by virtue of its appearance in the *Tischreden*.[2] The
analyst must therefore build his case on three or four
remarks of the aged Luther. To establish such a position from scanty evidence the psychiatrist will "bridge
lacunae with conjecture." Bainton charges that one

[1]Todd, Luther, pp. 5, 50; Schwiebert, Luther,
p. 109; V. H. H. Green, Luther and the Reformation (New
York: Capricorn Books, 1964), p. 28; Lau, Luther, p. 33.

[2]Roland H. Bainton, "Psychiatry and History: An
Examination of Erikson's Young Man Luther," in Psychohistory and Religion: The Case of "Young Man Luther," ed.
Roger A. Johnson (Philadelphia: Fortress Press, 1977),
p. 19; Bainton, "Luther's Life," p. 91.

"who constructs a pyramid of conjectures may be compared to God who made the world out of nothing."[1]
Rupp concurs with Bainton on this point by claiming
that the psychiatrist can make his point only by
abusing the evidence.[2]

In rejecting the psychological view Bainton
proposes that Luther's difficulties arose not from the
experiences of youth but rather from medieval religion.
Medieval religion produced tensions in Luther's soul
by playing alternately on fear and hope. Luther was
attracted to and repelled by God and ultimately came
to a new understanding of religion in order to calm
this tension.[3] Since Bainton's approach to Luther is
from the vantage point of the reformer's religious
development, it follows that Bainton would assume such
a position. As a man of religion Luther plunged into
periods of deep depression because of the inconsistencies of his inherited religion. In order to com-
pensate for these inconsistencies Luther finally rejected much of medieval religion. Ritter and Schwiebert agree with this explanation of the source of
Luther's *Anfechtungen* as does Lortz who terms the factors in medieval Catholicism against which Luther rebelled as "sub-Christian."[4]

---

[1]Bainton, "Psychiatry and History," p. 20.

[2]Rupp, Luther's Progress, p. 31.

[3]Bainton, "Luther in a Capsule," p. 4; Bainton, Here I Stand, p. 28.

[4]Ritter, Luther, pp. 21-2; Schwiebert, Luther,
p. 157; Lortz, "Luther's Intellectual Style," p. 33.
See also Joseph Lortz, "Reformatorisch und Katholisch
beim jungen Luther (1518-1519)" in Humanitas-Christiani-
tas: Walther V. Loewenisch zum 65. Geburtstag, ed. K.
Beyschlag, G. Maron, and E. Wölfel (Wittenberg: Luther,
1968), pp. 47-62.

By insisting that Luther's inner anguish originated in the problems of medieval Catholicism, Bainton presupposes a certain interpretation of medieval
religion. The medieval Christian, contends Bainton,
faced uncertainty as to his own standing before God
and as to his own future destiny. This particular
interpretation receives both popular and scholarly
treatment. Some scholars, however, question the validity of this interpretation.

For example, Steven E. Ozment claims that the
interpretation of medieval religion held by scholars
such as Bainton oversimplifies the religion of both
the Middle Ages and the Reformation. Ozment finds
that Luther departed from medieval thought only in the
appropriation of "by faith alone" to the tensions inherent in medieval religion.[1] Bainton states that
Luther came to a new view of God and Christ and thus
broke from late medieval religion. Ozment see an affinity between Luther's theology and that of medieval
mysticism.[2] Bainton contends that Luther's theology

[1]Steven E. Ozment, "Homo Viator: Luther and
Late Medieval Theology," in The Reformation in Medieval Perspective, ed. Steven E. Ozment (Chicago: Quad-
rangle Books, 1971), pp. 142-54. For an excellent
treatment of Luther and late medieval thought see Steven E. Ozmen, "Luther and the Late Middle Ages: The
Formation of Reformation Thought" in Transition and Revolution: Problems and Issues of European Renaissance
and Reformation History, ed. Robert Kingdon (Minneapolis:
Burgess Publishing Co., 1974), pp. 109-152.

[2]Heiko Oberman disagrees with both Bainton and
Ozment. Oberman argues that mysticism was a part of
Luther's understanding of the Gospel, and his relation-
ship to late medieval mysticism was "yes and no." See
Heiko A. Oberman, "Simil gemitus et raptus: Luther und

recaptured the vitality of primitive Christian life,
hence the affinity for Bainton is between Luther's experience and that of the first century church.

Bainton concludes his critique of the psychological interpretation by posing the thesis that
Luther's theological development "might have been just
the same if he had been left an orphan in infancy."[1]
Lau agrees: "The explanation of God's personal guidance, which naturally has no 'scientific' interpretation, remains for a Christian still the most illumina-
ting and most natural explanation."[2] Bainton maintains
that a psychoanalyst cannot envision the possibility
that Luther's motivation was anything except egocen-
tricity. Yet the very nature of Luther's dark night
of the soul is that the *Anfechtungen* arise inexplicably.
The source of Luther's struggles eludes the careful
historian. One must ultimately recognize that Luther
began with the religion and theology of his medieval
culture and there discovered difficulties to which
others were not similarly sensitive.[3]

The dominant approach which Bainton employs
in his interpretation of Luther centers around Luther's
religious consciousness. Bainton writes, "Luther was
an eternal Jacob, forever wrestling with the angel and

---

die Mystik" in The Church, Mysticism, Sanctification
and the Natural in Luther's Thought: Lectures Presented to the Third International Congress on Luther
Research, ed. I. Asheim (Philadelphia: Fortress Press,
1967), pp. 20-59.

[1]Bainton, "Luther's Life," p. 92.

[2]Lau, Luther, p. 55.

[3]Bainton, "Luther's Struggle," p. 18.

forever wresting a blessing."[1]   Bainton perceives the
importance of the *Anfechtungen* of Luther in that Luther
himself felt that they were important.   Luther verged
on saying that his inner conflicts were a mode of divine
revelation.   Bainton argues that those whose religious
nature predisposes them to fall into despondency and
rise into ecstacy may view reality from a perspective
unknown to most people.   It is a true perspective, and
when "the religious object has been once so viewed,
others less sensitive will be able to look from a new
vantage point and testify that the insight is valid."[2]
Such was the case for Luther according to Bainton.   The
Anfechtungen of his entire life forged a new perspective
on religion and on life; consequently, Luther's personal
struggle for faith is critical for understanding the
reformer.

       Bainton illustrates Luther's struggles by
placing him within the context of others who similarly
contended earnestly for their faith.   He writes:

> If one would discover parallels to Luther as the
> wrestler with the Lord, then one must turn to
> Paul the Jew, Augustine the Latin, Pascal the
> Frenchman, Kierkegaard the Dane, Unamuno the
> Spaniard, Dostoevski the Russian, Bunyan the
> Englishman, and Edwards the American.[3]

Thus one approaches Luther properly, maintains Bainton,
only when one approaches him through the dark night of
his soul.   The chief interest of Bainton in Here I
Stand is to understand the religious nature of Luther.
Bainton's thoroughgoing interpretation of *Anfechtungen*

---

     [1]Bainton, "Our Debt to Luther," Christian Cen-
tury 63 (23 October 1946): 1278.

     [2]Bainton, Here I Stand, p. 361.

     [3]Ibid., p. 385.

provides a perceptive and lucid analysis of the reformer's religious experience. Likewise Bainton's
treatment of the *Anfechtungen* places him squarely in
the tradition of Luther research which emanates from
Holl.

The Personal Dimension of Luther

The treatment of the personal dimension of
Luther's life reveals another distinctive element in
Bainton's approach to Luther. He presents Luther as
an extraordinarily gifted, unusually productive,
toweringly powerful personality. Yet he also presents
Luther as a very simple, approachable, and sensitive
individual. Acquiescing with Bainton in this approach,
Rupp provides the following description of Luther:

> Nobody ever wore his heart more on his sleeve
> than Luther, and there for all to see are his fun
> and tenderness, his deep love of his family and
> his home, his mighty prayers, and the vulgarity
> which prevents us thinking of him as some stained-
> glass figure, or cloying his memory with sickly
> romanticism.[1]

This is the picture of Luther which emerges in Bainton's
writings.

The examination of Bainton's treatment of the
personal dimension of Luther centers around three
emphases: 1) the "whole life" approach to Luther in
which Bainton correlates the "young" and the "mature"
Luther, 2) the domestic life of Luther, and 3) the
pastoral life of Luther.

In Here I Stand Bainton attempts to set forth
a development of Luther's entire life. The biographers
in the twentieth century who concentrate on the early
years of Luther generally deal with the period of time

---

[1] Rupp, Luther's Progress, p. 106.

from Luther's childhood to the Diet of Worms. Bainton's
study comprises a departure. Grimm remarks that one
significant aspect of Here I Stand is its attempt to
relate the young Luther to the mature Luther. Moreover, Bainton's work points out that little has been
done in this century toward developing an understanding of the Luther of 1530-1546.[1]

Bainton structures his Luther biography in a
framework inclusive of the development of the reformer
from his entrance into the monastery to the time of
his death. Luther's childhood bears examination only
for the purpose of explaining his decision to become
a monk.[2] Bainton interprets Luther's religious development through the monastic years, the break with Rome,
and the formation of the evangelical faith. He depicts Luther's achievements of reform as they progressed through the years of his maturity. Bainton
perceives a continuity throughout Luther's life by
which he unites the young and the mature Luther.

The synthesizing element which Bainton uses
to correlate Luther's entire life is the phenomenon
of *Anfechtung*. Bainton contends that the conflicts
and travailings of Luther for his faith were lifelong.
Some scholars, he points out, do not grant this continuity. They grant that Luther experienced continuous
depressions, but the character of these depressions
altered after the evangelical discovery in 1513.

---

[1]Harold J. Grimm, "Luther Research Since
1920," The Journal of Modern History 32 (June 1960):
118.

[2]Bainton, Here I Stand, p. 22. Here Bainton
states: "Childhood and youth will be drawn upon only
to explain the entry into the monastery."

Bainton recognizes that there is a serious problem in Luther interpretation in explaining the continuation of *Anfechtungen* after 1513. Heinrich Boehmer asserts that the struggles of Luther's later years differ sharply from those of his earlier years. The first disturbances related to his faith, contends Boehmer, while the latter disturbances related to his profession. Boehmer argues that as a young man Luther struggled with "spiritual temptations," yet after 1513 he suffered primarily from "worry over his work, grief over the frivolity and moral shortcomings of the evangelical princes and lords, and disillusionment over the ingratitude and sensuality of the masses."[1]

This distinction has no validity in Bainton's view. He says that the "sharp differentiation between the *Glaubensanfechtungen* of the early period and the *Berufsanfechtungen* of the latter appears to me thoroughly unsound."[2] Luther experienced both types of conflicts throughout his life. Luther was never liberated from the struggle for his faith. Hovland agrees with Bainton in this judgment, maintaining that the struggle for faith plagued him to the very last year of his life.[3] Bainton states his position clearly as follows:

> We cannot escape the plain fact that Luther's evangelical experiences of 1513 did not clear up his religious difficulties for the remainder of his days. The understanding of the text, "The just shall live by faith," which had come to him as a

---

[1]Heinrich Boehmer, Road to Reformation: Martin Luther to the Year 1521, trans. John W. Doberstein and Theodore G. Tappert (Philadelphia: Muhlenberg Press, 1946), p. 93.

[2]Bainton, "Luther's Life," p. 76.

[3]Hovland, "Luther's Biblical Exegesis," p. 46.

flash on the Damascus road, left no tangible relic
to which one could return at will.[1]
The writings of Luther in his later years make it
abundantly clear that the doubts of his youth continued
to haunt him.

    Bainton demonstrates the continuity of strug-
gles throughout Luther's life by depicting the ever-
present nature of anxiety in the reformer. For example he contends that Luther experienced melancholia
before his entrance into the monastery and at different intervals during his monastic years. Luther's
Ninety-Five Theses contained the "cries of a wrestler
in the night watches." During his stay at the Wartburg Castle Luther battled spiritual unrest, and
after his return to Wittenberg one finds Luther dealing again with *Anfechtungen*. Even in his final years
Luther faced inner turmoil. Bainton asserts that the
mature Luther's sermons on all the troubled spirits
in the Bible are essentially autobiographical.[2] Bainton concludes that Luther "was not suffered like Jacob
to escape with only one wrestling with the angel and
much of the vehemence of Luther's polemic arose from
the struggle to convince himself."[3]

    The persistence of spiritual struggles emerges
as the dominant method by which he relates the young
Luther to the mature Luther, thus providing a continuity
to the reformer's life. Although he proposes continuity to Luther's religious life, Bainton does see
a dichotomy between the young and mature Luther.

[1]Bainton, "Luther's Struggle," p. 14.

[2]Bainton, Here I Stand, pp. 83, 194, 220;
Bainton, "Luther's Struggle," p. 15.

[3]Bainton, "Luther's Life," p. 77.

The first phase of Luther's life grew out of
his search for a gracious God which resulted in a break
with Rome. The second phase of his life began when
other reformers emerged and situations developed which
placed Luther in a position of resisting petrified
tradition on one hand and unbridled innovation on the
other.[1] Yet Bainton is inconsistent in his attempt to
distinguish a point which divides these two phases of
Luther's life. In The Age of Reformation he states
that the condemnation at Worms divides Luther's career.
In Christendom and Here I Stand he contends that Luther's return to Wittenberg from the Wartburg marks
a division in Luther's career.[2] Despite variations in
dating Bainton divides Luther's life into the initial
period of revolt from Rome and the final period of
the development of the evangelical faith.

Other biographers generally note a dichotomy
in Luther's career along the lines which Bainton pursues, yet the point of division evokes disagreement.
Schwiebert sees a watershed event in the Leipzig Debate, but also notes that a division could be the
writing of the Augsburg Confession. Although Todd
claims that it is impossible to pinpoint any event as
a cleavage in Luther's career, he does give much attention to Luther's meeting with Cajetan as a significant

---

[1]The Encyclopedia of the Lutheran Church,
s.v. "Luther," by Roland H. Bainton.

[2]Roland H. Bainton, The Age of the Reforma-
tion (Princeton, N.J.: Van Nostrand, 1956), p. 35;
Roland H. Bainton, Christendom: A Short History of
Christianity and Its Impact on Western Civilization,
2 vols. (New York: Harper and Row, 1966), 2:22; and
Bainton, Here I Stand, p. 215.

event promoting division. Ritter considers the Reformation writings of 1520 as the break in Luther's
career, while Lau and Green choose the Diet of Worms
as the point of departure for the second phase of
Luther's life.[1] Some Luther scholars refuse to make
any such division in Luther's life (i.e., no "young"
and "mature" Luther) but instead lean toward interpreting Luther strictly along the lines of his theological development. For example, Kenneth Hagen
writes:

> Rather than trying to find in Luther an abrupt
> reversal from a "Catholic" position to a "Lu-
> theran" one, it would be better to say that
> Luther develops in a more organic way on par-
> ticular issues as the occasion and his exegeti-
> cal work demand.[2]

Bainton would agree that an organic development in
Luther's life did transpire, but he rejects the attempt
to interpret Luther exclusively along the lines of his
theological development apart from the historical
events of the sixteenth century. Bainton clearly
shows that Luther's theological development precipitated a break with Rome and thus demanded the formulation of an evangelical faith.

The final years of Luther's life from the
Augsburg Confession to his death usually receive little attention from biographers. Bainton indicates:
"There is a measure of justification for this comparative neglect because the last quarter of Luther's

[1]Schwiebert, Luther, pp. 282, 413, 437; Todd,
Luther, pp. 103, 151; Ritter, Luther, p. 99; Lau,
Luther, p. 92; and Green, Luther, p. 86.

[2]Kenneth G. Hagen, "Changes in the Understanding of Luther: The Development of the Young Luther," Theological Studies 29 (September 1968): 492-3.

life was neither determinative for his ideas nor crucial for his achievements."[1] His ideas were mature,
his church established, and his associates could continue the work which he began. In his final years
Luther became "prematurely an irascible old man, pet-
ulant, peevish, unrestrained, and at times positively
coarse."[2]

From these final years Bainton draws three
examples which demonstrate this judgment. He discusses Luther's approval of the bigamy of Philip of
Hesse, Luther's attitude toward the Anabaptists and
the Jews, and his polemics against the papists and
the emperor. Considering Luther's writings of this
period, Bainton finds substantial reasons for the
brevity of treatment given these years by biographers.
However, in defense of Luther, Bainton writes:

> Luther's later years are, however, by no
> means to be written off as the sputterings of a
> dying flame. If in his polemical tracts he was
> at times savage and coarse, in the works which
> constitute the real marrow of his life's endea-
> vor he grew constantly in artistic creativity.[3]

During this period Luther continued to improve his
biblical translation and he continued to develop his
religious and ethical principles. Likewise his sermons and biblical commentaries took on a rich quality.
Bainton chooses not to ignore this final chapter of
Luther's life, for these years epitomized the passion
as well as the piety which marked every phase of his
life.

---

[1] Bainton, <u>Here I Stand</u>, p. 373.

[2] Ibid.

[3] Ibid., p. 383.

Through the treatment of Luther's whole life
one observes a distinctiveness in Bainton's perspective on Luther. He unites the life of Luther with the
theme of *Anfechtungen*. He writes, "Faith was no pearl
to be mounted in a gold setting and gazed upon at
will. Faith was ever the object of an agonizing
search."[1] Bainton delineates the course of this search
in the life of Luther the rebel against Rome as well
as in the life of Luther the builder of the evangelical faith.

Another explicit direction taken by Bainton
in his portrait of Luther is the presentation of Luther's domestic life. Bainton deems this facet of
Luther's life important for the understanding of the
personal dimension of Luther. Many biographers frequently cast Luther in the role of reformer, theologian, and ethicist; however few scholars accentuate
the domestic relations of Luther. Bainton gives attention to this subject in order to provide a well-
balanced view of Luther. Todd also insists that such
a view of Luther demonstrates graphically his sensitivity, his openness, and his kindness.[2] Bainton's
attention to Luther's domestic life arises in part
from a broader interest which Bainton has in the historical aspects of the home, the family, marriage, and
women. Several journal articles and monographs by
Bainton exhibit this specific concern.[3]

[1]Bainton, "Luther's Struggle," p. 14.

[2]Todd, Luther, p. 239.

[3]See for examples of this the following works:
Roland H. Bainton, "Marriage and Love in Christian
History," Religion in Life 17 (Summer 1948): 391-403;

Bainton states that Luther's marriage was the
most unpremeditated and dramatic witness of his principles. If Luther could not reform all of Christendom,
"at any rate he could and did establish the Protestant
parsonage."[1]

According to Ritter the importance of his decision to marry is that it reflects a definite change
in Luther. Luther's marriage shows that the former
monk was settling into an earthly life, assuming responsibilities radically new for a medieval churchman.[2]
Bainton likewise stresses the change which marriage
brought to Luther. Yet Bainton argues that Luther's
views of marriage were not unique: "This whole picture [of marriage] was carried directly over from the
Middle Ages, in which Catholic sacramentalism and
agrarian society tended to make of marriage an institu-
tion for the perpetuation of families and the preserva-
tion of properties."[3] Luther knew little of romantic
love; his motivation for marrying Katherine von Bora
arose from less than amorous intentions.[4]

Roland H. Bainton, What Christianity Says About Sex,
Love and Marriage (New York: Association Press, 1957);
Roland H. Bainton, Women of the Reformation, 3 vols.
(Minneapolis: Augsburg Publishing House, 1971-77);
and Roland H. Bainton, The Office of the Minister's
Wife in New England (Boston: Harvard University, 1955).

[1]Bainton, Here I Stand, p. 286.

[2]Ritter, Luther, p. 173.

[3]Bainton, Here I Stand, p. 299.

[4]Ibid., p. 288. Here Bainton lists Luther's
three reasons for marrying: "to please his father,
to spite the pope and the Devil, and to seal his witness before martyrdom."

Bainton discerns a change in Luther's view of
marriage. In his early polemics, Luther reduced marriage
to the basest physical level. After his own marriage,
however, Luther viewed marriage in a different light,
referring to it as a "school for character." The
Church of the Middle Ages regarded the monastery as
the training ground of virtue and the surest way to
heaven. Luther rejected this path to salvation, but
believed in the value of the Christian virtues of patience, charity, and humility, which he believed would
develop in the "school for character."

Bainton interprets Luther as somewhat irre-
sponsible in family affairs, especially in the area of
financial duties. One point at which Luther was most
helpful was in his interest in gardening. Luther sup-
plied his family with fresh produce from his garden;
Green points out that Luther's love of gardening
emanated from his peasant-farmer heritage.[1] Although
Luther was far from ideal in many aspects of family
life, Bainton notes Luther's strength in his relation-
ships with Katie and with his children. Luther's love
for and dependence on Katie grew continually, and Bainton often accentuates the simple marital joy of their
companionship.[2]

One unusual perspective of Luther evolved
from his home life, viz., the writing of the *Tischreden*.
This collection of notes taken down by friends and
students presents a view of Luther which delights

---

[1]Green, Luther, p. 127.

[2]Bainton, Here I Stand, pp. 201-2; Roland H.
Bainton, Women of the Reformation in Germany and Italy
(Minneapolis: Augsburg Publishing House, 1971), pp. 29-30.

Bainton. "Luther ranged from the ineffable majesty
of God the Omnipotent to the frogs in the Elbe. Pigs,
popes, pregnancies, politics, and proverbs jostle one
another."[1] The personal dimension of Luther emerges
clearly in the Table Talks, depicting both the power
of his theology and the coarseness of his vulgarity.

    Bainton shows the tenderness and sensitivity
of Luther perhaps best in the brief narratives which
he relates concerning Luther and his children. For
example, Bainton describes the scene in Luther's home
when Luther's fourteen year old daughter Magdalena
passed away. He writes:

> And Luther reproached himself because God
> had blessed him as no bishop had been blessed
> in a thousand years, and yet he could not find it
> in his heart to give God thanks. Katie stood
> off, overcome by grief; and Luther held the child
> in his arms as she passed on. When she was laid
> away, he said, "*Du liebes Lenichen*, you will rise
> and shine like the stars and the sun. How strange
> it is to know that she is at peace and all is
> well, and yet to be so sorrowful."[2]

Luther's personal sensitivity, treated lightly by many
biographers, is treated with appreciation by Bainton.

    From the perspective of historiography, this
presentation of Luther is distinct. Bainton attempts
throughout his Luther writings to display the personal
dimension of Luther, and in his treatment of Luther's
home life this motif clearly emerges. Bainton portrays
not only the powerfully courageous Luther at Worms
but also the tenderly compassionate Luther at home.
Biographers of Luther tend to stress Luther's activity
in the realms of religious debate and reform while

---

[1] Bainton, Here I Stand, p. 295.

[2] Ibid., p. 304.

they tend to deemphasize Luther's influence in the
realm of domestic life. Bainton accentuates Luther's
influence on the home; he writes that the "Luther who
got married in order to testify to his faith actually
founded a home and did more than any person to determine the tone of domestic relations for the next four
centuries."[1] Thus one attractive perspective of Bainton's portrait of Luther is his involvement with the
common affairs of home life.

Another emphasis Bainton gives to Luther's
personal dimension is Luther's work as a preacher and
expositor of the Bible. He tends to find in Luther's
sermons and biblical expositions a key method by which
one understands not only Luther's theology but also
his personality and vocation. Biographers generally
accent the content of Luther's sermons as indicative
of his thought. Bainton finds Luther's sermons significant not only as a source of his thought but also
as an indication of his personal creativity and innovation.

According to Bainton, the centrality which the
Reformation gave to the sermon arises to a great degree from the significance which Luther gave to the
spoken Word.[2] The preeminence of Luther as a preacher
emerged in part from the integrity which he gave to
the office of preaching. Bainton points out that Luther's sermons ranged in theme from the sublimity of

[1]Ibid., p. 298.

[2]Ibid. Bainton writes that "Luther held
that salvation is through the Word and without the
Word the elements are devoid of sacramental quality,
but the Word is sterile unless it is spoken."

God to the greed of a sow.[1] The profundity as well as
the humanity of Luther emerged in his preaching.

Bainton appears unique among contemporary
biographers in the interest he gives to Luther's homiletical innovations. One such innovation is Luther's
use of direct discourse. Bainton says, "Luther is in
many respects a unique figure in his generation and
not the least in the way in which he introduced direct
speech into his sermons on Biblical passages."[2] Emula-
ting the discourses of biblical personalities (e.g.,
conversations between Job and his friends) Luther freely originated conversations or interjected what he would
have said had he been in certain biblical situations.
This characteristic of his preaching is quite distinctive in the sixteenth century, and Bainton questions
if Luther had any literary models from which he developed this style of preaching. He finds no parallel
in the preaching of other reformers such as Calvin,
Zwingli, Cranmer, and Knox. Bainton does claim that
medieval antecedents such as the biblical dramas could
have influenced Luther's style.

Bainton notes that Luther developed a personal affinity with many people of the Bible. For example, Bainton writes that Luther "steeped himself in
Scripture until he virtually became Abraham, . . . and
he brooded over the meaning of Scripture until his
heart leapt into flame."[3] Luther projected himself

---

[1] Bainton, Here I Stand, pp. 350-1.

[2] Roland H. Bainton, "Luther's Use of Direct
Discourse," in Luther Today, Martin Luther Lectures,
vol. 1 (Decorah, Iowa: Luther College Press, 1957),
p. 13.

[3] Bainton, "Bible and the Reformation," p. 29.

into the experience of biblical persons, he thought
their thoughts, and he felt their feelings. Luther
marvelled at the courage of Noah, and he experienced
vicariously the sufferings of Joseph, Noah, and Christ.
Bainton states:

> Luther in dealing with Scriptures became
> oblivious to time. The experiences of biblical
> characters were his and his were theirs. That
> is why one will find references to events of his
> own day in his commentaries at the most unexpected
> points.[1]

For Luther the setting of the Bible was often in his
own section of Germany: Palestine became Thuringia
and the distance from Nazareth to Bethlehem was that
from Saxony to Franconia.[2] Because of this close
identity which Luther maintained with the Bible, the
sermons of Luther exude the character, feelings, and
personal traits of the reformer. Thus Bainton finds
Luther's sermons of distinct importance in formulating
a portrait of Luther the person.

Schwiebert and Green interpret Luther primarily as a preacher and biblical exegete. Lortz claims
that as a preacher Luther encountered the Scriptures
with a power seldom matched in history.[3] Hovland, like

---

[1] Roland H. Bainton, "The Bible in the Reformation," in The Cambridge History of the Bible, 3
vols., ed. S. L. Greenslade (Cambridge: University
Press, 1963), 3:23.

[2] [Martin Luther], The Martin Luther Christmas
Book With Celebrated Woodcuts By His Contemporaries,
trans. and ed. Roland H. Bainton (Philadelphia: Fortress Press, 1948), p. 11.

[3] Schwiebert, Luther, p. 618; Green, Luther,
p. 149; Lortz, "Luther's Intellectual Style," p. 24.

Bainton, claims that Luther came to see the Bible as
a collection of biographies of persons who had suffered *Anfectungen*.[1] No biographer of Luther, however, gives the prominence to the sermons of Luther
that Bainton does.

Bainton quotes Luther's preaching extensively.
For example, in Here I Stand Bainton devotes a chapter
to Luther's work as a preacher. The majority of this
chapter consists of excerpts from Luther's sermons
on the Nativity and on Jonah. Several articles by
Bainton consist of selections from Luther's sermons
connected by Bainton's cursory remarks. Moreover,
Bainton produced two books of Luther's sermons. Luther's Meditations on the Gospels (1962) contains a
collection of Luther's sermonic works arranged under
nine different topics relating to the life of Jesus.
Likewise The Martin Luther Christmas Book (1948) em-
bodies a selection of Luther's sermons on the Nativity.

Bainton notes that the prodigious homiletical
tasks which characterized Luther's life paralleled
his work as a biblical translator. Most biographers
join Bainton in assessing Luther's translation of the
Bible into German as a most significant achievement.
Bainton calls the work Luther's noblest achievement,
both as an outstanding vernacular translation and as
a book of religion. He says,

> Not only is the work a monument of the German
> tongue, it is also a great book of religion.
> Many passages pulsate with the life of one who
> for himself could say, "out of the depths have
> I cried unto Thee," and having experienced de-
> liverance could exclaim, "My soul doth magnify
> the Lord."[2]

---

[1]Hovland, "Luther's Biblical Exegesis," pp. 48-9.

[2]Bainton, Age of Reformation, p. 35.

Ritter echoes the sentiments of Bainton and finds the
genius of Luther's translation in his remolding of
the Scriptures to touch the depths of the German soul.
Even Grisar, whose biography is usually highly critical
of Luther, considers the translation a literary monu-
ment.[1] Although Bainton indicates that most points
in Luther's life evoke scholarly disagreement in interpretation, the appraisal of Luther's work as a
biblical translator brings perhaps the closest point
of scholarly unanimity.

     The pastoral work of Luther demands the atten-
tion of Bainton for several reasons. Preaching was a
major part of Luther's duties at Wittenberg, and consequently it occupied much of his time. Likewise Luther
gave preeminence to the role of the preacher and thus
worked toward perfecting his own pulpit ministry.
Bainton also maintains that Luther's sermons provide
a significant avenue by which the historian can approach
the personality, theology, and vocation of Luther. A
further reason for Bainton's interest lies in the fact
that Luther's sermons were influential beyond the confines of the Castle Church in Wittenberg. Through
frequent publications they became accessible to churches,
universities, and homes throughout Germany and hence
served as a key medium for the dissemination of both
Luther's ideas and his influence. For reasons such as
these Bainton finds the study of Luther's sermons
significant for the biographer.

Conclusion

     Several historiographical considerations
emerge in assessing Bainton's Luther writings. The

---

[1]Ritter, Luther, p. 133; Grisar, Luther, p. 424.

initial consideration centers around the clearly-de-
fined approach which Bainton employs to interpret
Luther, viz., that one understands Luther most properly as a man of religion who struggled for faith.
The essence of Luther's religious struggles lies in
the concept of *Anfechtungen*; the preeminence given to
the analysis of the meaning and significance of Luther's *Anfechtungen* is the clue to Bainton's overall
treatment of Luther. Bainton is certainly not unique
among Luther scholars in his portrayal of the *Anfechtungen* as determinative for Luther. Most Luther biographers since Holl recognize the presence of inner
conflicts in Luther, and several biographers understand the conflicts as vitally significant for interpretation. Yet Bainton's stress on the importance of
the spiritual temptations throughout Luther's life
does provide a significant contribution to Luther
studies.

Bainton's approach leads to a second consideration in his Luther writings. His emphasis on Luther's
religious conscience as the starting point of interpretation carries with it the significant corollary
that he rejects other interpretations of Luther. Approaches to Luther which interpret him as a German
nationalist or as a schismatic monk provide Bainton
little satisfaction in developing a portrait of Luther.
Bainton also strongly opposes those scholars who interpret Luther from the perspective of psychohistory.
These scholars interpret Luther by the use of depth
psychology, and approach him through the delineation
of his psychological development.

Likewise Bainton's religious approach to
Luther distinguishes him from those scholars who

interpret Luther as a heretic deviating from the Roman
Church. This perspective of Luther, held traditionally
by Catholic historians, portrays Luther as an aberrant
schismatic and quite often casts Luther in a negative
light.

A third school of interpretation stresses the
external forces at work in Luther's life as most significant. These scholars stress for example economic
factors, social factors, or nationalistic factors as
the primary consideration for interpreting Luther and
the Lutheran revolt. Bainton's approach to Luther via
religion places him in sharp disagreement with this
sociological school of thought. Therefore, from an
historiographical perspective, Bainton falls within
the category of scholars who perceive Luther's faith
as the beginning point of Luther interpretation.

A third consideration is the sense of "confessional detachment" evident in Bainton's Luther writings.
Bainton does not interpret Luther for the purpose of
providing an apologetic for Lutheranism, nor does he
assess Luther for polemical purposes. Scholars such
as Lau and Ritter are German Lutherans who perceive
Luther from the perspective of that particular religious
heritage. Likewise the work of Grisar represents scholarship directed toward a polemical portrait of Luther.
Bainton appears detached from such perspectives, and
hence approaches Luther for the primary purpose of
understanding Luther's religious conscience.[1]

---

[1]Bainton describes himself as a "Gentile in
the courts of the Lord" by being a non-Lutheran scholar
whose specialty is Luther studies. See Roland H.
Bainton, "The Aarhus Conference," in Luther Today, Martin Luther Lectures, vol. 1 (Decorah, Iowa: Luther College Press, 1957), p. 27.

Bainton remarks that upon the publication of
Here I Stand, many Continental scholars sought to determine what his *Standpunkt* was as a Luther scholar.
These scholars generally determined that Bainton's
Standpunkt was that of a Quaker interested in religious
experience. To this assessment of his own position
Bainton agrees. He states that ultimately his interest
is in Luther's religious development, and Here I Stand
reflects this interest.[1]

Bainton's concentration on Luther's religious
quest rather than on a theological idea is the clue to
Bainton's confessional detachment. Consequently Bainton portrays Luther in the context of other men whose
lives epitomized a marked religious sensitivity and
a powerful passion for God. Bainton portrays Luther
not from the standpoint of the "founder" or the "cor-
rupter" of modern faith, but as the *homo religiosus*
earnestly wrestling for his own salvation.

---

[1]Roland H. Bainton, "An Interview," tape-recorded interview conducted by Parker Rossman (Waco,
Texas: Creative Resources, 197-).

CHAPTER IV

THE LEFT WING WRITINGS

The writings by Bainton on the left wing of
the Reformation comprise the most creative segment of
the entire Bainton corpus. Bainton points out that
scholars neglected left wing studies for many generations because confessional interests guided most historians. Such scholars, writes Bainton, "preferred to
investigate the groups to which they themselves be-
longed rather than to delve into the records of a lost
cause."[1] According to Bainton, one value of the study
of the left wing is that it allows the historian to
understand the Catholic and Magisterial Reformation
groups better.

Bainton points to another value of studying
the left wing. He states that it is in left wing research that the historian discovers one clue among
others to the spiritual cleavage between Germany and
"the West." In Germany during the Reformation era,
the radicals experienced severe suppression, yet in
England radical Protestantism gained a foothold. Bainton contends that it was the people of radical persuasion who did much "to fashion the temper of England and
America."[2]

---

[1]Roland H. Bainton, "The Left Wing of the Re-
formation," in Studies on the Reformation, Collected
Papers in Church History, series 2 (Boston: Beacon
Press, 1963), p. 129.

[2]Ibid.

Bainton's interest in the left wing as a
generic group emerges from his own contention that
this expression of Christianity has made a valuable
contribution to Western culture. He states that the
most direct influence Anabaptism made on history is
the "demonstration of the power of the segregated
Church to maintain its identity and continuity over
the course of four centuries."[1] A further contribution of Anabaptism centers on the question of religious toleration. Bainton points out that when the
Church became "atomized" the alternative to religious
liberty was mutual extermination. Bainton thus draws
a direct correlation between the rise of left wing
sentiments in the sixteenth century and the rise of
the issue of toleration.

Interest in religious toleration is a major
emphasis in Bainton's writings. With the aid of a
Guggenheim fellowship in 1926, Bainton studied for
a year in selected European archives. This study
centered on four figures of the left wing movement.
Bainton explains that his original plan was to bring
out a single volume on four heretics of the sixteenth
century,

> who fled from the Inquisition in four countries
> to the refuge of the Swiss cities, only there to
> fall foul of the Calvinist regime. The four were
> Castellio from France, Ochino from Italy, Joris
> from Holland, and Servetus from Spain.[2]

---

[1]Roland H. Bainton, "The Anabaptist Contri-
bution to History," in Studies on the Reformation,
Collected Papers in Church History, series 2 (Boston:
Beacon Press, 1963), p. 202.

[2]Roland H. Bainton, "Foreword," in Studies on
the Reformation, Collected Papers in Church History,
series 2 (Boston: Beacon Press, 1963), p. vi.

The sources proved so prolific that Bainton published
four separate monographs, one on each radical. The
original plan to publish one volume took form years
later when Bainton treated the four radicals in a
larger context, viz., in the book The Travail of Religious Liberty. The present chapter discusses Bainton's
interpretation of the left wing as a whole, and then
analyzes his discussion of the four radicals.

Bainton and Anabaptist Historiography

        The term "left wing" of the Reformation is a
characteristic trait of Bainton's categorization of
Reformation patterns. The debate as to the proper
term of classification is secondary for Bainton. He
writes:

> But more important than the terminology is
> the recognition that the Reformation was too com-
> plex and too much in flux for any precise clari-
> fication. Whether one speaks of the left wing or
> of the *radical Reformation*, the allocation of
> persons and movements will vary according to the
> point chosen through which to draw the line of
> demarcation.[1]

The Reformation was inchoate, hence any categorization
becomes highly interpretive and tends toward oversim-
plification.

        Bainton points out that the variety of issues
which historians use to categorize the Reformation
leads to very different results. If the issue is the
teaching on the sacraments, then Zwingli moves to the
left; if the issue is the doctrine of the Church, then
the Anabaptists move to the right. Likewise if the

----

[1]Bainton, "Left Wing," p. 119.

issue is the doctrine of the Trinity, then the Socinians
are all alone on the left.[1]

The line of demarcation used by Bainton for
his own categorization is the issue of Church-state
relations. He contends that the left wing includes
those who separated the Church from the state and who
rejected the use of the civil arm in matters of religion. These groups also shared common ideas on the
sacraments, the creeds, and on the organization of the
Church. The groups to which Bainton refers and which
make up the left wing of the Reformation are in chronological order as follows: the Zwickau prophets,
Thomas Müntzer, the Swiss Anabaptists, the Melchiorites,
the Mennonites, the Hutterite Brethren, the Schwenck-
felders, and the Socinians.[2]

The terminology and categorization employed
by Bainton have drawn much criticism from other Reformation scholars. James Stayer claims that the
term "*the* Reformation" is highly ambiguous theologi-
cally, and thus the language about its left and right
wings becomes "quick-silver in the hands of the interpreter."[3] This judgment is borne out by a survey of
contemporary writings in this area of Reformation research. Some scholars reject Bainton's designation of
a "left wing." For example, George H. Williams discounts the use of "left wing" claiming that the term

---

[1]Ibid., p. 120.

[2]Ibid., p. 121.

[3]James M. Stayer, Werner O. Packull, and Klaus
Deppermann, "From Monogenesis to Polygenesis: The
Historical Discussion of Anabaptist Origins," The
Mennonite Quarterly Review 49 (April 1975): 93.

is not "wholly felicitous." Such a term, writes
Williams, gives prominence to the religio-political
principles shared by almost all peoples. The term,
however, depends upon the political parlance of recent parliamentary history during which the separation
of Church and state was a "leftist" cause.[1]

The term "left wing" is not technically correct according to Williams, especially if the historian
uses the criterion of Church-state separation as the
primary issue of demarcation. Williams points out
that not all of the so-called "left-wingers" were
adamant separationists, e.g., the cases of Balthasar
Hubmaier and Thomas Müntzer.[2] The term most satisfying
to Williams is the "radical Reformation." Bainton
calls into question Williams's terminology, and notes:

> This usage has the merit of substituting one word
> for two but does not simplify or clarify the sit-
> uation. A radical reformation implies a conserva-
> tive reformation, and a reformation implies a body
> to be reformed so that one still has three groups:
> the Catholics, the Lutherans and related bodies,
> and the radicals.[3]

In discussing both Williams's and Bainton's usage of
terms, Paul Peachey notes that the designation "left

---

[1]George H. Williams, "Introduction," in Spiritual and Anabaptist Writers, Library of Christian Classics, vol. 25 (Philadelphia: Westminister Press, 1957),
pp. 21-22.

[2]Ibid. On page 22 Williams explains: "Though
Anabaptists, Spiritualists, and Evangelical Rationalists
differed among themselves as to what constituted the
root of faith and order . . . all three groups within
the Radical Reformation agreed in cutting back to that
root and in freeing church and creed of what they regarded as the suffocating growth of ecclesiastical
tradition and magisterial prerogative. Precisely this
makes theirs a 'Radical Reformation.'"

[3]Bainton, "Left Wing," p. 119.

wing" comes closer to a Marxist interpretation of Anabaptism than does the designation "radical Reformation."[1]

    Several contemporary Reformation scholars em-
ploy theology rather than Church-state relations as
the point of demarcation and hence propose the use of
the term "right wing." Kenneth R. Davis claims that
from a strictly theological standpoint Anabaptism was
more "right wing" than left and more conservative than
radical. Davis finds this conservatism in the use of
the medieval ascetic tradition in Anabaptist theology.[2]
Stayer contends that there is a growing consensus in
Anabaptist historiography to use the terminology of a
"right wing." He points out that scholars must use
this term with extreme caution since the theology of
early Anabaptism is quite multifaceted. Stayer does,
however, find a typology based on theological lines
more convincing than one shaped by Church-state issues.[3]

    Critically assessing his own terminology of
"left wing" Bainton states that any reform movement
with a degree of stability may appears as a *via media*
between two extremes. On one side is the body whom
the reformers are seeking to reform, and on the other

[1] Paul Peachey, "Marxist Historiography of the Radical Reformation: Causality or Covariation?" Sixteenth Century Essays and Studies 1 (June 1970): 1, note 1.

[2] Kenneth R. Davis, Anabaptism and Asceticism: A Study in Intellectual Origins (Scottdale, Pennsylvania: Herald Press, 1974), p. 297.

[3] Stayer, "Monogenesis," p. 91. Stayer points to the fact that many Anabaptist scholars find more theological affinity between the Anabaptists and Luther than between the Anabaptists and Zwingli.

side is the unstable fringe. If the unstable fringe
ever becomes stable, it would then confront another
more radical periphery. This was the case with the
Anabaptists. Bainton writes that "curiously some of
the Anabaptists whom Luther branded en masse as fanatics
discovered such diversities within their own ranks that
they too were found to be in the middle way."[1] For
example, Schwenckfeld said that he stood in the middle between the Lutherans and the Zwinglians while
Pilgrim Marpeck claimed that he was the *via media*
between the Lutherans and Schwenckfeld.[2] Consequently
Bainton is keenly aware of the relativity of such attempts at categorization, yet he employs the terminology
of "left wing" in his typology of the Reformation.

Within the left wing of the Reformation Bainton discerns two main groups, the Anabaptists and the
Free Spirits. In this division, the Free Spirits represents a generic group of reformers who did not fit
the Anabaptist mold. Of the Free Spirits Bainton
states: "It [the Free Spirits group] was so amorphous,
varied, and vague that it can better be described as a
tendency than as a movement. The characteristic notes
were mysticism and rationalism."[3] Williams uses a
similar grouping of reformers; he calls his divisions
the Anabaptists and the Spiritualists.[4]

---

[1]Roland H. Bainton, "Luther and the *Via Media*
at the Marburg Colloquy," in Studies on the Reformation, Collected Papers in Church History, series 2
(Boston: Beacon Press, 1963), p. 47.

[2]Bainton, "Left Wing," p. 119.

[3]Roland H. Bainton, The Reformation of the Sixteenth Century (Boston: Beacon Press, 1952), p. 123.

[4]Williams, "Introduction," pp. 19-40.

Some scholars reject the dichotomy evident in
Bainton's and Williams's classification. One such
scholar, Robert Friedmann, sees a "concrete Biblical
Spiritualism" among the Anabaptists and thus finds the
dichotomy specious.[1] Walter Klaassen, although uncom-
fortable with the division between Anabaptists and
Free Spirits, admits the historical necessity for such
a classification. He regards the left wing of the Reformation as a "collection of variations on a theme
of the separation of Scripture and Spirit."[2]

Bainton finds a commonality among all the
groups which made up the left wing. There are five
main ideas which he sees as appearing and reappearing
in varying combinations among these groups. The first
of these ideas is the concern for ethics. The left
wing reformers felt that the Lutheran revolt failed
to produce an adequate transformation of life. Bainton tersely states that "the kernel of Anabaptism was
an ethical urge."[3] The Anabaptists located the problem
in the Lutheran doctrine of the Church. The inclusion
of all members of society in the Church by virtue of
infant baptism rather than on the basis of inner conviction and moral living was the root of the problem.
Harold Bender agrees with Bainton's emphasis on an
ethical commonality among Anabaptists. Bender sees
the "newness of life" as the chief concern of

------

[1] Robert Friedmann, "Recent Interpretation of
Anabaptism," Church History 24 (June 1955): 138; see
also Walter Klaassen, "Spiritualization in the Reformation," Menninite Quarterly Review 37 (April 1963):
77.

[2] Klaassen, "Spiritualization," p. 77.

[3] Bainton, The Reformation, pp. 96-97.

Anabaptists.[1] Likewise Klaassen claims that many Anabaptists reacted against the Lutheran reform because
of its ethical sterility. He writes: "The doctrine of
sola fide, as they heard Luther preach it, appeared to
them to be merely an intellectual concept because it
did not call for a change in the style of life."[2]

A second idea common to Anabaptists was primitivism. Bainton points out that the accent on primitivism marks all reform movements. The general term
denoting this urge is restitutionism. The question for
Bainton is the degree to which the restitution is to
take place: how far back chronologically does one
go? For Luther, the Church should return to the period
before Boniface III; for the Anglicans the Church
should return to the period before and inclusive of
the Fourth Ecumenical Council. Yet for the left wing,
the Church should fashion itself after the apostolic
times alone. No other period had the priority that
this one did for the Anabaptists.[3] Robert Friedmann
claims that the idea of restitution within the left
wing of the Reformation was for the first time discussed

---

[1]Harold Bender, "The Anabaptist Vision," in
The Recovery of the Anabaptist Vision, ed. Guy F.
Hershberger (Scottdale, Pennsylvania: Herald Press,
1957), p. 40.

[2]Walter Klaassen, "The Nature of the Anabaptist Protest," The Mennonite Quarterly Review 45
(October 1971): 297.

[3]Bainton, "Left Wing," p. 123; Roland H.
Bainton, Hunted Heretic: The Life and Death of Michael
Servetus, 1511-1553 (Boston: Beacon Press, 1953: reprint ed., Gloucester, Mass,: Peter Smith, 1978),
p. 137.

in Bainton's essay "Changing Ideas and Ideals in the
Sixteenth Century" (1936). Regardless of the question
of Bainton's primacy in this area, the idea of primitivism as developed by Bainton has become a major tool
of interpretation for left wing studies.[1]

An emphasis on eschatology comprises a third
idea common to all Anabaptists. Bainton contends that
the thinking of the radicals in this respect emanated
from the movements and men of the late Middle Ages,
especially the Spiritual Franciscans and Joachim of
Fiore. Anabaptist eschatology also grew out of the
strong Biblical orientation of the left wing groups,
according to Bainton. Perhaps most important, however,
was the fact that Anabaptist sects found a heightened
eschatology to be quite compatible with their concept
of the Church.

Late medieval movements also influenced the
Anabaptists on the fourth common idea which Bainton
terms anti-intellectualism. Inheriting the thought of
the *Devotio Moderna* and the Spiritual Franciscans, the
left wing basically rejected the technical theological
speculations of medieval thinkers. The radicals
favored the example of the penitent thief on the cross.
His salvation occurred without any knowledge of the
substance and persons of the Godhead, transubstantia-
tion, or predestination.[2]

The final idea which characterized Anabaptists
was a conviction of the necessity of Church-state separation. Bainton says, "The left wing was united in its

---

[1]Friedmann, "Recent Interpretations," p. 149.
note 17.

[2]Bainton, "Left Wing," pp. 125-6.

demand for the separation of Church and state."[1] For
some radicals the division between Church and state
was so sharp that it required withdrawal from the world.
For most radicals the stress was directed to what
Bainton terms "inner worldly asceticism."

Bainton's interpretation of the common threads
which run through the left wing movement agrees with
the interpretation of Bender. Likewise Friedmann, in
his essay "Recent Interpretations of Anabaptism" (1955),
enunciates many of the same points found in Bainton.

Thus the terminology, categorization, and the
approach to Anabaptism via common themes mark Bainton's
work on this phase of the Reformation. Bainton's studies represented a new approach to Anabaptism by historians, and his treatment of the left wing groups
helped to augment the burgeoning interest in Anabaptism
in the first half of the twentieth century.

The period of time during which Bainton published many of his left wing studies was an era of Anabaptist historiography dominated by the work of Harold
Bender. Werner Packull asserts that much of the current
respectability of Anabaptist studies arises from the
"vision of Harold Bender and his generation."[3] Packull

[1]Ibid., p. 127.

[2]Bender, "Anabaptist Vision," p. 42; Robert
Friedmann, "Recent Interpretations," pp. 132-51. This
approach to Anabaptism represents a previous generation's method of interpretation. Contemporary scholars
are hesitant to find commonality in the broad spectrum
of Anabaptism. A thorough discussion of this approach
follows in the next section of the chapter, pp. 121-26.

[3]Werner O. Packull, "Some Reflections on the
State of Anabaptist History: The Demise of a Normative
Vision," Studies in Religion 8 (1979): 313.

states that he prefers to use the term "Bender generation" rather than "Bender school" or "Goshen school"
because non-Mennonites like Robert Friedmann, George
Williams, Franklin Littrell, and Bainton contributed
significantly to the image of Anabaptism current in
the middle of the twentieth century. Bainton's work
added significantly to the historical recovery of
Anabaptists and it is appropriate to include him in
the Bender generation of Anabaptist scholarship.

One major difference between the Bender generation and contemporary Anabaptist historiography
centers on the question of Anabaptist origins. The
assumption of the monogenesis of Anabaptism was normative for the Bender generation whereas the recognition of the polygenesis of Anabaptism is characteristic
of current historiographical thought.[1] An examination
of Bainton's view of Anabaptist origins shows his affinity with the Bender interpretation.

Bainton proposes that Anabaptism originated
through a breach with Zwinglianism. The break with
Zwinglianism came through the disillusionment of many
of the more radical thinkers with the visible effects
of the reform.[2] Bainton writes that "Anabaptism originated in the Protestant fold . . . . It was in the
circle of Zwingli that Anabaptism arose."[3] He contends

[1]Stayer, "Monogenesis," p. 84.

[2]Roland H. Bainton, "Changing Ideas and Ideals
in the Sixteenth Century," in Early and Medieval Christianity, Collected Papers in Church History, series 1
(Boston: Beacon Press, 1962), p. 168.

[3]Roland H. Bainton, "The Church of the Restoration," Mennonite Life 8 (July 1953): 136.

that one dominant motivation of the early Anabaptists
was to carry the program of restoration to its radical
conclusion. Here Bainton shows his affinity with Bender, who concluded that the Anabaptists enlarged the
visions of Luther and Zwingli by giving body and form
to their ideas. Anabaptism set out to achieve reform
in actual experience.[1]

Although Bainton finds medieval antecedents
to the Anabaptist movement, he contends that the initial
impulse of the left wing came from Luther. The radicals
of the Reformation almost uniformly went through a
Lutheran stage followed by a migration toward Zwinglianism and finally to a sectarian position.[2] Klaassen
echoes the conclusion of Bainton on Anabaptist origins:
"Anabaptism was without question a Reformation movement
rooted both in Zwinglian as well as in Lutheran Protestantism."[3]

The idea of a monogenesis of Anabaptist origins
finds little credence among contemporary Anabaptist
scholars. In the 1960s a reaction surfaced against
what Stayer calls an "overly idealized Anabaptist historiography."[4] This reaction produced a more complex
and technical approach to Anabaptist studies. Packull
maintains, "It is a sign of maturation that the history
of Anabaptism has become uncomfortably complicated even
for specialists."[5] Packull characterizes the present

---

[1]Bender, "Anabaptist Vision," p. 37; see Bainton, The Reformation, p. 95.

[2]Bainton, "Changing Ideas and Ideals," p. 165;
see Bainton, "Anabaptist Contribution," pp. 199-200.

[3]Klaassen, "Spiritualization," p. 71.

[4]Stayer, "Monogenesis," p. 103.

[5]Packull, "Reflections," p. 313.

state of Anabaptist studies as scholarship lacking a
normative vision. He finds within contemporary research three dominant approaches to the question of
Anabaptist origins: 1) the polygenesis of Anabaptism, 2) the modified monogenesis of Anabaptism, and
3) the revolutionary beginnings of Anabaptism.

Scholars such as Stayer, Klaus Deppermann,
and Claus-Peter Clasen argue for the polygenesis of
Anabaptist origins. Stayer tersely describes the
thought of this group of scholars when he writes:

> The history of Anabaptist origins can no longer
> be preoccupied with the essentially sterile
> question of where Anabaptism began, but must
> devote itself to studying the plural origins of
> Anabaptism and their significance for the plural
> character of the movement.[1]

Clasen augments the view of polygenesis through his
identification of the major historical Anabaptist sects,
while John H. Yoder offers a correction to the extreme
compartmentalization of Anabaptism into autonomous
regional groups.[2]

A second trend in contemporary scholarship,
embracing a modified monogenesis, sees several Anabaptist groups emerging perhaps independently of each
other in different localities but with a homogeneity
of religion. Davis finds the quest for holiness as

---

[1]Stayer, "Monogenesis," p. 85. In Anabaptists
and the Sword (Lawrence, Kansas: Coronado Press, 1972),
Stayer proposes that there are distinctive intellectual
histories of several Anabaptist groups based on the
doctrine of the sword.

[2]Claus-Peter Clasen, Anabaptism: A Social History, 1525-1618 (Ithaca, N.Y.: Cornell University Press,
1972), pp. 32-36; John H. Yoder, "'Anabaptists and the
Sword' Revisited: Systematic Historiography and Undogmatic Non-resistants," Zeitschrift für Kirchengeschichte
85 (1974): 126-39.

the dominant concern binding early Anabaptists together.[1]

Under this same rubric of modified monogenesis
is the group of scholars proposing that Anabaptism originated apart from both Catholicism and Protestantism.
Klaassen's Anabaptism: Neither Catholic nor Protestant
(1973) argues for the idea of Anabaptism as a different
way of approaching Christianity.[2] Likewise Hans Hillerbrand proposes that the early Anabaptists pursued a
"different" approach to Christianity. Summarizing a
discussion of Anabaptist affinity with Protestantism
and Catholicism, Hillerbrand states, "The postulate of
Anabaptism as a Christian tradition in its own right
may be the answer to our problem."[3]

A third approach to Anabaptist origins takes
seriously the revolutionary character of Anabaptist beginnings. This approach admits of different degrees
of interpretation. For example, several scholars simply find social and political overtones as well as new

---

[1]Kenneth R. Davis, "The Origins of Anabaptism:
Ascetic and Charismatic Elements Exemplifying Continuity
and Discontinuity," in The Origins and Characteristics
of Anabaptism, ed. Marc Lienhard (The Hague: Martinus
Nijhoff, 1977). This collection by Lienhard is an excellent source of contemporary Anabaptist thought on the
problem of origins. In this same vein see Umstrittenes
Täufertum 1925-1975: Neue Forschungen, ed. Hans-Jurgen
Goertz (Gottingen: Vondennoeck and Ruprecht, 1977).

[2]Walter Klaassen, Anabaptists: Neither Catholic
nor Protestant (Waterloo, Ontario: Conrad Press, 1973).

[3]Hans J. Hillerbrand, "Anabaptism and the Reformation: Another Look," Church History 29 (December
1960): 418. See also Hans J. Hillerbrand, "Origins of
Sixteenth Century Anabaptism: Another Look," Archiv für
Reformationsgeschichte 53 (1962): 152-80.

religious ideas in the discontent of the early radicals.
Abraham Friesen shows that Marxist historiography of
the left wing of the Reformation casts all Anabaptists
into the impoverished classes of the sixteenth century.
The Anabaptism revolt was *de facto* a revolt of the lower
classes. This interpretation follows closely the lines
of Marxist ideology.[1] Bainton had already evaluated
this particular interpretation of Anabaptism in his
response to H. Richard Niebuhr's Social Sources
of Denominationalism: "Men in the sixteenth century
became Anabaptists not because they were disinherited,
but were disinherited because they became Anabaptists."[2]
The Anabaptists were not revolutionaries in a violent
sense, contends Bainton. Yet both their reluctance to
participate fully in society and their pacifism were
extremely subversive to society as a whole. By virtue
of their religious commitments, the Anabaptists chal-
lenged the very basis of civil as well as religious
society.[3]

    The three approaches to Anabaptist origins
reviewed above depict in a cursory manner the growing
complexity of left wing historiography. The general
agreement among scholars of the Bender generation on
the issue of Anabaptist origins has dissolved into a
more diverse historiographical approach by contemporary

---

[1]Packull, "Reflections," pp. 318-19; Abraham
Friesen, "The Marxist Interpretation of Anabaptism,"
Sixteenth Century Essays and Studies 1 (June 1970):
34. See also Abraham Friesen, Reformation and Utopia:
Marxist Interpretation of the Reformation and its
Antecedents (Wiesbaden: F. Steiner, 1974).

[2]Bainton, "Changing Ideas and Ideals," pp. 165-6.

[3]Bainton, "Restoration," p. 139.

researchers. Packull states that the trend away from
the Bender interpretation derives from a shift in
interest from theological conceptions and their intellectual or spiritual pedigree to the socio-political
function of religious ideas. In a summary treatment
of the current status of left wing research Packull
writes:

> The demise of Bender's "normative" vision, which
> constitutes one of the major features of Anabap-
> tist history in the seventies, must be seen in
> a larger context. It reflects the process of
> professionalization, with its accompanying multi-
> plication of perspectives, as well as shifts in
> focus which Anabaptist research shares with cur-
> rent trends in Reformation history.[1]

In assessing Bainton's understanding of the
left wing of the Reformation, one can place him within
a school of thought which is no longer current. Although Bainton's left wing writings continue to have
significance, other scholars have developed, questioned,
or reinterpreted the sources differently, and have arrived at significantly different conclusions.

The Four Radicals
Michael Servetus: The Heretic as Martyr

Bainton's interest in Michael Servetus emanates
from the larger context of Bainton's interest in the
history of toleration. Bainton sees the study of Servetus as the study of the radical effects of religious
intolerance. In the opening chapter of Hunted Heretic
Bainton states, "In this day, religious liberty is in
peril. This study may be revealing as to the reasons

---

[1]Packull, "Reflections," p. 314.

why men persecute and the reasons why, as Christians,
they should not."[1]

Bainton considers the death of Servetus as
the event which precipitated the toleration controversy of the sixteenth century. Likewise the death
of Servetus epitomizes for Bainton the manner by
which both Protestants and Catholics dealt with religious dissent. He writes:

> Michael Servetus has the singular distinction
> of having been burned by the Catholics in effigy
> and by the Protestants in actuality. This coinci-
> dence of itself would have secured for him no more
> than a niche in the hall of eccentrics were it not
> that his martyrdom came to have a significance ex-
> ceeding that of perhaps any other in his century--
> because it served as the occasion for the rise in
> volume and intensity of the toleration controversy
> within Protestantism. This is the essential reason
> for recounting again--just four hundred years after
> his execution--the story of his life and death.[2]

Bainton has produced in Hunted Heretic what
is perhaps the standard biography of Servetus. This
book interprets the life of Servetus from the perspective of his religious development and contains a
lengthy bibliography of works on Servetus. Another
biographical treatment is John F. Fulton's Michael
Servetus: Humanist and Martyr. Earl Morse Wilbur provides what Bainton calls "an admirable treatment of
Servetus" in A History of Unitarianism, volume one.
The most recent biography is that by José Barón Fer-
nández entitled Miguel Servet: Su vida y su obra.

---

[1] Bainton, Hunted Heretic, p. 4.

[2] Ibid., p. 3. Bainton published the biography
of Servetus on the four hundredth anniversary of Servetus's execution.

Bainton also published a collection of primary documents on Servetus which appeared in volumes 44 and
45 of the Archiv für Reformationsgeschichte.

The consideration of Bainton's treatment of
Servetus pursues two general themes. These are as
follows: 1) the approach to Servetus as a man of religion, and 2) the emphasis of Bainton on the trial and
death of Servetus. The following discussion centers
around these two themes in order to assess Bainton's
approach to Servetus.

Scholars view Servetus from a variety of perspectives. Some interpret him within the context of
the history of medicine, stressing his work as a phys-
ician. Others study Servetus from the perspective
of his importance as a geographer or as a pioneer in
the field of biblical criticism. Bainton approaches
Servetus as a man of religion and stresses his religious development as paramount for a proper understanding of the Spaniard. To Bainton, "Servetus was
not primarily a speculative thinker, but a man of
intense personal religion . . . ."[1]

Several examples will illustrate the ubiquity
of this theme. Commenting on a passage taken from
Servetus's On the Errors of the Trinity Bainton asserts
that Servetus was wrestling with more than the theological abstrusities of medieval trinitarian speculation.
Servetus was dealing with questions which transcended
the problem of the Moors and the Jews. He was struggling
with the immensities of the issues of all men's relationship

---

[1]Roland H. Bainton, "Michael Servetus and the
Trinitarian Speculation of the Middle Ages," in Autour
De Michael Servet Et De Sebastien Castellion, ed.
Bruno Becker (Haarlem: H. D. Tjeenk and Zoon N. V.,
1953), p. 30.

with the Eternal. Bainton writes, "The question was
. . . how he should stand for all eternity before
the ineffable splendor of the Divine Majesty."[1]

     In another context Bainton discusses Serve-
tus's work as an editor of a tract written by the distinguished medical humanist Symphorien Champier. The
editorial comments of Servetus included in the tract
had much to do with theological matters. Bainton observes: "Servetus was a smoldering Savonarola--or
better might one say an Anabaptist prophet in dis-
guise, covertly pronouncing doom upon a stiff-necked
and adulterous generation."[2] Moreover in his general
assessment of Servetus's writing Bainton states that
Servetus's style "is marked by bold speculation and
by passionate outbursts of lyrical piety."[3] Bainton
thus begins with the assumption that Servetus was a
man deeply sensitive to and highly involved in matters
of religion.

     On the question of the sequence of Servetus's
religious development Bainton confesses ignorance.
The sources simply do not indicate the progress of his
religious life. Rather than attempting to chronicle
a sequence of development, Bainton proposes that the
best the historian can do is to examine the various
sources which influenced the thought of Servetus.
Therefore the pattern of Bainton's discussion is to
trace the intellectual roots which produced Antitrinitarian thought in Servetus.[4]

----

[1]Bainton, Hunted Heretic, p. 49.

[2]Ibid., p. 106.

[3]The Mennonite Encyclopedia, s.v. "Servetus,
Michael," by Roland H. Bainton.

[4]Bainton, "Trinitarian Speculation," p. 45.

Bainton criticizes traditional treatments of Servetus because they were intent on approaching his theology as true or false, orthodox or unorthodox. The point of historical interest for Bainton is to identify the sources which coalesced in the life of Servetus and which influenced him toward Antitrinitarianism. He says, "Only after we understand this are we in a position to raise the question of values."[1]

Bainton identifies two prominent streams of thought converging on Servetus in his early years: Erasmianism and chiliasm. He points out that at the age of fourteen Servetus came under the influence of Erasmus.[2] Servetus also was influenced by medieval chiliasm, mediated perhaps through Protestant writings. Bainton observes that the severe indictments against the pope by the young Servetus demonstrate that he had imbibed "if not the virus of the Protestants, then the scathing apocalypticism of the Spiritual Franciscans . . . ."[3] Of these two influences, Erasmianism and chiliasm, Bainton writes:

> Servetus is a fascinating figure because he brought together in a single person the Renaissance and the left wing of the Reformation. He was at once a disciple of the Neoplatonic Academy at Florence and of the Anabaptists.[4]

---

[1]Roland H. Bainton, "The Present State of Servetus Studies," Journal of Modern History 4 (1932): 78.

[2]Bainton derives this position from the fact that Servetus served with Juan de Quintana, a Franciscan minorite who was a doctor of the University of Paris and a man of Erasmian spirit.

[3]Bainton, Hunted Heretic, p. 20.

[4]Ibid., p. 4.

Regardless of the impact which these two streams of
thought had on Servetus, Bainton discerns a third influence which perhaps proved most significant.

As a young student at Toulouse Servetus confronted the problem of the Moors and the Jews. If
Christianity were the revelation of God, why did
these people refuse to believe? Bainton claims that
no sensitive and inquiring Spaniard could escape concern for this issue. The great stone of stumbling,
writes Bainton, was the doctrine of the Trinity.
Servetus wrestled with this theological doctrine not
from speculative concerns but rather out of practical
necessity. Much to the amazement of Servetus, there
was little if anything within the Scriptures about
the Trinity.[1]

Bainton devotes much attention to the question of the formulation of Servetus's Antitrinitarian
thought. Bainton suggests that it was the study of
the Scriptures which provided Servetus's initial impulse toward Antitrinitarianism. Jerome Friedman
agrees with this interpretation, and specifically
he argues that it was a "new" approach to the Bible
which led Servetus toward his ultimate position on
the Trinity. Servetus saw revelation as progressing
through the Old and New Testaments. Therefore Christ
was simply a step in the revelatory plan. Friedman
writes: "If indeed Servetus was an antitrinitarian,
a millenarian, a restorer of pristine Christianity,
he was so because he was primarily an exegete of
divine history."[2] Bainton contends that Servetus's

---

[1]Ibid., pp. 13-14.

[2]Jerome Friedman, "Michael Servetus: Exegete of
Divine History," Church History 43 (December 1974): 469.

impassioned Biblical studies employed the textual
criticism introduced by the Renaissance exegetes.   In
the person of Servetus, writes Bainton, is the beginning of scientific Biblical criticism.   Earl Morse
Wilbur's earlier study concludes that hailing Servetus as a precursor of modern Biblical criticism
highly overestimates his work.[1]

     Woven into Servetus's thought Bainton finds
strands of deep devotion and simple piety.   Despite
these personal qualities, Bainton also finds a caustic
treatment of medieval scholasticism.   Servetus strongly
rejected the formulations of the medieval thinkers.
Bainton concludes: "With devastating glee he despoiled
their arsenal of riddles to demolish the ramparts of
orthodoxy."[2]

     The assault by Servetus on the traditional
view of the Trinity necessitated his withdrawal from
Catholic lands.   The reconstruction of his own views
made his residence untenable also in Protestant lands.
In Bainton's view the theology of Servetus made him
an outcast in European society.   What was it about
Servetus's theology which caused such universal ostracism?   Bainton summarizes the questionable formulation
as follows:

---

[1]Roland H. Bainton, What Is Calvinism?"
Christian Century 42 (12 March 1925): 352; Earl Morse
Wilbur, A History of Unitarianism, 2 vols. (Boston:
Beacon Press, 1945), 1:130.

[2]Bainton, "Trinitarian Speculation," p. 45;
see Roland H. Bainton, Travail of Religious Liberty:
Nine Biographical Studies (Philadelphia: Westminister
Press, 1951; reprint ed., Hamden, Conn.: Shoe String
Press, 1971), p. 77.

God [is] universally diffuse in the form of
light. Christ is the eternal self-expression
of this God. He too is manifest as the Light
of the World, irradiating all things visible
with the luster of the divine. Jesus, however,
was a man with whom this Christ was conjoined
at a point in time to produce the Son of God.
The Son, therefore, was not eternal. This
was the point which Catholics and Protestants
alike considered intolerable. For if the Son
were not eternal, they argued, the Father
also would not be eternal, since there cannot
be a father without a son.[1]

Bainton claims that such was the position, developed
out of religious devotion and practical concern, which
finally led to Servetus's execution.

Bainton's interpretation of Servetus's thought
follows the traditional lines developed by Adolf von
Harnack. Harnack argued that the medieval Nominalist
school directed a subversive criticism against the
doctrine of the Trinity. The authority of the Church
prevented this criticism from reaching full fruition,
but when Renaissance humanism extinguished that authority, the Nominalist critique of the Trinity came into
full bloom. Bainton assents to this thesis, claiming
that Servetus was the bridge from scholastic skepticism
to the sectarian repudiation of the doctrine of the
Trinity in the sixteenth century.[2]

---

[1]Roland H. Bainton, "Burned Heretic: Michael
Servetus," Christian Century 70 (28 October 1953):
1230.

[2]Roland H. Bainton, "New Documents in Early
Protestant Rationalism," in Studies on the Reformation,
Collected Papers in Church History, series 2 (Boston:
Beacon Press, 1963), p. 137; Adolph von Harnack, His-
tory of Dogma, 7 vols., trans. Neil Buchanan (New York:
Russell and Russell, 1958), 7:122-32.

Servetus's submission to the authority of the
Church weakened as he came under the influence of
Protestant criticism of the Church; thus he could not
accept as valid that which appeared philosophically
false. Bainton therefore interprets Servetus as a
vital link in the development of Antitrinitarian speculation. Through Servetus, argues Bainton, the "acids"
of late scholasticism influenced the Antitrinitarians
of the Reformation era.[1]

Friedman finds the clue to Servetus's thought
in Hebrew influences rather than in reaction to late
medieval scholasticism. He claims that Servetus attempted to build a case for Jewish Christianity.
Hebraic thought heavily influenced Servetus in theology,
exegesis, and mysticism. These Jewish ideas were fun-
damental to his Christian beliefs. The problem with
Servetus, according to Friedman, was that he misunderstood both early Christian development as well as
the Jewish sources. Friedman interprets Servetus's
religious thought as being dependent on one main
tradition, i.e., Hebraic thought. Bainton interprets
Servetus within the welter of Renaissance and Reformation thought, heavily influenced from a diversity of
sources.[2]

Bainton's approach to Servetus as a man of
religion centers on Servetus's Antitrinitarian thought,
its development and its consequences. Yet another

[1]Bainton, The Reformation, p. 46; Bainton,
"Trinitarian Speculation," p. 46.

[2]Jerome Friedman, "Michael Servetus: The
Case for Jewish Christianity," Sixteenth Century
Journal 4 (April 1973): 108-10.

means by which Bainton depicts Servetus as a man of
religion is in the assessment of Servetus's discovery
of the pulmonary transit of blood. The significance
of this discovery gives Servetus a place for all time
in the annals of medicine according to Bainton. Yet
it was not scientific questions which compelled Servetus toward this medical breakthrough. Why was it,
Bainton asks, that Servetus disclosed his findings in
a work on theology? The answer, he contends, lies in
certain presuppositions which Servetus shared with his
time, although Servetus applied them in a manner pecu-
liarly his own.[1] Bainton lists three reasons for
Servetus's interest in the circulation of blood: 1) the
Renaissance spirit which stressed the cohesiveness of
the universe, 2) the belief that the immanent animating
force is a dynamic and creative energy, the very being
of God, and 3) the problem of personal salvation.[2]

Servetus imbibed the tradition which held
that physiology, psychology, and theology were inti-
mately bound, and the place of their conjunction was
man. Bainton finds that as a Renaissance man Servetus
sought the answer to his personal salvation in the
transit of blood. His questions, maintains Bainton,

---

[1]Roland H. Bainton, "Michael Servetus and
the Pulmonary Transit of Blood," Bullentin of the
History of Medicine 25 (January-February 1951): 5.
A full discussion of the physiological and theological import of Servetus's discovery is in this article. See also Roland H. Bainton, "The Smaller Circulation: Servetus and Colombo," Sudhoffs Archiv für
Geschichte der Medizin und der Naturwissenschaften
24 (1931): 371-74.

[2]Bainton, "Pulmonary Transit," p. 5.

differed only in vocabulary from those of Luther on how
to find a gracious God. Fulton agrees with Bainton in
this interpretation. He claims that Servetus wrote
more as a theologian than as a physiologist when he
wrote on blood circulation. He was more interested
in the course traveled by the spirit than in the path
of the blood.[1]

Bainton explains Servetus's understanding of
the relationship of blood to the question of salvation:
in the Biblical account God breathed the soul into
man, thus injecting into man's being the divine principle. In a physiological sense, respiration correlates
with the purification of the blood. Hence Servetus
grasped the meaning of the Hebrew doctrine that the
soul is in the blood. The locus of God in man is in
the soul, and consequently the inspiration of the Holy
Spirit within man brought about the divine rebirth in
man.[2] Bainton explains:

> Here is the Renaissance faith in the unity
> of all reality. Servetus drew no compartmental
> lines. With the Victorian poet he would have
> said that he who understands the flower in the
> crannied wall is able to understand what God and
> man are . . . . He who really understands all
> that is involved in the breathing of man has
> already sensed the breath of God.[3]

[1]Bainton, Hunted Heretic, p. 125; John F.
Fulton, Michael Servetus: Humanist and Martyr (New
York: Herbert Reichner, 1953), pp. 36-37.

[2]Bainton, "Pulmonary Transit," p. 6.

[3]Bainton, Hunted Heretic, p. 127. Williams
argues that Servetus's real interest was to show that
the Spirit, entering the blood system by the nostrils,
makes plausible physiologically the doctrine of the
virgin birth of Christ. See George H. Williams, The
Radical Reformation (Philadelphia: The Westminister
Press, 1962), p. 337.

Servetus's involvement in the physiological research
on the pulmonary transit of blood is secondary to his
involvement with the soteriological struggles for a
peace with God.

Bainton approaches Servetus as a man often
obsessed with religious concerns and always sensitive
to the questions of his own existence. This dominant
theme surfaces in Bainton's thorough treatment of
Servetus's development of Antitrinitarianism as well
as in Bainton's handling of Servetus's work as a
pioneer in the field of blood circulation. Moreover
Servetus's religion is an underlying assumption in the
extensive treament which Bainton gives to Servetus
as a martyr.

The martyrdom of Servetus is the second theme
characterizing Bainton's biographical treatment. The
subtitle of his biography of Servetus, The Life and
Death of Michael Servetus, points to this emphasis on
the importance of the life and death of Servetus.
Two full chapters in the book deal with this final
episode in the Spaniard's career. The trial and
death of Servetus are volatile issues among scholars.
Writers on this episode usually gravitate toward
judgment of one party and sympathy for the other, e.g.,
judgment on Servetus as unorthodox and sympathy for
Calvin as justified. The approach by historians to
this series of events usually reflects their historiographical bias, and such is the case for Bainton. Bainton defends Servetus on the grounds of freedom of conscience while he attacks Calvin for his intolerance.

Servetus died as a heretic. Bainton accepts
no other interpretation of Servetus's death. The
Council at Geneva convicted him on two counts:

Antitrinitarianism and anti-paedobaptism. There is
absolutely nothing about any political offense in
Servetus's conviction, claims Bainton. He died *de
facto* because he disagreed too sharply with Calvin's
theology. Bainton interprets the trial of Servetus
as a conflict between two diverse views of God and
man. Calvin stressed the ineffable sovereignty of
God and the depravity of man; Servetus held to the
immanence of God and the deification of man.[1] Williams
concurs on this point, stating that on the highest
level the struggle was "passionately theological."
From a wider perspective Richard Nürnberger contends
that the conflict between Calvin and Servetus was a
personification of the conflict between the Renaissance
and the Reformation. Taking still a different view is
Friedman who finds Servetus indicted because he was
neither Protestant nor Catholic. Servetus developed
a distinctly separate approach to Christianity compared
with the traditions of his day and for this he came
into fatal conflict with Calvin.[2]

Bainton firmly contends that Calvin's theology
alone determined the ultimate decision in the Servetus

---

[1] Bainton, Hunted Heretic, pp. 195, 207.

[2] Williams, Radical Reformation, p. 609;
Richard Nürnberger, "Calvin and Servet: Eine Begegnung
zwischen reformatorischem Glauben und modernem Un-
glauben im 16. Jahrhundert," Archiv für Reformationsgeschichte 49 (1958): 201-2; Jerome Friedman, "The
Reformation Merry-Go-Round: The Servetian Glossary of
Heresy," Sixteenth Century Journal 7 (April 1976): 73.
Nürnberger's position is somewhat distinct in that he
sees the theological struggle as mainly Christological
in nature.

affair. Execution of heretics was necessary for Calvin
in order to vindicate the honor of God. One particular
school of thought attempts to justify Calvin's treatment of Servetus on the grounds that Servetus was in
collusion with the Geneva Libertines. The stability
of the Geneva regime was at stake, thus justifying
Calvin's severe strictures against Servetus. On Servetus's alleged Libertine connection Bainton states
that there is not "a shred of contemporary evidence."
The accusation of sedition on the part of Servetus is
totally without foundation.[1]

The arguments for Servetus's association with
the Genevan Libertines usually takes three forms:
1) Servetus plotted to overthrow the regime of Calvin
with the aid of the Libertines, 2) the Libertines
sought to bring about Servetus's acquittal, and 3) the
Libertines communicated with Servetus concerning his
acquittal to the end of his trial. Bainton thoroughly
refutes all three of these points.[2] One does not need
to invoke the arguments concerning the Libertines to
explain Calvin's opposition to Servetus, writes Bainton. The honor of God was at stake. Bainton summarizes
his position on this issue very tersely when he writes,
"Servetus rejected Calvin's view of the trinity and
infant baptism. For that he died."[3]

Bainton's judgment of Calvin is harsh. Since
Bainton studies Servetus from the perspective of the

---

[1]Bainton, "What Is Calvinism?" p. 352; Roland
H. Bainton, "Servetus and the Genevan Libertines,"
Church History 5 (1936): 146.

[2]Bainton, "Genevan Libertines," p. 141.

[3]Bainton, "What Is Calvinism?" p. 352.

history of toleration, Bainton sharply criticizes Calvin's intolerance. Hence Bainton interprets Calvin
as the "peak of Protestant intolerance" and Servetus
as the "victim of Protestant persecution." Bainton
frequently points out the "coldness" of Calvin's personal dealings with Servetus. More extreme than Bainton is Fulton who states that Calvin "murdered his
enemy" and never repented of the crime.[1]

As to the significance of Servetus's death,
Bainton states that it posed the question of religious
liberty for the evangelical churches in an unprecedented
manner. Perhaps, as Bainton notes, it was the cruelty
of the execution which precipitated the intensity of
the toleration controversy.[2] Wilbur contends that according to a sixteenth century document (In haereticis
coercendis by Mino Celso, 1577) many orthodox Christians who witnessed the burning of Servetus converted
to his position because of Servetus's courageous spirit.
Fulton calls the execution "barbaric" and refers to
the trial and death of Servetus as "one of the most
farcical [stages] in man's struggle for his freedom."[3]

Bainton points out that the modern researcher
finds the execution of Servetus appalling, especially

---

[1]Fulton, Servetus, p. 36. Bainton indicts Calvin as a heresy hunter and severely judges him from this
perspective. See Bainton, "What Is Calvinism?" p. 351.

[2]Bainton, Hunted Heretic, p. 214. In Travail
and Hunted Heretic Bainton provides a graphically detailed account of the execution.

[3]Wilbur, Unitarianism, 1:181; Fulton, Servetus,
p. 35. On page 46 Fulton states that Servetus "has taken
his rightful place among those gallant spirits who paid
the supreme price for what they held as truth."

on the tenuous basis of Servetus's alleged crime. However, Bainton states, such an execution should not
shock the twentieth century reader. He says:

> The story of Calvin and Servetus should demon-
> strate for us that our slogans of liberty need con-
> tinually to be thought through afresh. The severity
> of Calvin was born of zeal for truth and even con-
> cern for the victim. Death itself seemed to him not
> too harsh a penalty for perversion of the truth of
> God. Today any of us would be the first to cast a
> stone against Calvin's intolerance; and seldom do
> we reflect that we who are aghast at the burning of
> one man to ashes for religion do not hesitate for
> the preservation of our culture to reduce whole
> cities to cinders.[1]

Herein lies a clear statement of Bainton's bias and
concern in his treatment of the trial and execution of
Servetus.

Bainton casts Servetus in the role of a man of
religion, radical in his theological formulations, but
devotedly sincere in his religious motivation. Bainton
interprets the trial and execution of Servetus as a
breach of Servetus's own freedom of conscience. A
strong sense of advocacy underlies all of Bainton's
Servetus writings. He studies Servetus not simply out
of historical curiosity but out of a deep personal commitment to the ideals of freedom of conscience and
religious toleration.

Sebastian Castellio: The Heretic
as Remonstrator

In the history of toleration, Sebastian Castellio ranks as an eminent representative of the sixteenth

---

[1]Bainton, Hunted Heretic, p. 214. A personal
letter from Bainton to Fulton contains these same sentiments. See Fulton, Servetus, p. 7.

century argument for religious liberty. In the life
and thought of Castellio, Bainton finds a prophetic
voice of one whose protest against intolerance contained the seeds of modern assumptions on the issue
of toleration. Bainton terms Castellio the "champion
of religious liberty." He interprets Castellio, whose
ideas were heretical in the sixteenth century, as vin-
dicated by the progress of history toward freedom of
conscience. Bainton's interest in Castellio focuses
on the arguments for religious liberty set forth by
Castellio; hence Bainton is concerned with Castellio's
thought.

Bainton acknowledges that Castellio is a
relatively unknown figure of the Reformation era.
Such historical anonymity is in Bainton's assessment
quite beneficial because Castellio is one of the few
fortunate persons whose life escaped distortion at the
hands of historians. "Not infrequently," writes Bainton,

> the forgotten are resuscitated only in order to
> serve the purpose of some party after the order
> of Melchisedek which has come to feel the need
> of a geneology and pitches upon a likely personage
> of the past in order to make him a symbol and an
> instrument of propagation.[1]

No party, however, claims Castellio as a progenitor and
hence he is neglected.

Castellio is the only radical of the four
studied thoroughly by Bainton whose life is not a subject of a full-length biography. Instead Bainton produced three major articles on Castellio's life and

---

[1] Roland H. Bainton, "Sebastian Castellio:
Champion of Religious Liberty," in Studies on the Reformation, Collected Papers in Church History, series
2 (Boston: Beacon Press, 1963), p. 139.

thought. These articles are as follows: "Sebastian
Castellio, Champion of Religious Liberty, 1515-1563,"
"Sebastian Castellio and the Toleration Controversy of
the Sixteenth Century," and "Sebastian Castellio: The
Heretic as Remonstrant." Bainton also produced an unpublished monograph on Castellio's ideas of toleration
entitled "Religious Liberty and Religious Knowledge."
Moreover Bainton translated into English one of Castellio's major works, Concerning Heretics.

A standard biographical treatment of Castellio
is a dated work in French by Ferdinand Buisson, Sebastien
Castellion (1892). A treatment of Castellio's ideas
of toleration comprises Castellioniana, Quatre Etudes
sur Sebastien Castellion et L'Idee de la Tolerance.
Several monographic works appear in Autour de Michel
Servetus et de Sebastien Castellion. The most recent
biography (1963) is in Polish, entitled Sebastian Castellion by Waldemar Voise.

Since Bainton's approach stresses Castellio's
thought, this discussion will center on Bainton's interpretation of the ideas presented in Castellio's
writings. This section examines Castellio's protest
against religious intolerance, followed by an examination of his arguments for freedom of conscience.

Bainton claims no knowledge of Castellio's
conversion to Protestantism. He offers the conjecture
that Castellio perhaps witnessed the suffering and
martyrdom of a Protestant refusing to recant before
Catholic authorities, or perhaps he listened to fer-
vent Huguenot psalm-singing. Bainton proposes that
Catholic intolerance precipitated Castellio's initial
interest in the Protestant position. The sources of

his early life indicate only that Castellio went into exile in Strassburg and that later he became a school-master in Geneva.[1] Williams is more specific; he asserts that Castellio converted to Protestantism after reading Calvin's Institutes.[2]

As to the early influences on Castellio, Bainton discerns two movements which deeply tinctured his thought. One was Renaissance humanism and the other was mysticism. Both of these advocated a non-dogmatic approach to religion. Castellio imbibed the ethical relativism of Erasmus and the mystical piety of Sebastian Franck. Bainton states that "the ability to effect a combination [of these two movements] is itself an instance of breadth and balance."[3] Some scholars argue that Castellio was definitely no mystic, yet Bainton claims that through Franck's influence Castellio "had been warmed to the core."[4]

Castellio directed his plea for religious liberty against the intolerance of Calvin and Theodore Beza exemplified in the execution of Servetus. On the significance of the Servetus affair for Castellio's thought in particular and the toleration controversy in general Bainton states:

---

[1]Bainton, Travail, p. 98; Bainton, "Champion," pp. 147-8.

[2]Williams, Radical Reformation, p. 627.

[3]Bainton, "Champion," p. 160. See also Roland H. Bainton, "Sebastian Castellio and the Toleration Controversy of the Sixteenth Century," in Persecution and Liberty: Essays in Honor of George Lincoln Burr (New York: The Century Company, 1931), p. 185.

[4]Bainton, "Toleration Controversy," p. 198.

[T]he stake of Servetus is more crucial because
it became the *cause célèbre* of the toleration
controversy, and Sebastian Castellio is responsible for making it that by his spirited protest
which continued to reverberate even after
oblivion had engulfed the author.[1]

Castellio's concern for humanity and his spirit of
critical inquiry with regard to the Scriptures dis-
posed him to reject both the cause of Servetus's execution and the method of death. From his rejection,
contends Bainton, came the writing of Concerning Heretics. H. Liebing claims that Castellio's position
against Calvin solidified because of Castellio's
friendship with David Joris, an interpretation dis-
counted by Bainton.[2]

Calvin employed the doctrine of predestination
to justify the persecution of heretics. Such a position contended that God would allow execution only to
those condemned to eternal death. Bainton states that
Castellio recoiled against this position. He claimed
that Castellio's rationalistic argumentation showed
that if God had condemned some to eternal death, then
persecution had no point. If the object of persecution were to save souls, then extermination would not
change the immutable decree.[3] Bainton compares the
theological alignments of Calvin and Castellio. For
Calvin God was arbitrary and sovereign, a law unto
Himself. Castellio held that God was merciful and
forgiving. Calvin contended that man was a worm;

---

[1]Bainton, "Champion," p. 142.

[2]Die Religion in Geschichte und Gegenwart,
s.v. "Castellio (Castalio, Chatillon), Sebastian,"
by H. Liebing.

[3]Bainton, "Champion," pp. 144-5, 175.

Castellio proposed that man was a worm "with great
expectations, capable of perfectly obeying God."[1]

In the protest of Castellio against Calvin
Castellio raised four points demonstrating the futility
of persecution. These are as follows: 1) persecution
cannot beget a man in Christ, 2) persecution leads
some to hypocrisy, 3) persecution advertises heresy,
and 4) persecution evokes sedition among the populace.[2]

Bainton finds the distinction which Castellio
made between essentials and non-essentials as most
significant. His distinctions were "destined to play
an enormous role in the entire struggle for religious
liberty . . . ."[3] Castellio had certain tests by
which he relegated to the adiaphora many of the points
about which persecution was raging. Bainton states
that in Castellio's system, a doctrine was essential
only if it were knowable, clear, and reasonable. Consequently Castellio confronted the problem of religious
epistemology.

The relationship which Bainton finds in Castellio's thought between faith and knowledge is a key
to understanding Castellio's entire argument. Bainton
writes: "Castellio to my knowledge was unique in ad-
dressing himself to the problem of knowledge in relation to the problem of liberty."[4] Castellio introduced

---

[1] Bainton, "Toleration Controversy," pp. 192-4.

[2] Bainton, "Champion," pp. 177-8.

[3] Bainton, _Travail_, p. 113.

[4] Roland H. Bainton, "Freedom, Truth and Unity:
Reflections on the Renaissance," in _Early and Medieval
Christianity_, Collected Papers in Church History, series
1 (Boston: Beacon Press, 1962), p. 244. For a thorough

a new perspective to the toleration controversy by
claiming that faith and knowledge were mutually
exclusive.

Castellio discerned three sources of knowledge:
experience, revelation, and reason. The first two of
the above depend upon the third for clarification and
elaboration. Hence Bainton observes that on "this
basis many of the traditional dogmas of the faith are
incapable of conclusive demonstration and lie in the
realm not of knowledge but of faith."[1] Bainton contends that Castellio proceeded to inquire more precisely into the question of religious truth and its
limits. Castellio asserted that to recognize the
limits of what one can know is as important as to
affirm what one does know. This type of rational inquiry into the faith-knowledge issue is for Bainton
critical in the controversy over religious persecution.

Bainton places Castellio's separation of faith
from knowledge within the larger context of the history
of ideas. Castellio, he claims, revived an ancient
distinction representing two levels of certainty.
Bainton comments that "Castellio is doing little more
than elaborating the view of Cicero, and the whole
picture of reason [in relation to faith] is a combination of the early patristic logos doctrine with
Ciceronean strands."[2] Williams also asserts that on

discussion of this point see Roland H. Bainton, "Religious Liberty and Religious Knowledge," article prepared for a festschrift honoring D. C. Macintosh but
not included in the book. 193-? (Typewritten.)

[1]Bainton, The Reformation, p. 216.

[2]Bainton, "New Documents," p. 134.

this point Castellio represents a significant divergence from the views of most of the radical Reformers.
Comparing Castellio's views to Luther's, Williams
writes that

> the reason of the interpreter [of Scripture] oc-
> cupied in Castellio's ethical theism the place
> of Christ as the *opus Dei* in Luther's theology.
> *Ratio* and *spiritus* replaced Luther's *sola fides*
> and *sola scriptura.*[1]

In summation of Castellio's argument Bainton
states:

> The practical consequence for religious liberty
> to be drawn from this type of rationalism was
> obviously the inappropriateness of persecution in
> the interests of dogmas which cannot be positively
> known. Castellio held that we simply do not know
> enough to persecute.[2]

Bainton interprets Castellio on this point as saying
that the very fact of controversy proves that the matter in dispute is not clear.[3]

Bainton interprets Castellio as the progenitor
of ideas which germinated through the succeeding generations in the cause of religious liberty. In Castellio
he locates a sixteenth century prophet of liberty whose
thought transcended his own generation. Bainton sees

---

[1]Williams, Radical Reformation, p. 827.

[2]Bainton, "Champion," p. 168. For a treatment
of this position see Roland H. Bainton, "Church History
and Progress," in Education for Christian Service (New
Haven: Yale University Press, 1922), p. 260.

[3]Bainton claims that this idea of freedom
espoused by Castellio emerged in the writings of John
Locke. Although tenuous, the connection between Castel-
lio and Locke has great significance for the British-
American position on religious toleration. See Roland
H. Bainton, "Sebastian Castellio and the British-Ameri-
can Tradition," in Studies on the Reformation, Collected
Papers in Church History, series 2 (Boston: Beacon
Press, 1963), pp. 182-4.

Castellio's treatment of faith and knowledge, emanating
from the distinction between essentials and non-essentials, as paramount in the intellectual achievements
of Castellio.

Bainton maintains that the most radical point
in Castellio's teaching was his relativizing of conscience. This became, according to Bainton, the "common coin of liberalism."[1] In Castellio's day, the
objective law of God overpowered the inner feelings
of the individual. Yet Castellio held that righteous-
ness was inward, making morality a subjective matter.
Loyalty to what one thinks is right became for him the
ultimate principle of truth. Bainton states that Servetus died for telling the truth, i.e., he said what
he believed. In Castellio's argument, external force
should not constrain a person to deny his own conscience.
Thus Bainton points out that Castellio defined a heretic simply as "one with whom we disagree."[2] Hans
Guggisberg concurs with Bainton's assessment of this
argument by Castellio. Guggisberg writes that Castellio
held that nobody had the right to force the conscience
of another person, and certainly not to persecute
or kill him for reasons of religious disagreement.[3]

This interpretation of Castellio's position
leads Bainton to an evaluation of the role of error.

---

[1]Bainton, Travail, p. 119.

[2]Bainton, "Champion," p. 169.

[3]Hans R. Guggisberg, "Sebastian Castellio on
the Power of the Christian Prince," in The Responsibility
of Power: Historical Essays in Honor of Hajo Holborn,
ed. Leonard Krieger and Fritz Stern (Garden City, N.Y.:
Doubleday and Company, 1967), p. 64.

Here then we have an enunciation of the rights
of error as a stage in the quest for truth.
Error is not the goal, but honest error is
nearer to the truth than dishonest correctness.[1]

Castellio protested against Calvin's handling of the
Servetus affair not because Castellio agreed with Servetus's theology. Instead Castellio honored the rights
of the individual conscience, and held sincerity of
conviction more important than correctness of doctrine.

Although Bainton speaks of the integrity of
this position on the freedom of conscience, he also
points out that this is the weakest point in Castellio's entire argument. To illustrate his criticism
Bainton notes the examples of men in the sixteenth
century like Poltrot who assassinated the Duke of
Guise, Jacques Clement who stabbed Henry III, and
Balthazar Gerard who shot William of Orange. "These
men met Castellio's test that they should be ready to
die for their convictions," states Bainton. "They
were quite prepared to die provided that they were
able first to kill."[2] Bainton asks if the state should
respect such a conscience. Unfortunately Castellio
never dealt with this problem. Bainton thus offers
the conjecture that Castellio would hold to the inviola-
bility of the conscience only as long as it does not
violate another persons's liberty.

Bainton estimates the impact of Castellio's
entire argument for toleration as a watershed in
modern thought on this issue. He writes that Castellio

---

[1]Roland H. Bainton, "The Struggle for Religious
Liberty," in Studies on the Reformation, Collected
Papers in Church History, series 2 (Boston: Beacon
Press, 1963), pp. 219-20.

[2]Bainton, "Toleration Controversy," p. 204.

"set going an agitation that runs in a direct line to
the English Act of Toleration."[1] Rufus Jones, in a
dated article on Castellio, agrees with this assessment as does Guggisberg. Guggisberg ventures that
Castellio's thought

> stands at the beginning of an intellectual tradi-
> tion at whose end we find the catalogue of the
> Rights of Man. The significance of Castellio's
> contribution . . . [is] no longer questioned by
> modern scholarship.[2]

If one considers Bainton indicative of modern scholarship on Castellio, then the significance of Castellio
is indeed unquestioned.

Bainton's treatment of Castellio reflects a
twofold approach. One approach is from the perspective
of the history of toleration. The other is from the
perspective of the history of ideas. The approaches
are interrelated. As a proponent of toleration himself, Bainton is interested in the arguments put forth
by Castellio for a cause to which Bainton adheres.
Likewise as a historian Bainton finds the significance
of Castellio to be in his thought. This latter point
merits further consideration.

Bainton wrote no biography of Castellio as
he did for the other three radicals. This is significant in that Bainton finds Castellio's thought more
important than his life. Bainton's writings on Castellio, although biographical in form, are patterned
as an intellectual portrait of the man. He places
Castellio within the larger context of the history of
ideas, relating his thought to Ciceronian and patristic

---

[1] Bainton, _Travail_, p. 97.

[2] Guggisberg, "Castellio," p. 65. Rufus Jones,
"A Forgotten Hero of the Reformation," _The Constructive
Quarterly_ 1 (June 1913): 423.

ideas and to modern concepts of the freedom of conscience. Bainton appears most like an historian of
ideas in his Castellio writings. The meticulous care
which he gives to delineating Castellio's thought contrasts with the cursory narration which he gives to
Castellio's life. Whereas Bainton's emphasis on Servetus is on his trial and execution, the emphasis for
Castellio is on his thought. Consequently Bainton aptly discloses his historiographical approach in the rec-
ognation that Castellio is "the heretic as remonstrant."

Bernardino Ochino: The Heretic as Exile

A third radical of interest to Bainton is the
Italian Bernardino Ochino of Sienna. Bainton indicates
two reasons for his concern for Ochino. First, Ochino
is significant for the issue of religious liberty.
Bainton places Ochino within the context of the history
of toleration by using Ochino's life of exile as an example of the consequences of religious intolerance.

The argument is often made that banishment is
more suitable a punishment for heresy than the penalty
of death. This argument is one-sided, claims Bainton,
in light of the hardships which exile often brings for
the heretic. Ochino endured five different exiles during
his life; Karl Benrath describes Ochino as a man "tossed
about the world like a ball." Bainton sees Ochino's
life as a situation where "the fox had no hole and the
bird no rest."[1] This protracted insecurity ultimately
clouded Ochino's spirit.

---

[1]Karl Benrath, Bernardino Ochino of Sienna:
A Contribution Towards the History of the Reformation,
trans. Helen Zimmern (New York: Robert Carter and Brothers, 1877), p. 297; Bainton, Travail, p. 149.

A second reason for Bainton's interest in
Ochino lies in Ochino's spiritual odyssey. Ochino
began his life as a Franciscan, an order which Bainton
notes had criticized quite fervently the Crusades of
the Middle Ages. Bainton casts the Franciscan Ochino
in the role of a mystic who became the target of cru-
sading religious intolerance in the Reformation era.
Within the welter of sixteenth century Christendom
Ochino passed from Catholicism to Calvinism and finally
to Anabaptist sentiments.

Bainton produced two works on Ochino, the
more thorough being his book <u>Bernardino Ochino Esule</u>
<u>e Riformatore Senese del Cinquecento</u>.[1] The other is
"Bernardino Ochino: The Heretic as Exile" which forms
a chapter in Bainton's <u>Travail of Religious Liberty</u>.
Twentieth century treatments of Ochino's life are sparse.
Karl Benrath's <u>Bernardino Ochino of Sienna</u> is a dated
but comprehensive work which examines Ochino in the
context of the Reformation in Italy. Father Cuthbert
treats Ochino's early life in volume one of <u>The Capu-</u>
<u>chins</u>. The most recent discussion of Ochino's life is
an article by Philip McNair entitled "Ochino's Apology:
Three Gods or Three Wives?"[2]

[1]For the unpublished English manuscript of
this book see Roland H. Bainton, "Bernardino Ochino
of Sienna," Yale Divinity Library, New Haven, Conn.
(Typewritten).

[2]McNair concentrates on a theological discussion of Ochino's thought; therefore, he develops a
brief biographical sketch of Ochino. See Philip Mc-
Nair, "Ochino's Apology: Three Gods or Three Wives?"
<u>History</u> 60 (October 1975): 353-73.

Bainton narrates the life of Ochino as a leading Capuchin in Italy, and he delineates in a lengthy discussion the course by which Ochino came to embrace Protestant thought. Yet Bainton's emphasis centers on the significance of Ochino's exile necessitated by his Protestant convictions, and in this voluntary banishment Bainton discerns a symbolic event which set the tone for the remainder of Ochino's life. Bainton writes:

> From the heights of the Alps he looked back upon his native land, where he had labored for more than half a century. He was fifty-six. Behind him lay the sunlight playing upon the Bay of Naples, the silhouette of Sienna against an evening sky, daybreak over Fiesole, conversations on heavenly themes with distinguished men and aristocratic women, churches packed and throngs in tears, the pope, the emperor, and dozens of cardinals hanging upon his words--all this behind. Before him lay bleaker lands and unknown tongues, struggling refugee congregations, and all the insecurity of religious revolution.[1]

In this statement Bainton establishes the perspective of Ochino as the exile, whose truthfulness to his conscience led him to a life of perpetual wandering.

Bainton describes the difficulties of banishment in empathetic terms. Cuthbert, however, finds Ochino's exile worthy of an apostate from the Church. He asserts that Ochino's defection from the Capuchins was the "saddest and most desperate" chapter in the history of the Capuchin Reform of the sixteenth century. Cuthbert denounces Ochino as a hypocrite, and he contends that the tragedy of Ochino's exile lay in the suffering which his departure caused for the Capuchins. Benrath's view, on the other hand, approximates Bainton's perspective: there is "something

---

[1]Bainton, _Travail_, p. 157.

deeply tragic" in the fact that Ochino's Protestantism compelled him to abandon his homeland and to sacrifice his life's work in order to find peace of conscience.[1]

Ochino's conversion to Protestantism brought persecution and awakened Ochino to the problem of religious liberty, according to Bainton. The shift to Protestant convictions exposed a character trait in Ochino which Bainton deems significant for the understanding of the radical. Bainton discerns in the Protestant Ochino the trait of an "incorrigible individualist," and he calls him a "prima donna." An individualist forced from his native environment out of necessity, Ochino formulated a doctrine of religious toleration which came into conflict with the major religious groups on the Continent. Ochino, like Castellio, distinguished between the essentials and the non-essentials in religion. He asserted that no person should suffer persecution nor extermination for error in the adiaphora. Moreover, in the case of religious essentials, the offender must recognize that the article in question is indeed essential for the faith.[2]

Bainton finds in Ochino a sensitivity to the issue of toleration which surpassed all other thinkers in his own generation. "Ochino was more discerning than any of his contemporaries with regard to the

---

[1]Father Cuthbert, The Capuchins: A Contribution to the History of the Counter-Reformation, 2 vols. (New York: n.p., 1928; reprint ed., Port Washington, N.Y.: Kennikat Press, 1971), 1:139-40; Benrath, Ochino, 298.

[2]Bainton, Travail, p. 168; Bainton, "Ochino," p. 182.

problem of conscience. The persecutors contended that
no conscience has any right save a right conscience."[1]
Ochino considered that every individual's conscience
should be granted appropriate respect. This is essentially the position of Castellio, yet Bainton notes
that Ochino refined the question. Ochino raised the
tedious question of "conscientious tyrannicide"[2] which
means he recognized the problems inherent in unrestrained freedom of conscience. Bainton claims that
Ochino "is first to have raised a problem when others
did not sense its existence."[3] No other scholar of
Ochino's works appears to make this judgment held by
Bainton.

        If Ochino leaned toward an absolute freedom
of conscience, then how did he stand in regard to persecution? Bainton answers that for Ochino persecution
was futile because of a determinism both of intellect
and of faith. An individual cannot fully assent to
a doctrine which he rejects intellectually. Moreover
faith is a gift of God induced only by prayer. Bainton
writes, "Knives and spears are of no avail. If the
magistrate have recourse to these he may increase
heresy by making martyrs."[4] The magistrate simply
may drive the weak to hypocrisy by forced assent, and
he may drive the strong to inflexibility. In essence,
contends Bainton, Ochino claimed that persecution of
heresy may destroy a heretic before he has the opportunity to repent.

---

[1]Bainton, Travail, p. 171.

[2]Ibid.

[3]Ibid., p. 172.

[4]Bainton, "Ochino," p. 183.

Bainton proposes that Ochino's view of religious liberty had little impact on his own generation
or the cause of the Reformation, except in England.
When exiled from Augsburg, Ochino fled to England.
How far Ochino's thought influenced Cranmer and the
course of the English Reformation is a matter of
debate. Bainton contends that Ochino may have influenced Cranmer's movement toward a Zurich-type
Protestantism.[1]

Rather than casting Ochino in the role of an
influential figure on the Reformation, Bainton portrays him as one overpowered by the intolerance of
the Reformation. The impact of intolerance forced
Ochino to spend his entire life as a Protestant so-
journer and ultimately precipitated in Ochino a keen
disillusionment with the Reformation. Like Erasmus,
Bainton states, Ochino became disillusioned at the
violence and the intolerant extremes of the Reformation. Ochino suffered great discomfort in every
succeeding confrontation with the Church, both Catholic
and Protestant. In Italy, Ochino's Protestant ideas
precipitated his summons to Rome where he would certainly face imprisonment or death. Exile to Protestant Europe offered no better life. Bainton writes:

> At Geneva he had seen a Church State, a holy
> commonwealth, a select community based upon the
> Word of God. At Augsburg he had witnessed four

---

[1]Ibid., p. 137; Roland H. Bainton, "Feminine
Piety in Tudor England," in Christian Spirituality:
Essays in Honor of Gordon Rupp, ed. Peter Brooks
(London: S.C.M. Press, 1975), pp. 195-6. Besides
this debatable influence on England, Bainton sees
Ochino as having a degree of influence on Antitrini-
tarian thought. A later section of the chapter deals
with this question.

religions side by side with a moderate Lutheranism
in the ascendant. In England he was to watch the
birth pangs of a national Church.[1]

In each of these locations Ochino had suffered rejection and ostracism. From each he ultimately fled persecution.

Near the end of Ochino's life when he was
living in Zurich the disillusionment became intense.
Bainton writes, "Ochino had come to realize like Jere-
miah that to demolish the high places is not to bring
in the covenant written . . . on hearts of flesh."[2]
Having demolished his faith in Catholicism, Ochino
recognized that the freedom offered by Protestantism
held no better promise to the dissident. Bainton
herein deplores the practice of banishment. As a
form of religious intolerance it is a harsh and de-
bilitating punishment for the dissenter, but it is
also an ineffective method of dealing with a believer's
conscience.

In addition to interpeting Ochino as an exile
Bainton's treatment of Ochino emphasizes Ochino's
religious odyssey. Bainton correlates Ochino's wanderings as an exile with his wanderings as a man of
faith: he describes Ochino's religious life as a
pilgrimage from the Capuchins to Anabaptism.

Bainton finds throughout Ochino's life the
underlying strands of Franciscan thought. Initially
nurtured as a Franciscan monk, Ochino was strongly attracted to the mystical tradition within Franciscanism.
He was never to abandon his grounding in mysticism.

---

[1]Bainton, Travail, p. 163.

[2]Bainton, "Ochino," p. 187.

Bainton states that Ochino was the perfect exemplifica-
tion of the medieval saint, "austere, emaciated, frail
. . . with the rapt and ethereal look of a Moses de-
scending from the Mount . . . ."[1]

Ochino was a great preacher. Bainton calls
Ochino "the Savonarola of his generation in Italy,"
an appellation used also in Benrath's description of
Ochino. His sermons were characterized by marked
diction and vibrant emotion. His "ravishing voice"
melted his hearers. Ochino represented Franciscan
preaching at its best. His preaching was so powerful
that the cities of Italy vied for his services. Williams claims that when Ochino spoke he did so with
"terrifying directness." Benrath writes that Ochino
could "move stones to tears." Because of his unusually
gifted ability to sway the masses in preaching, Ochino
commanded the adoration of Italy's most prominent
citizens. Bainton states that everywhere Ochino was
"the lion of the aristocracy."[2]

As a conscientious monk, Ochino devoted himself not only to the task of preaching but also to
the discipline of study. Bainton characterizes him
as a man with a keen and inquiring mind. As such he
was open to diverse intellectual currents in sixteenth
century Italy, among which was the stream of Erasmian
thought mediated through Juan de Valdéz. Ochino came
under Valdéz's influence and through Valdéz he came

---

[1]Bainton, "Champion," pp. 159-60; Bainton,
Travail, p. 150; Benrath, Ochino, p. 21.

[2]Bainton, Travail, p. 150; Williams, Radical
Reformation, p. 540; Benrath, Ochino, p. 21; Bainton,
"Ochino," pp. 21, 40, 157.

into contact with Protestant thought. Gradually
Ochino embraced Protestantism. This interpretation
by Bainton parallels that of Philip McNair, Cuthbert,
and Benrath.[1] The evangelical doctrines of grace
surfaced in Ochino's preaching and ultimately made
his stay in Italy untenable.

      From Italy he went to Geneva. There, Bainton
claims, Ochino embraced Calvinism almost in its entirety. The reason for this was that Calvin, without
knowing it, approximated the tradition of Franciscan
illuminism. Bainton notes:

> The scorn of the Erasmian Valdéz for external
> austerities had not weaned the spiritual Fran-
> ciscan from an admiration for ascetic rigor and
> zeal for the literal pattern of the primitive
> church. The Protestants had abandoned monas-
> ticism only in order to impose the counsels of
> perfection on the entire Christian community
> . . . ."[1]

Hence Bainton finds Ochino welcoming the religious
positions espoused by the Geneva Calvinists. According to Bainton there was no theological breach between
Ochino and Calvin which precipitated Ochino's departure
from Geneva. Apparently the departure grew out of
Ochino's financial needs which could not be met in
Geneva. Ochino's move from Geneva to Augsburg continued the series of transitions and exiles which
characterized his life.

      Bainton describes the influence which these
travels had on Ochino. One significant effect was
Ochino's confrontation with more radical forms of

---

[1]McNair, "Ochino's Apology," p. 360; Cuthbert,
Capuchins, p. 134; Benrath, Ochino, p. 68.

[2]Bainton, "Ochino," p. 93.

Protestantism, notably Antitrinitarianism. This phase
of Ochino's religious development is a point of contention among Ochino scholars. Bainton acknowledges
that some of Ochino's contemporaries considered him
Antitrinitarian, but there is no proof in any source,
contends Bainton, that Ochino did in fact move toward
Antitrinitarian thought.[1] Benrath agrees with Bainton's
position, stating that Ochino never doubted the doctrine of the Trinity. However, McNair claims that
from the years 1555 to 1562 Ochino "seems to have
been reoriented by Sozini's subtle and speculative
spiritualizing." The point of departure for Ochino,
writes McNair, may have been the execution of Servetus.[2]

        Earl Morse Wilbur maintains that Ochino's
writings "furnished a complete arsenal of arguments"
against the doctrine of the Trinity. The Socinians
later adopted these arguments with little change or
addition. Yet Wilbur does not propose that Ochino
ever fully accepted Antitrinitarianism, although he
was a kindred spirit. Wilbur states in A History of
Unitarianism that "Ochino was perhaps better entitled
than any other than we have mentioned, to be regarded
as a pioneer of the movement whose history we are
following."[3]

        Although Bainton denies charges of Antitrini-
tarian thought in Ochino, he does point out that Ochino

---

[1]Bainton, Travail, p. 174.

[2]Benrath, Ochino, p. 182; McNair, "Ochino's
Apology," p. 361.

[3]Wilbur, Unitarianism, 1:257.

may have influenced the Antitrinitarian doctrine of
the Atonement:

> One notes here also echoes of the Scotist
> view that God might equally well have chosen
> any other way of saving men. Thus the lines
> from Scotus and Valdéz ran through Ochino to
> the Racovian catechism of the Socinians.[1]

Williams agrees with Bainton here, finding a common
thread from Valdéz to Ochino and to Sozini.[2]

Bainton depicts the final stages of Ochino's
religious development by showing his growing closeness
to Anabaptism. Bainton finds the Anabaptist emphasis
on the spirit, the attempt to restore primitive Christianity, ascetic living, and the objection to war as
points of agreement with Ochino's later thought.
Drawing together the religious influences of Ochino's
life, Bainton writes:

> Much of Anabaptism would accord with his own
> lifetime attitudes. The way for Anabaptism
> had been in some measure prepared by the reli-
> gious movements of the Middle Ages and the
> Moravian group reckoned the Fraticelli among
> their spiritual ancestors.[3]

Ochino's roots in Franciscan mysticism and austerity
prepared the way for a shift to some forms of Anabaptism.

Bainton says that Ochino, in his later years,
had become the prophet of the inward word. "On
nothing external, not on the Book, not on the spoken
word does religion depend, but on the voice of God
within the heart."[4] Hence Bainton finds a continuity

---

[1]Bainton, _Travail_, pp. 174-5.

[2]Williams, _Radical Reformation_, p. 14.

[3]Bainton, "Ochino," p. 228.

[4]Ibid., p. 188.

throughout the diverse religious stages of Ochino's
life in the mystical piety of Franciscanism. Here
Bainton sees a common theme uniting Ochino's religious life from his beginning as a Capuchin to his
final association with Anabaptism.

In Bainton's Ochino writings several motifs
common to many of Bainton's writings are prominent.
For example, Bainton's advocacy for religious toleration is clear in his description of Ochino's experiences.

Another motif to emerge in the Ochino writings
is Bainton's interest in the question of religious
experience. Bainton speaks positively of the hearty
devotion of the Franciscans. He interprets Ochino from
the perspective of Ochino's relationship with God.
Closely related to this motif is another theme which
appears in Bainton's work on Ochino: he casts Ochino
in the role of an indomitable individualist. He sees
Ochino as a person faithful to his own convictions
and as one willing to suffer hardships for the cause
of freedom of conscience.

David Joris: The Heretic as Hypocrite

A fourth radical deemed significant by Bainton
for the history of toleration is David Joris. Bainton finds Joris interesting because of Joris's mystical
approach to toleration and because his behavior demonstrated Castellio's thesis that all too readily persecution turns a heretic into a hypocrite.[1]

Bainton's David Joris, Wiedertäufer und Kämpfer für Toleranz im 16. Jahrhundert, is the only

---

[1]Bainton, Travail, p. 125.

biography on Joris written in the twentieth century.[1]
Bainton states that he had the opportunity in 1926 of
studying the Jorist papers preserved in the Universitäts-
bibliothek at Basel. Bainton has published several
Jorist documents including eight letters in his article
"Williams Postell and the Netherlands." Likewise in
Concerning Heretics (the translation by Bainton of
Castellio's work on toleration) Bainton includes his
translation of "The Pleas of David Joris for Servetus."[2]
Works by other scholars on Joris are scant. The most
complete work on Joris's life besides Bainton's biography is the article "David Joris und seine Gemeinde
in Basel" by Paul Burckhardt.[3]

Bainton describes Joris as a Hollander and as
an Anabaptist of a very eccentric variety. Joris's
enthusiasm for religion matched his unconventional
methods of propagating the faith. Bainton states, "Er
war ein eifriger Beter, ein unermüdlicher Mahner, ein
fesselnder, wenn auch unmethodischer Lehrer."[4] In

---

[1]This monograph is available only in German.
The unpublished English manuscript appears under the
title "David Joris: A Refugee from the Netherlands,"
Yale Divinity Library, New Haven, Conn. (Typewritten.)

[2]The English translation of this letter appears also in Bainton, Hunted Heretic, pp. 206-7.

[3]Paul Burckhardt, "David Joris und seine
Gemeinde in Basel," Basler Zeitschrift für Geschichte
und Altertumskunde 48 (1949): 5-106.

[4]Roland H. Bainton, David Joris, Wiedertäufer
und Kämpfer für Toleranz im 16. Jahrhundert (Leipzig: M.
Heinsius Nachfolger, 1937), p. 61. "He was an eager wor-
shipper, an indefatigable admonisher, a captivating although unmethodical teacher." This translation and all
those following are the writer's translations.

interpreting Joris's life Bainton finds no consistency to his prophetic teachings.

He see an early Joris imbued with the belief
that he has a messianic calling. However, Bainton
points out that at Basel a change occurred in Joris's
messianism which radically moved him toward mysticism.
As a young radical in Holland, Joris contended that
the Holy Spirit spoke directly to him in Dutch. During
this period of his life, writes Bainton, ecstatic experiences, visions, and apocalypticism marked Joris's
religion. Yet as a heretic in hiding in Basel, Joris
gravitated toward a pronounced mysticism, rejecting
de facto the ecstacy and apocalypticism of his younger
days. Describing Joris's life in Basel, Bainton
claims: "Joris war weit entfernt von dem Tage, wo
der Heilige Geist holländisch gesprochen hatte."[1]
Thus Bainton perceives a distinct cleavage in Joris's
career precipitated by the flight of the heretic
from Holland to Basel.

Bainton's interpretation of Joris centers on
the theme of Joris as a hypocrite. The chapter divisions of David Joris are significant. The two sections of this book are entitled respectively "Die
Prophet in den Niederlanden" and "Der Basler Ketzer-
prozeß ." The thread which Bainton follows is the
emergence of the hypocrite.

Bainton considers the religious environment
of the Netherlands as highly influential on the early
thinking of Joris. Joris grew to manhood, states

[1]Bainton, Joris, p. 81. "Joris was widely
removed from the day when the Holy Spirit had spoken
in Dutch."

Bainton, in a time of exceptional religious ferment.
Only in the Netherlands could one find "such a juxta-
position of an intensely orthodox foreign administrator
in clash with a populace widely addicted to Protestantism of the most radical type."[1]   Bainton locates several sources of influence which had an impact on Joris.
Melchior Hoffman, the "father of Anabaptism" in the
Netherlands, was a major influence on him.   Likewise
the mystical thought of such works as the Imitatio
Christi and the Theologia Deutsch deeply influenced
Joris's religion.   Bainton also notes that the larger
context of international events of the sixteenth century influenced his thought.

Bainton perceives Joris's thought as a *via
media* in Holland between the Münsterites on one hand
and the followers of Menno Simons on the other.   By
adopting a position between these two forms of Anabaptism, Joris secured for himself a wide following.[2]
Joris, in Bainton's interpretation, developed a new
form of Anabaptist thought which gained some degree
of acceptance in Holland.   Joris's Anabaptism reflected chiliastic thought, and at the Anabaptist

_____

[1]Bainton, Travail, p. 126.

[2]Bainton, Joris, pp. v-vi.   Here Bainton
writes: "Joris' Stellungnahme zwischen diesen beiden
Gruppen sicherte ihm eine weite Anhängerschaft, die
es ihm ermöglichte, schließlich das Leben eines
wohlhabenden Mannes im fernen Basel zu führen, von
wo aus er eine umfassende schriftstellerische und
seelsorgerliche Tätigkeit entfaltete."

Conference in Bucholt in 1535 the strong mystical
tendencies of Joris began to show.[1]

Soon after this conference, Joris had what
Bainton regards as a life-changing experience. Joris
had visions of himself as the "third David." In these
visions Joris saw the three Davids as King David, Christ
the Son of David, and David Joris. The first David
was a type, the third an ambassador. The role of the
third David "was transmuted into that of the purga-
tive stage of the mystic and resembled therefore
greatly the mission of the Suffering Servant of
Isaiah."[2] The result of these visions was the assumption of a strongly messianic role in the work of Joris.

Bainton approaches these visions as a point
of departure for Joris's religious ideas. Such an
experience increased both the radicalness of Joris's
sect and the resentment of the Dutch authorities.
Bainton, however, is careful not to stress the radical
nature of Joris's own messianic thinking. The blending of Joris's mysticism with his messianic ideas
had the effect of muting the intense apocalypticism
which characterized some of the members of the Joris
sect. Bainton contends:

> Ein weiterer, noch wichtigerer Gesichtspunkt
> für das Verständnis von Joris ist der, daß von

---

[1]Bainton, _Travail_, pp. 128-9. Bainton contends that at this conference Joris spiritualized
all the controversial points, thus winning him many
followers.

[2]Ibid., p. 131. A terse discussion of this
vision appears in Bainton, _Joris_, pp. 30-31.

Anfang an sein Messianismus durch seinen Mystizismus
gemäßigt wurde."[1]
Yet the mysticism of Joris did not deter him from the
prophetic course which he felt he must pursue.

Bainton shows that Joris's pursuit of his messianic role brought upon the sectarian leader the threat
of persecution from the authorities. This, in turn,
led him to champion religious liberty. "One is not
amazed," writes Bainton, "that the head of an under-
ground religious association, wandering for five years
with a price on his head, should have been an advocate
of religious liberty."[2] In Joris's advocacy of religious toleration Bainton emphasizes the significance
of Joris's mysticism. Bainton's own writings on
religious toleration argue that there are two positions which lean most strongly toward religious freedom: rationalism and mysticism.[3] Castellio is for
Bainton an example of the rationalist's view of toleration; Joris is an example of the mystic's view.

In Joris's pleas for liberty he emphasized a
doctrine of God common to many mystics. "Basic was
his picture of God as impartial and unrestricted, ex-
tending his grace to all creatures and refusing to be
bound by all man-made lines of land or sect."[4] Likewise

[1]Bainton, Joris, p. 34. "A further more important point for the understanding of Joris is that
from the beginning his messianism was moderated by
his mysticism."

[2]Bainton, Travail, pp. 134-5.

[3]For a discussion of this position see Bainton, "Changing Ideas and Ideals," pp. 168-9.

[4]Bainton, Travail, pp. 134-5.

the concept of faith entertained by Joris contained
the mystic's disdain for confessional uniformity.
Faith for Joris was not assent to an article but
instead was an experience of the spirit. Bainton
points out that this line of thought eliminates the
role of the magistrate as the judge of religious
competency.

There are certain dangers inherent in the
mystics' argument. Bainton points out that too much
emphasis on the spirit can lead to a different form
of intolerance such as that of the Münsterites "who
grasped the sword under inspiration."[1] Yet Bainton
observes that the emphasis on the inwardness of religion generally has the effect of making outward con-
formity unnecessary. If such freedom of conscience
predominated, how could one identify a heretic?
Castellio had claimed that a heretic is simply "one
with whom we disagree." Joris defined a heretic, as
Bainton points out, as an unregenerate person. Bainton asks, "wer ist dann ein Ketzer? Der wahre Ketzer
ist der, der die neue Geburt nicht empfangen hat."[2]
For Bainton, the significance of Joris's argument
lay in the consistent emphasis on personal experience
over against propositional unanimity.

In Joris's life in the Netherlands Bainton
stresses two factors significant for Joris's attitude
toward religious liberty. One factor, Joris's messianism, made him a heretic sought by the authorities.

---

[1]Ibid., p. 137; Bainton, _Joris_, pp. 45, 83.

[2]Bainton, _Joris_, p. 84. ". . . . who is then
a heretic? The real heretic is the one who has not
received the new birth."

The other factor, Joris's mysticism, undercut the
basis for persecution. Joris's ideas on religious
toleration thus developed out of his own personal
experience.

The prospect of spending a lifetime of avoid-
ing the authorities had little appeal to Joris. Hence
Joris, after several years of furtive and clandestine
activity in the Netherlands, moved to Basel and there
established a life under the name of Jan van Brugge.
Whereas Bainton considers Joris's ideas on toleration
as the most significant development in the Netherlands
period of his life, he considers the life of hypocrisy
lived by Joris as the most significant aspect of the
Basel period.

Due to the wide following of Joris in the
Netherlands, he accumulated considerable wealth. In
Basel he lived the life of a writer in comfort and
quiet. Joris painted, played with his children, and
devoted much time to the affairs of the soul.[1] Con-
trasting the lifestyles between Joris in Basel and his
followers in the Netherlands, Bainton writes that "the
third David was basking under his vines and fig trees
while his followers still confronted the Philistines
in the Netherlands."[2]

Bainton contends that many persons condemned
Joris for such hypocrisy. Two such persons mentioned
by Bainton are Joris's son-in-law, Nicholaes Blesdijk,
and William Postell. Postell earlier had esteemed
Joris for his "religious illumination" but rejected

---

[1]Ibid., pp. v, 61.

[2]Bainton, _Travail_, pp. 144-5.

him for living a life of ease.[1] Bainton mentions that,
in an essay on Postell, Sigrid Stahlmann argues against
Postell's appreciation for Joris. Stahlmann claimed
that the Jorist sect esteemed Postell, but Postell himself never entertained any attachment to Joris.[2]
Nevertheless, Bainton points out that Joris's life in
Basel elicited caustic criticism from Postell on the
grounds of hypocrisy.

Bainton further contends that during the residence in Basel Joris "softened" the messianic views
of earlier years. As Joris grew older, he grew less
attached to messianic pretensions and more drawn
toward the mystical life. Bainton interprets Joris's
development toward mysticism as precipitated by necessity. Persecution in Holland led him to Basel, and
mysticism in his Basel years led him to conceal his
true identity. Joris made a cloister of his own
heart. For him the inward cross became more important
than the outward.[3] Paul Burckhardt argues with Bainton's position that Joris's messianic pretentions
diminished in Basel. Instead Burckhardt sees a consistency in Joris's messianism throughout his life.[4]

---

[1]Roland H. Bainton, "William Postell and the
Netherlands," in Studies on the Reformation, Collected
Papers in Church History, series 2 (Boston: Beacon
Press, 1963), p. 186. In this article Bainton includes
several letters as primary source evidence to demon-
strate the connection between Joris and Postell.

[2]Ibid., p. 185.

[3]Bainton, Travail, pp. 141-2, 145.

[4]See Bainton's analysis of the question of
consistency in Bainton, Travail, p. 263.

Joris rationalized his life in Basel on the
basis of his views of the positive and negative
characteristics of Christianity. Bainton contends
that the mature Joris did not reject the concept of
a suffering church, but rather Joris interpreted suffering as the negative characteristic of Christianity.
The positive characteristic was love. Summarizing
Joris's view of love Bainton writes:

> Dies ist das negative Kennzeichen. Das positive
> ist Liebe, die ihren Ausdruck findet in Langmut,
> Sanftmut und Demut, wie die Langmut und Sanftmut
> Christi.[1]

Bainton points out that the life of Joris in Basel
had more affinity with the positive than the negative
characteristic of Christianity.

Bainton states that Joris died in Basel,
where the authorities never discovered his true identity. It was not until months after Joris's burial
that his hypocrisy came to light. Only then was action
taken against Joris. Bainton describes the burning
of Joris's exhumed body and the forced recantation of
all known Jorists in Basel. At the conclusion of
this discussion Bainton offers the following conjecture:

> One can imagine Sebastian Castellio walking
> home on that thirteenth day of May [the day of
> the auto-da-fe] and reflecting upon the singular
> demonstration of the truth of his contention that
> persecution can turn a heretic into a hypocrite.[2]

---

[1] Bainton, _Joris_, p. 87. "This [suffering] is
the negative distinguishing characteristic. The positive distinguishing characteristic is love which found
its expression in patience, gentleness, and humility,
as the patience and gentleness of Christ."

[2] Bainton, _Travail_, p. 148.

In this comment Bainton restates his own interpretation
of Joris. Persecution had not succeeded in making
Joris orthodox. Instead it drove him into anonymity
in Basel to live as a hypocrite, denying externally
the sentiments of his conscience.

One point at which Bainton departs from his
standard biographical approach is in the categorization
of Joris's life. Bainton proposes a disparity between the young Joris and the mature Joris. This
methodology is distinctively different for Bainton.
Generally he proposes a continuity of thought in the
characters whom he studies. For example, he asserts
a continuity of thought in Erasmus, a continuity of
the *Anfechtungen* in Luther, and a continuity of
mystical piety in Servetus. Such an approach distinguishes Bainton from other Reformation scholars. In
the case of Joris, however, Bainton discovers a definite difference between Joris's life and thought in
the Netherlands period and in the Basel period. This
perspective, based on Bainton's interpretation of the
primary sources, differs from Burckhardt's position
which proposes a continuity of messianic thought in
Joris. Hence in the Joris writing Bainton displays
an interpretation distinct from his other biographical
works.

Conclusion

The writings on the left wing of the Reformation comprise the most extensive area of Bainton's
Reformation corpus. The assessment of these writings
will focus on three major considerations. The themes
evident in the left wing writings provide insight into
the general historiographical approaches employed by
Bainton in the entire Reformation corpus.

The conceptual category, "left wing," came
into common usage due in part to Bainton's adoption of
the term in his own works. Although use of the term
now draws scholarly criticism from some historians,
Bainton's employment of the category "left wing of
the Reformation" pointed the way toward including a
vast and diverse movement under a generic topic.
Bainton's work on the left wing also provided an important impetus to the scholarly research in this
burgeoning field of study: many of his students
worked in this field.

Bainton also produced creative monographic
works on the four radicals. The work by Bainton on
each of these heretics remains standard in the field.
For example, the biography of Servetus is the single
scholarly writing on the life of Servetus available
in English. Moreover, Hunted Heretic (published in
French as Michel Servet, hérétique et martyr, 1511-
1553) ranks internationally as a standard work of
twentieth century Servetus scholarship.

The Castellio writings, like the Servetus
works, are foundational writings. Although few works
deal with the life and thought of Castellio, Bainton's
three monographic articles are standard works on
Castellio. Bainton's translation of Concerning Heretics adds to the significant original work done on
this sixteenth century heretic.

The Ochino and Joris writings by Bainton are
indeed groundbreaking works. These two sixteenth century figures elicit little scholarly attention, and
as a result there is a dearth of writings on both of
them. Bainton's Bernardino Ochino, although still
unavailable in English, is one of few writings on
Ochino's life. The interpretive work on Ochino is

as yet unchallenged by contemporary scholars. <u>David
Joris</u> is the only biography on Joris available in
any language. Certainly in the case of Joris, Bainton is attempting to rescue an unknown figure from
historical oblivion. Bainton's interest is in the
unheralded prophet, in the exploited religious
groups, and in the hearty souls hidden in historical
anonymity. It appears as a historiographical concern
of Bainton's to do justice to such people in his own
writings.

In the area of Anabaptist research, Bainton
falls within the scope of Bender's influence. Bainton's left wing writings are significant because of
the contribution they make toward the positive attitude
and burgeoning integrity of Anabaptist studies during
the middle years of the twentieth century. For example,
Bainton's work on Anabaptist contributions to history,
on Anabaptist origins, and on Anabaptist thought all
contributed to dispelling the idea of Anabaptism as
the unstable and violent fringe of the Reformation.
Likewise, Bainton's conceptualization of primitivism
within the context of restitution became a standard
interpretive approach for many scholars. Bainton's
Anabaptist writings reflect the larger interests of
the Bender generation. The strength of that school
of thought was its emphasis on the positive contributions of Anabaptist traditions; its limitation was its
simplistic approach to a highly complex pheonomenon.

Perhaps the most prominent theme pursued by
Bainton with the left wing is his underlying advocacy
for toleration. Bainton studied the four radicals
because of their significance for the history of
toleration. Appeals to religious liberty and freedom

of conscience emerge repeatedly in Bainton's treatment of the left wing in the sixteenth century, and he repeatedly critiqued the alternatives: the inadequacy of persecution, the inhumanity of extermination, and the injustice of intolerance.

In many instances Bainton becomes less than objective due to his own sympathies with religious liberty. He uses his historical writings as a platform from which to address issues of personal interest.

A similar personal interest is his concern for the broader questions of freedom of conscience. Examples of his work on this issue in the historical materials are his writings on Castellio and Ochino. Both of these men dealt with freedom of conscience, and Ochino especially raises for Bainton the volatile issue of conscientious tyrannicide. This interest by Bainton is more than historical curiosity. It is an interest born from his own struggle with these same issues precipitated by his pacifism.

CHAPTER V

THE HISTORIOGRAPHY OF ROLAND H. BAINTON

Underlying Assumptions
View of History

There is no thorough development of Bainton's
philosophy of history in any of his writings. One
must reconstruct Bainton's view of history by synthesizing the numerous comments about the nature of history scattered throughout Bainton's writings. Bainton's understanding of history includes the major
ideas of progress, causation, and rhythms of history.
These ideas are the most clearly discernible and most
distinctive concepts in his philosophy of history.

In his book Yesterday, Today, and What Next?
Bainton distinguishes three different philosophies of
history. One is the philosophy of fate and fortune,
a second is the philosophy of a cyclical pattern, and
a third is the philosophy of progress. The philosophy
of fate and fortune is occasionally convincing according to Bainton. For example, he points out that
Luther escaped arrest by the Catholic authorities
through what Bainton calls a "fluke." Likewise Bainton draws from his own personal experience in claiming
that he once escaped death simply by fortune.[1] As a

---

[1]Roland H. Bainton, Yesterday, Today, and
What Next? (Minneapolis, Minn.: Augsburg Publishing
House, 1978), pp. 18, 20.

workable philosophy of history, however, the idea of
fate and fortune provides little satisfaction for
Bainton.

Bainton is also sharply critical of the cyclical philosophy of history. He writes that the examples
of the waxing and waning of the moon and the changing
of the seasons "when used as analogies for human history falter because in each case it is the same moon,
the same planet, the same earth which repeats its
course."[1] The merit of this view of history is in its
idea of the recurrence of patterns. Bainton contends
that any philosophy, religion, or ethos which profoundly influenced a generation and then diminished
will eventually revive to influence later generations.
Bainton's chief criticism of this idea of history lies
in its deterministic view of life. If the entire
structure of the universe revolves in an unchanging
framework there can be no creativity and there can be
no spontaneity in man. The philosophy of progress is
most appealing to Bainton.

His earliest publication (1922) was an article
entitled "Church History and Progress." In this article Bainton states:

> The hope of achievement is the spur of ef-
> fort. Nothing so slackens the speed of the racer
> as the fear that he may run in vain. The Chris-
> tian minister is willing to spend and be spent so
> long as he believes that the world may be bettered.[2]

What justification does Bainton give for this confidence in progress? He contends that for liberal

---

[1] Ibid., p. 21.

[2] Roland H. Bainton, "Church History and Progress," in Education for Christian Service (New Haven:
Yale University Press, 1922), p. 245.

Protestantism faith in progress supplanted the chiliastic hope. This is true for Bainton's own concept of
history. To believe in progress, he writes, one must
have an assurance that there is a future. Bainton
centers his belief in both progress and the future
around an optimistic view of man by which he proposes
a this-worldly chiliastic vision of the amelioration
of mankind.

A clear example of Bainton's belief in progress in history is in his writings on the history
of toleration. In response to the question, "Has man
progressed morally?" Bainton states that the history of religious toleration depicts the gradual progress of man from acute intolerance to widespread
toleration. Although admitting that toleration remains tenuous in every generation, Bainton finds that
twentieth century men interpret the idea of freedom
of conscience as a self-evident truth.[1]

Progress is not a constant in Bainton's view
of history. He notes that degeneration is also a
factor of history. The fact of degeneration does not
negate the ultimate progress of history. Bainton
states,

> Sometimes decline is real, but a stage in prog-
> ress. Sometimes it may be progress itself, be-
> cause the original ideal was undesirable, or
> pursued with more heat than light.[2]

There is no determinism in Bainton's idea of progress.
He contends that one generation may gain while the

---

[1]Roland H. Bainton, "The Anabaptist Contribution to History," in Studies on the Reformation, Collected Papers in Church History, series 2 (Boston:
Beacon Press, 1963), pp. 199, 205-6.

[2]Bainton, "Progress," p. 262.

succeeding generation may decline. Yet ultimately
mankind may overcome certain evils and may register
certain gains by transcending the confines of particular cultures. In a summary statement Bainton says,
"We have no reason to assume that the future will
afford no advances over the present."[1]

Bainton graphically frames his thesis of the
progress of history by proposing that progress comes
by "volcanic eruptions" each of which carries mankind
farther along. Every age, he states, requires the
eruption of new streams of commitment and achievement.
Bainton writes:

> There is no inevitable progress. We stand where
> we now are because of the efforts of those of
> whom the world was not worthy. Only a like ef-
> fort will save us from . . . the short-sighted
> vindictiveness of our time. Progress depends
> upon a new eruption that shall send forth molten
> streams of living flame.[2]

Hence Bainton affirms that progress rests on the ability and the decision of man. Progress is possible
ultimately because of the innate capacity of man to
overcome injustice and to ameliorate society. Bainton's view of progress shows the influence of early
twentieth century liberalism on his thinking. He
holds to an optimistic view of history, and he has
great confidence in man's ability to achieve goodness.

The consideration of Bainton's understanding
of causation in history indicates that he avoids any
monocausationalism. He operates carefully with the

----

[1] Roland H. Bainton, "Burned Heretic: Michael
Servetus," Christian Century 70 (28 October 1953): 70.

[2] Bainton, "Progress," p. 266.

understanding that events occur in the context of interaction among numerous factors within culture.
Seldom does Bainton show any cause-effect relationship, but instead he interprets events as arising
from various historical phenomena which act as conditioning factors. Bainton sees culture as organic
with each factor conditioning all others.

His historical writings are replete with
examples of this understanding of causation. In a
discussion of the causes of the Reformation Bainton
delineates the economic, social, political, and religious developments of late medieval years which set
the stage for the Reformation. Concluding that the
religious situation was the most significant factor
in inaugurating the Protestant movement, Bainton
states:

> The Reformation was not derived from any of
> these movements, however much its course may have
> been conditioned by them . . . . The Reformation
> was above all else a revival of religion. So
> much is this the case that some have looked upon
> it as the last great flowering of the piety of
> the Middle Ages.[1]

Another example is Bainton's interpretation
of Servetus's embracing of Antitrinitarianism. Bainton gives much emphasis to Servetus's religious ideas,
but points out that many other factors conditioned the
movement away from Trinitarianism. In Hunted Heretic
Bainton thoroughly examines the social, political,
and intellectual influences on Servetus. Likewise
Bainton points out the significance of the sixteenth
century Zeitgeist and the late medieval trinitarian

---

[1]Roland H. Bainton, The Reformation of the
Sixteenth Century (Boston: Beacon Press, 1952), p. 3.

speculation as formative for Servetus. All of these
factors, contends Bainton, are necessary to understand the emergence of Antitrinitarian thought in
Servetus.

A third example evidences itself in Bainton's
interpretation of the pacifism of Erasmus. Some scholars argue for an environmental interpretation of
Erasmus's pacifism based on the fact that Erasmus grew
to manhood in the small state of Holland. This factor
is significant, claim some scholars, when contrasted
with the fact that the power politics of Machiavelli
emerged from an Italy which was the center of war,
conquest, and ruthless diplomacy. Bainton denies
that the pacifistic sentiments of Erasmus allow such
a singular explanation. He finds numerous factors
influencing Erasmus's pacifism such as Erasmus's concept of Christian brotherhood, the pacifism of some
classical writers, the Hellenic ideal of the unity of
mankind and Erasmus's own conviction of the folly of
war. In Bainton's assessment, the historian cannot
isolate one influence as determinative for Erasmus's
pacifism to the exclusion of all other influences.

This rejection by Bainton of a single cause
for historical phenomena places him in the company of
many contemporary historians. Maurice Mandelbaum
asserts that historians must take into account the
whole complex pattern of influences which form the
cultural context of history. Likewise Jacques Barzun
and Henry Graff propose that history does not reveal
the causes of any event, but instead shows only the
conditions attending the emergence of an event.
Wallace Ferguson states that "an increasingly large
number of historians" contend that all elements of
a civilization relate to one another as "parts of a

total configuration."[1] Bainton writes: "The sum of
the matter is that causation is exceedingly difficult
to assess. One can do no more than offer a plausible
conjecture."[2] In Bainton's writings the "plausible
conjectures" of causation emerge only after his due
consideration of diverse conditioning factors within
the context of a historical period of time.

      A notable characteristic of Bainton's view of
history is his concept of the rhythms of history. He
proposes that history moves in a pattern of rhythms,
oscillating from one ideal to another or from one
emphasis to another. Describing this pattern of history Bainton states that the law of rhythm leads one
to expect that any valid element in Christianity, if
obscured in one generation, will reappear in the
next. He points out that when complexity is dominant
there is a move toward simplicity. Likewise when
simplicity proves an impoverishment, there is a trend
toward complexity. Periods of division give way to
periods of solidarity, and period of sectarianism
dissolve into periods of uniformity.[3]

---

[1]Maurice Mandelbaum, The Anatomy of Historical
Knowledge (Baltimore: The Johns Hopkins University
Press, 1977), p. 140; Jacques Barzun and Henry F.
Graff, The Modern Researcher, 3rd ed. (New York: Har-
court, Brace and World, 1977), p. 143; Wallace K.
Ferguson, The Renaissance in Historical Thought: Five
Centuries of Interpretation (New York: Houghton Mifflin
Company, 1948), p. 392.

[2]Bainton, Yesterday, p. 49.

[3]Roland H. Bainton, "Friends in Relation to
the Churches," in Christian Unity and Religion in New
England, Collected Papers in Church History, series 3
(Boston: Beacon Press, 1964), p. 60; Roland H. Bainton,

In the concluding section of Christendom Bainton points out the numerous manifestations of this
pattern of oscillation. For example, he notes the
zeal of the first century church, the apathy of the
second century church, and the resurgence of spirit
in the third century. The history of Christian mis-
sions is one of the ebb and flow of missionary interest. Christian art oscillated from simplicity to complexity and back to simplicity. Theology moved from
a primitive kerygma to Medieval Scholasticism and back
to the simplicity of Reformation thought.[1]

One rhythm of history discussed by Bainton
in Yesterday, Today, and What Next? is the "failures
of success and the successes of failure." He points
out that when the Church became successful in uniting
the medieval world, the seeds of failure became ap-
parent. The extreme wealth of the medieval church inaugurated problems heretofore unknown to the Church.
Ultimately wealth brought on by success served as a
corrosive element on the medieval Church. As to the
success of failure, Bainton points to the life of
Christ. The ministry of Christ appeared doomed by
the crucifixion, yet this "failure" led to the success of procuring the salvation of mankind.[2]

In defense of this concept of the rhythms of
history Bainton claims that the history of the Church

Christendom: A Short History of Christianity and Its
Impact on Western Civilization, 2 vols. (New York:
Harper and Row, 1966), 2:179.

[1]Bainton, Christendom, 2:197.

[2]Bainton, Yesterday, pp. 38-42.

is not simply a "seesaw." One cannot forget, he writes,
that revival is never simply a repetition. Neither is
the rhythm of history simply a muted cyclical view of
history. Renewal is also a "re-creation." Even a
"zig-zag" admits of a forward movement.[1]

One may ask of Bainton: What is the dynamic
behind these rhythms in history? What is the force
which moves history on this course? He offers no
answer as to the dynamic force behind history. Bainton gives much attention to the religious impulse in
society. He sees the religious factor as dominant in
the lives of men such as Luther, Erasmus, Servetus,
and Ochino. Likewise he finds religion to be the chief
concern which motivated the Protestant movement. Yet
Bainton does not contend, as do some pietistic historians, that God is the dynamic power behind history.
For Bainton, the answer to the question of the dynamic
of history transcends any empirical observation. Bainton summarizes his position succinctly: "The rhythms
of history belong to the inexplicable."[2]

View of the Christian Faith

Bainton provides no thorough delineation of
his own religious experience or of his own theological
persuasion. Underlying his historical writings, however, is a discernible concept of the Christian faith.
From a variety of statements provided within the context

---

[1]Bainton, Christendom, 2:197.

[2]Roland H. Bainton, "Changing Ideas and Ideals
in the Sixteenth Century," in Early and Medieval Christianity, Collected Papers in Church History, series 1
(Boston: Beacon Press, 1962), p. 157.

of his works one can assemble a basic understanding of
Bainton's view of the Christian faith.

In the article "Unity, Utrecht, and Unitarians"
Bainton describes his own understanding of the essence
of Christianity. He says:

> Christianity affirms that the way of life is
> through death, the way to joy through sorrow, the
> way to fulness of life through sacrifice. This
> is the doctrine of the cross. Eternal life lies
> beyond tragedy. Here is the most distinctive,
> the most offensive and the most ineradicable note
> in Christianity. Those who deny the cross have
> cut adrift from the Christian tradition. Chris-
> tianity with starker realism than any other re-
> ligion has looked with unaverted face upon the
> ugliest tragedy of history and has seen there the
> emergence of triumph and eternal life.[1]

This statement discloses in capsule form the faith of
Bainton.

Several influences converge in Bainton's life
to serve as formative factors on his personal understanding of Christianity. One influence of profound
importance is the close relationship of Bainton and
his father. In Pilgrim Parson Bainton speaks frequently of the significance of his father's life, his
father's theological alignment, and his father's social
ethics. The influence of his father ranks as perhaps
the most profound factor both in Bainton's religious
conscience and in his vocational inclination.

A second influential factor was Bainton's
lifelong involvement with Yale Divinity School. Bainton writes that he embraced the critical approach to
religious studies during his student years at Yale.

---

[1]Roland H. Bainton, "Unity, Utrecht, and the
Unitarians," in Christian Unity and Religion in New
England, Collected Papers in Church History, series
3 (Boston: Beacon Press, 1964), p. 53.

He describes the threefold motif of scholarship at
Yale, viz., piety, the Enlightenment, and the Reformation. These three emphases emerge as significant
in Bainton's understanding of Christianity.

A third influence on Bainton's concept of
Christianity emerges in his social involvement. Bainton's pacifism during two world wars, his advocacy of
liberty of conscience, and his participation in ecumenical endeavors demonstrate the ideals which he embraces.

Bainton's view of the Christian faith centers
on three characteristic elements of his religious understanding: 1) personal piety, 2) the historic nature
of Christianity, and 3) sectarian involvement.

The piety of Bainton emanates from his belief
that Christianity should emulate the life of Christ.
The positive attributes of Christ, writes Bainton, are
compassion, tenderness, and the absence of hate. On
the cross Christ forgave even those who persecuted him.
Bainton asks, "Where in all history before him is
there anything comparable?"[1] In the life of Christ
Bainton finds significant the absence of self-centered-
ness. Of Christ's selfless attitude Bainton states,

> I would stress . . . the concrete leader of a
> little band who with a towel over his arm sank
> to his knees before a basin of water and in the
> role of a slave washed the grime from the feet
> of peasants.[2]

The piety of Bainton finds an affinity with the quiet,
tender, and compassionate Christ whose life centered
on service to others.

---

[1]Bainton, Yesterday, p. 86.

[2]Ibid.

Likewise Bainton's piety entails an emphasis
on the spiritual nature of Christianity. His positive
assessment of this aspect of Erasmus's life reveals
Bainton's sympathies with this expression of Christianity. The Christian faith for Bainton depends not
on externals but on the inward relationship of man
with God. Descriptive of this aspect of his faith is
a statement by Bainton concerning the ordinances of
the Church. He says, "This, however, is plain:
neither water nor the lack of water, neither bread
nor the lack of bread is so significant as the com-
munion of the spirit. . . ."[1]

The inward experience of faith aligns closely
with another aspect of Bainton's piety. Inner struggles for the faith appear to mark Bainton's piety. He
finds a great personal affinity with Luther on this
point. Speaking of Luther's struggles Bainton says
that "all of us today are engaged in a struggle for
faith and our concern is not so much with the disease
as with the cure . . . . Luther's faith is our quest."[2]
The struggles of which Bainton speaks are those of a
modern man dealing with questions of doubt and unbelief. He contends that faith is never easy to grasp,
and thus modern man encounters the same difficulties
as did Luther.

> Confronted by the self-emptying of God, modern
> man stands on no other ground than that of Lu-
> ther. For neither can faith be easy. For neither

---

[1]Bainton, "Friends," p. 69.

[2]Roland H. Bainton, "Luther's Struggle for
Faith," in Studies in the Reformation, Collected Papers
in Church History, series 2 (Boston: Beacon Press, 1963),
p. 13. For more on Bainton's struggles see Bainton,
Yesterday, p. 50, and Bainton, "Anabaptist Contribution,"
p. 207.

need it be impossible. That Luther, feeling as
acutely as we all the difficulties, could yet
believe--this may help our unbelief.[1]
Hence Bainton's interest in Luther's *Anfechtungen* is
more than mere historical curiosity.

Another facet of Bainton's piety revolves
around Bainton's positive view of life. He asserts
that two words characterize the Jewish-Christian attitude toward life: affirmation and discipline. As
to Bainton's affirmation of life, one notes his social
activism. He contends that life is good and that
society is worthy of Christian involvement and influence. Social activism may produce results which
come to fruition generations after one lives. This is
part of the hope of the Christian witness for Bainton.
As to Bainton's concept of a disciplined life, one
notes an example in his total abstinence from alcohol.
Bainton based his abstinence on two New Testament
teachings which are as follows: 1) the body is the
temple of the Holy Spirit, and 2) the strong should
accommodate themselves to the weak.[2]

Thus a significant factor in Bainton's view
of the Christian faith is personal piety. His piety
reflects the tradition in Christianity of the quiet
but hearty spirits earnestly contending for the faith.

A second characteristic of Bainton's concept
of Christianity is his understanding of the historic

---

[1][Martin Luther], The Martin Luther Christmas
Book With Celebrated Woodcuts By His Contemporaries,
trans. and ed. Roland H. Bainton (Philadelphia: Fortress Press, 1948), pp. 12-13.

[2]Roland H. Bainton, "Total Abstinence," Christianity Today 2 (7 July 1958): 3, 6.

nature of the Christian faith. He claims that the essential character of Christianity rests upon what God
did in the fifteenth year of Tiberius. Christianity
centers on the Christ event and on the quality of
life and faith engendered by this event. Writing of
the Christ event Bainton states,

> In Him God the inscrutible became God the dis-
> cernible. . . . God was in Christ reconciling
> the world unto himself. Therefore Christianity
> is forever anchored in the past.[1]

The Christ event yields full meaning, according to
Bainton, only to those who experience an absolute
commitment to Christ.

The historic nature of Christianity demands
that ultimately faith must rest upon the Biblical norm.
There is a strong Biblical orientation in Bainton's
view of Christianity. He states that Zwingli "uttered
a sound word" in calling for a return to the basics of
the Bible. Elucidating this position Bainton states
that anyone who seeks to discover the secret of Christianity inevitably goes to the Biblical witness because Christianity emerged from the incarnation of
God in Christ at a definite point in history. The
Bible is a record of this central event.[2]

---

[1]Roland H. Bainton, "The Bible and the Reformation," in Five Essays on the Bible: Papers Read at
the 1960 Annual Meeting of the American Council of
Learned Societies (New York: American Council of
Learned Societies, 1960), p. 22. See also Roland H.
Bainton, "Man, God, and Church in the Renaissance,"
in Early and Medieval Christianity, Collected Papers
in Church History, series 1 (Boston: Beacon Press,
1962), p. 196.

[2]Roland H. Bainton, "The Enduring Witness,"
Mennonite Life 9 (April 1954): 90; Roland H. Bainton,
Here I Stand: A Life of Martin Luther (New York: Abing-
don-Cokesbury Press, 1950), p. 60.

Bainton's insistence on the historicity of Christianity and his adherence to the Biblical witness do not mean that he interprets the events of Christ's life from a literal perspective. Instead Bainton approaches the Bible as a critical scholar. An example of this approach appears in his treatment of the resurrection accounts. He expresses doubts as to the historicity of the resurrection based on his own critical examination of the sources. The testimony of the witnesses, he says, reflects the credulity of the first century thus weakening the factual nature of Christ's resurrection. He writes that whatever the nature of the resurrection, Christ is forever alive to give assurance of immortality and strength.[1]

Bainton finds in the Incarnation a statement of the potentialities of mankind. God's historical participation in the life of man provides a solid ground for confidence in the abilities of man. A positive anthropology marks Bainton's view of Christianity, emerging in part from his interpretation of the historical nature of the Christ event. Speaking of man's potential Bainton writes, "And let it not be forgotten that the angel and the ape make their abode in the same individual. Ours to hope, pray, and labor for a loftier race."[2]

A third characteristic of Bainton's view of the Christian faith is his sectarian involvement. His denominational affiliation was twofold, being a member of the Congregational Church and an affiliate member of the Society of Friends. He writes of this dual

---

[1]Bainton, Yesterday, pp. 76-7.

[2]Ibid., p. 37.

participation by stating, "My wife and I commonly at-
tend first Friends meeting and then a Congregational
service."[1] Several of his writings depict his preference for the sectarian expression of Christianity.
Bainton's pacifism aligns him with the Quakers as
does his propensity for the uniqueness of the Friends'
witness. He sees the Friends' interpretation of
Christianity as distinctive in four ways: 1) the
service of worship is unique, 2) the involvement of
the total membership in the Society's affairs is distinct, 3) the equality of women is notable, and 4) the
peace testimony is valid.[2]

Bainton's own understanding of Christianity
finds an affinity with the historic theological themes
enunciated by the left wing churches. Bainton's belief in the validity of the witness of suffering and
martyrdom reflects a sectarian ideal. His concepts
of freedom of conscience and pacifism likewise reflect
the ideals of the left wing churches. Bainton's personal discipline, his affinity for a simple expression
of the faith, and his unadorned lifestyle are also
marks of this expression of Christianity.

One aspect of the sectarian witness has little
credence with Bainton. The practice of withdrawal
from society by groups such as the Hutterites and the
Mennonites draws his sharp criticism. He claims that
withdrawal takes the easy way out of the complexities
and dilemmas of modern life. Of the practice of withdrawal Bainton writes;

> Such a course appears to me to be justified only
> on one or two assumptions. The first is that our

---

[1] Bainton, "Friends," p. 68.

[2] Ibid., p. 67.

society is utterly hopeless, that it can never be
Christianized nor even ameliorated in a Christian
direction. This is an assumption which for my-
self I am not prepared to make.[1]

Bainton rejects any expression of Christianity which
refuses to accept the responsibility of social activism
or of ethical involvement.

The sectarian alignment does not cause Bainton to disdain other traditions of Christianity. He
has actively participated in ecumenical work and
claims that the "genius of our time is distinctly
ecumenical."[2] Bainton states that the reason he never
left the Congregational Church to align fully with
the Society of Friends is because of his hope that
Congregationalism may serve as a key to ecumenical
adherence within Christendom.[3]

Thus Bainton's sectarian involvement, his
view of the historicity of Christianity, and his
personal piety are marked characteristics of his understanding of the Christian faith. Taken together
these emphases form the underlying conceptual framework from which Bainton practices his faith, and
they affect the way he produces his historical writings.

The underlying assumptions of Bainton with
regard to history and to Christianity significantly
influence his historiography. These two broad assumptions comprise the bedrock upon which he structures
his historical writings, and they likewise form the

[1]Bainton, "Anabaptist Contribution," pp. 205-6.

[2]Roland H. Bainton, "The Sectarian Theory of
the Church," Christendom 11 (Summer 1946): 387.

[3]Roland H. Bainton, "Congregationalism: The
Middle Way," Christendom 5 (Summer 1940): 354.

framework within which he deals with the historical
phenomena of the Church. His concepts of history and
of Christianity direct his interpretations of men
and movements of the past. These concepts also shape
the subject matter of many of his works. His selected
subjects derive in part from the basic assumptions from
which he operates as an historian.

Distinct Historiographical Themes
Pacifism

Bainton defends the propriety of his advocacy
for pacifism in his writings when he asks, "[W]hy
should not a historian be profoundly concerned over
behavior which threatens to bring an end to history?"[1]
Bainton's concern evidences itself in that his works
are replete with discussions of the issue of war and
peace. He finds no progress in man's attempt to
eliminate war. "There is no sense in comparing wars
as if progress consisted in growing nicer about killing
each other," states Bainton.[2] The one mark of progress
would be eliminating the temptation to fight wars of
any kind.

The position which Bainton assiduously advocates for a Christian is that of total disassociation
from war but not from political involvement. The
Christian pacifist must disdain conflict, yet he must
also respect the conscience of one who chooses not to
renounce war. Bainton argues that assent to any form

[1]Roland H. Bainton, Christian Attitudes Toward
War and Peace: An Historical Survey and Critical Re-
evaluation (New York: Abingdon Press, 1960), p. 16.

[2]Bainton, "Progress," pp. 249-50.

of armed conflict is inconsistent with the principles
of Christianity. He says, "The Christian must do more
than say 'no' to war. His vocation is to be, in the
words of George Fox, 'in that spirit which is above
all war and contention.'"[1] The New Testament reflects
little concern with power struggles. Instead the New
Testament speaks of the gentler virtues of love, joy,
peace, and longsuffering. Christ Himself said nothing
about massive retaliation. Hence Bainton's pacifistic
position centers on the emulation of the life of Christ.

Bainton treats the ideal of pacifism from a
historical perspective. He delineates the pacifism of
men and movements throughout the history of the Church.
He attempts to show that his own pacifistic sentiments
have a firm historical basis.[2]

Pacifism is the most consistent position
which a twentieth century Christian can embrace, he
says. Bainton advocates voluntary disarmament by the
United States, a move which no nation in history has
tried. Bainton contends that when the threat of retaliation ceases, nations hostile to America might
respond in a similar fashion. However, hostile nations
may also expand and ultimately dominate the United
States. Bainton proposes that possible Communist dom-
ination does not necessarily signal the defeat of American ideals. He writes:

---

[1]Bainton, War and Peace, p. 261.

[2]Bainton became a historian of the peace movement after his experience as a conscientious objector
in World War I. See Charles Chatfield, For Peace and
Justice: Pacifism in America 1914-1941 (Knoxville:
University of Tennessee Press, 1971), pp. 51-2.

> This only we know, that the spirit of man is
> resurgent, and that more than once in history
> the descendents of conquerers have looked upon
> themselves as spiritually the sons of the con-
> quered.[1]

Thus Bainton constructs his concept of pacifism on an
optimistic view of man and on his confidence in the
resiliency of the Christian witness.

In keeping with his Anabaptist sympathies,
Bainton contends that if pacifism leads to martyrdom
then death itself is a proclamation of the truth. He
maintains that if by defenselessness one forfeits sur-
vival, then the Christian response must be that sur-
vival is not the chief end of man. Life is a "precious
boon, but life is not to be had at any price."[2]
Bainton claims that it is better "to be wiped out than
to survive by sinking lower than beasts and barbarians."[3]

In his numerous writings on pacifism Bainton
frequently points out the difficulty encountered by
the conscientious objector. Those who refuse to accept
war as a viable alternative quite often face the same
haunting question as did Luther in his break with Rome,
i.e., the question, "Are you alone wise?" For Bainton,
this question is the most difficult for a pacifist
since it represents an acute trial of conscience.
When a nation foments war, the magistrate deems the
pacifist a traitor. Bainton argues that pacifism does
not pose a threat to a warring nation. Instead, the
integrity of a pacifist makes him "the finest citizen"
and the most effective civil servant in a post which

[1]Bainton, War and Peace, pp. 266-7.

[2]Ibid., p. 267.

[3]Bainton, Yesterday, p. 118.

he can accept in good conscience. Bainton states,
"Of all considerations the deepest is that conscience
is worthy of honor and is not lightly to be constrained."[1]
          Bainton's pacifism emerges in his obvious
sympathies with pacifists of previous ages. He speaks
positively of the pacifism of historical figures such
as Origen, Erasmus, Castellio, and the early Anabaptists. Pacifism is a theme which Bainton incorporates
throughout his historical writings. It appears even
in the survey Christendom. This motif is distinct in
Bainton's writings and thus establishes a method of
interpretation which distinguishes him from many other
historians. To understand Bainton's historiography
one must deal with the issue of pacifism which per-
meates his work.

Toleration

          A major theme of Bainton's writings is the
history of religious toleration. He claims that
religious liberty is an accomplished fact in the western world although its acceptance was lamentably slow.
The best arguments for toleration arose in the sixteenth century but the practice of religious liberty
did not occur until the nineteenth century. Bainton
comments that social change "is all too slow and gains
are not necessarily permanent."[2] Bainton points out
that a spirit of love alleviated the lot of the slave,
the sick, and the child. However, it required centuries to eliminate the temptation to exterminate the
heretic.

---

[1]Bainton, War and Peace, p. 162.

[2]Bainton, Yesterday, p. 34.

The concern for the history of toleration
pervades a large number of writings in the Bainton
corpus. Bainton's general method of writing on the
history of toleration has a twofold approach. One
approach is his interest in ideas which precipitated
arguments favorable to toleration. Another approach
is his study of figures involved in the quest for
religious liberty. The figures studied by Bainton
are either victims of intolerance or are exponents of
an intellectual position which augmented the case of
freedom of conscience. A terse analysis of these two
approaches to the issue of toleration will prove in-
structive.

The Renaissance inaugurated the spirit of
toleration according to Bainton. Three central ideas
significant for liberty emerged among Renaissance
thinkers. One idea, an acceptance of non-Christian
religions, muted the distinctiveness of Christianity.
When Renaissance thinkers allegorized the major tenets
of Christianity in an effort to produce unity among
people, they opened the door to modern ideals of
toleration.

Bainton discerns two further ideas propagated
during the Renaissance that strengthened the arguments for liberty. Reason and the religion of the
Spirit combined to give strong impetus to the concept
of toleration. Bainton uses these two ideas frequently as interpretive tools in his discussions of
arguments for religious liberty:

> Reason may cast doubt on the value of persecution,
> and the religion of the Spirit may give a new
> worth to human life so that to harm it would be
> repulsive.[1]

---

[1]Bainton, "Progress," p. 256.

Reason allowed a critical inquiry into the sources of
and arguments for religious orthodoxy. Spiritual
religion contended that the experience of the individual with God had precedence over both doctrinal
uniformity and theological precision. Bainton finds
these two ideas of paramount importance for religious
liberty.

Bainton also assesses the contribution of
four major figures of the Reformation era who formulated arguments which were to have lasting influence
on the history of toleration. These four figures
are Erasmus, Luther, Castellio, and Ochino.

Erasmus proposed a distinction between the
fundamenta, the essential dogmas, and the adiaphora,
the non-essentials. Bainton states that Erasmus was
the first to use this distinction extensively in the
interests of religious liberty.

Luther's basic contribution to religious
liberty was in the shift of attention from heresy as
a belief to the social problems created by heresy.
He attempted to show that heresy was a threat to the
social order. When heresy as a social threat proved
unreal, the "way was open to abolish the penalties."[1]

In the case of Castellio, Bainton finds another significant watershed in the toleration argument.
Bainton claims that Castellio was the first to address
questions of faith and knowledge in relation to religious freedom. Castellio held that faith and knowledge

---

[1]Roland H. Bainton, "Luther's Attitudes on
Religious Liberty," in Studies in the Reformation,
Collected Papers in Church History, series 2 (Boston:
Beacon Press, 1963), p. 44.

were mutually exclusive. One cannot empirically prove
tenets of faith, and one cannot know with ultimate
certainty the truth of religious dogmas. Hence one
does not know enough to persecute.

Bainton sees a step of progress from Castellio's thought to Ochino's. Castellio relativized
conscience, and Ochino dealt with the social concomi-
tants of unbridled freedom of conscience. Bainton
claims that Ochino was the only person of the sixteenth
century to deal with the question of conscientious
tyrannicide. Ochino pointed out the thin line between
freedom of conscience and social subversion in the
name of freedom. Bainton hails Ochino's significance
in dealing with this problem.

Bainton writes that through his career anger
towards historical intolerance has dissipated to sympathy for the intolerant. All too often, he states,
it is the saints who burn the saints.[1] Bainton uses
history to depict the significance of the issue of
freedom of conscience. He shows the impropriety of
intolerance exemplified in victims such as Ochino
and Servetus. Likewise he shows the strength of the
argument for toleration in men such as Castellio and
Erasmus. Ultimately Bainton proposes that twentieth
century man should learn from history the validity of
the ideals of liberty of conscience.

Bainton praises the contemporary practice of
religious freedom yet he also criticizes the motives
for present-day toleration. He attributes much of
contemporary toleration to the fact of indifference.
Commenting on Calvin and Servetus, Bainton says, "There

[1]Ibid., p. 20.

is after all something magnificent in the spectacle
of two men, the one ready to kill, the other to die
for his convictions . . ."[1] For twentieth century
man, Bainton claims that toleration should arise from
a commitment to the truth rather than from flippant
apathy toward religion.

As Bainton surveys the history of toleration,
he makes several historical judgments on the enduring
problem of religious freedom. He points out that in
the sixteenth century the great question was whether
a "house divided against itself" can stand. Experience demonstrates that two religions can exist side
by side amicably only if they think they can. Fur-
thermore Bainton claims that too much liberty of conscience may in fact lead to the disintegration of the
Church. Yet in a pluralistic society religious toleration provides the most enduring witness of the spirit
of Christ.[2]

A weakness of Bainton's works is his exces-
sive attention to the cause of toleration. Toleration
does constitute a major focus of his writings, but
often this emphasis appears obsessive. Quite frequently he uses events in the history of toleration
as illustrative material, and often he repeats the
narration of the same events. Bainton's writings

---

[1]Bainton, "Burned Heretic," p. 1231.

[2]Roland H. Bainton, Hunted Heretic: The Life
and Death of Michael Servetus 1511-1553 (Boston: Beacon
Press, 1953); reprint ed., Gloucester, Mass.: Peter
Smith, 1978), p. 75; Roland H. Bainton, "Sebastian
Castellio: Champion of Religious Liberty," in Studies
on the Reformation, Collected Papers in Church History,
series 2 (Boston: Beacon Press, 1963), p. 177.

on toleration as a whole become redundant at points
and display little creativity. At points he becomes
highly subjective and exchanges the mantle of critical
history for that of passionate advocacy. His writings
on toleration give little sympathy to the intolerant,
and often those such as Calvin became targets of Bainton's indignation. Bainton nears intolerance himself
in his propagation of the freedom of conscience. This
criticism does not discount the valuable contribution
Bainton makes to the history of toleration. It does,
however, point out the weakness of the historian whose
presuppositions conflict with his critical inquiry.

Concern for the Neglected

In his preface to Women of the Reformation:
In Germany and Italy Bainton states, "I have always
had an interest in those who have not had their due,
and devoted my earliest studies to the heretics of
the Reformation, who were persecuted alike by the
Catholics and the Protestants."[1] Bainton's writings
epitomize this underlying concern. His Reformation
writings are replete with the discussion of those
figures virtually ignored by many historians.

Perhaps most noticeable is Bainton's treatment of women in the Reformation. This interest by
Bainton perhaps characterized his entire career as a
Church historian, but the writings on women appeared
only in the latter years of his career. He writes
that his interest in women of the Reformation took on

---

[1]Roland H. Bainton, Women of the Reformation:
In Germany and Italy (Minneapolis, Minn.: Augsburg
Publishing House, 1971), p. 9.

a personal significance upon the death of his wife,
Ruth Woodruff Bainton. The writings on women, writes
Bainton, characterize those like his wife who was
"widely loved but little acclaimed."[1] He published
three volumes on women, each volume containing bio-
graphical sketches of women who participated in the
Protestant movement. Figures such as Katherine von
Bora, Isabella Bresegna, Marguerite of Navarre, and
Jadwige Gnoinskiej attract his scholarly attention.
Bainton maintains that the study of such women adds
a dimension to understanding the Reformation often
overlooked by Reformation historians.

He discounts the charge that the neglect of
women in the primary sources reveals a "male chauvinism" among historians. Bainton contends that "clerical
chauvinism is perhaps more accurate inasmuch as laymen,
like women, receive scant notice."[2] Women did not
suffer enslavement throughout the past as some contend. The historical sources reveal that women,
specifically those of the sixteenth century, simply
did not participate in the administrative functions
of the Church thus causing much of the historical
neglect. Bainton views women of the Reformation era
positively, pointing out that they were actively involved in the Protestant reform through multifaceted
endeavors.

---

[1] Roland H. Bainton, Women of the Reformation
From Spain to Scandanavia (Minneapolis, Minn.: Augsburg Publishing House, 1977), p. 9.

[2] Roland H. Bainton, "Feminine Piety in Tudor
England," in Christian Spirituality: Essays in Honor
of Gordon Rupp, ed. Peter Brooks (London: S.C.M. Press,
1975), p. 185.

An example of this positive interpretation
by Bainton is his treatment of Margareta Peutinger.
Peutinger wrote to Erasmus after the publication of
the 1519 edition of his New Testament. Her concern
was with a translation by Erasmus which Peutinger
felt was erroneous. Bainton writes:

> That the Erasmian reading is not confirmed by
> modern scholarship is irrelevant here. The
> point is rather that Margareta was in a position
> to compare the German, the Latin, and the Greek
> and to carry on a discussion with Erasmus quite
> on his own level.[1]

Such an example leads Bainton to question the assumption that women had little significance in the religious developments of the sixteenth century.

One critical problem Bainton confronted in
his research was the dearth of primary sources which
deal with women. He finds, however, that in itself
the lack of sources actually speaks highly of women
unchronicled by sixteenth century writers. He says
of his volumes on women:

> Perhaps the most revealing discovery is that
> no one of these sketches is a success story.
> Prophets always die disappointed because achieve-
> ments never equal aspirations. These women
> walked as seeing Him that is invisible sustained
> by faith that somehow their toils and troubles
> had a place in the grand design.[2]

These are examples of unchronicled figures of history.
Herein Bainton gives an account of those persons of
the sixteenth century who have not received their due.

Likewise Bainton's works on the left wing of
the Reformation are efforts to do justice to those who

---

[1]Roland H. Bainton, Erasmus of Christendom
(New York: Charles Scribner's Sons, 1969), p. 233.

[2]Bainton, Spain to Scandanavia, p. 12.

receive little attention from historians. Illustrative
of this effort are his biographies of Joris, Servetus,
and Ochino, each of which ranks as a significant treatment of radicals whose lives had attracted little
scholarly attention. The writings on Castellio likewise are groundbreaking works on a little-known
figure of history.

A further demonstration of this concern for
the unknown figures of history appears in Bainton's
article "The Anabaptist Contribution to History."
He states that the lives of multitudes of Anabaptists
were not of sufficient consequence to merit any attention. As an example Bainton lists the names of
Anabaptists arrested at Augsburg in 1528. After quoting
an abbreviation of a lengthy list of prisoners, he
states:

> Names, just names! Back of every one lay a
> history and after every one came a sequel, but
> we do not know what. Were they imprisoned,
> banished, beheaded, burned, drowned? The re-
> cord does not say. Before God they stand with
> no notice in the annals of man.[1]

The unnamed, unheralded, and unknown figures of history
captivate Bainton's scholarly attention.

Yet Bainton considers some of the most prominent figures of history as people who have not received
their due. He states that Erasmus has never been
properly treated. Since Erasmus founded no church nor
gathered any school of thought around him, his life
suffers neglect. Bainton maintains that the writing
of Erasmus of Christendom grew out of a concern to do
justice to this well-known but poorly treated figure
of history.

---

[1]Bainton, "Anabaptist Contribution," p. 207.

As a theme, this concern for the inadequately
studied people of history is prominent. Much of
Bainton's contribution to Church history emerges from
this unique concern. When assessing the entirety of
the Bainton corpus, one may ask: Why does Bainton devote his attention to Joris, to Isabella Zapolya, or
to Ochino? The answer lies in the perspective of
scholarship which Bainton brings to the study of the
Reformation. To understand Bainton's numerous writings
on that which is seemingly insignificant one must
understand his conviction that one does not need to
stand at the apex of fame to merit high tribute.
Bainton asserts that for the historian fame cannot
determine significance nor can anonymity deny importance.

Approach to the Reformation
Historical Method

Bainton's writings reveal a pronounced inclination toward empirical verification from the primary sources of the Reformation. Nonetheless this
positivistic orientation does not assure complete
objectivity for Bainton. Aware of his own presuppositions Bainton writes that no historian is free from
subjective proclivity.

Bainton claims that the modern historian seeks
to "fortify himself" by declaring his prejudices in
advance. Then in an effort to overcome his subjectivity the historian strains so conscientiously to
correct his prejudices that he forfeits objectivity.
Yet Bainton perceives a more subtle difficulty for the
historian who seeks objectivity:

> But a deeper difficulty is that we are not even
> aware of our prejudices because frequently they

are those which we share with our age. If we
are to recognize that they are prejudices, we
must engage in a comparison between the point
of view of our time and those of previous times.
Thus we invoke history to disclose to us our
presuppositions in the approach to history.[1]
Bainton thus approaches history by demanding objectivity, yet he recognizes that presuppositions influence every interpreter of history.

   His own subjectivity evidences itself when
he writes on issues of history which correlate to his
deeply-held personal convictions. For example, Bainton displays obvious subjectivity when he writes on
pacifism or on toleration. The basic historiographical
approach to the four radicals centers on his advocacy
of liberty of conscience. This subjectivity does not
negate the valuable historical research on these four
radicals, but it does demonstrate the presuppositions
pervading Bainton's works. Also notable at this
point is Bainton's treatment of Calvin. Castigating
the intolerance of Calvin, Bainton treats the Genevan
reformer with little historical objectivity.

   Despite the influence of presuppositions,
many of Bainton's works reflect his passion for objectivity. As a critical historian Bainton makes
careful and thorough use of primary source material.
His writings reveal the work of a historian who has
steeped himself in the sources. Even the interpretive essays of Bainton rely heavily on the sources.
He states that the "broader problems of interpretation

---

[1]Roland H. Bainton, "Interpretations of the
Reformation," in Studies in the Reformation, Collected
Papers in Church History, series 2 (Boston: Beacon
Press, 1963), p. 105.

of any period depend for the verification and progress
on documentary evidence."[1] Progress in the field of
Reformation research, he writes, demands the constant
quest for new sources and the dissemination of such
sources in modern critical editions.

An excellent example of Bainton's careful use
of sources is in his treatment of Luther's Table Talks.
He notes that many scholars misuse the *Tischreden* by
treating it in the same manner as they treat Luther's
writings. Bainton's essay "Luther on Birds, Dogs,
and Babies" demonstrates Bainton's critical analysis
of the Table Talks. Bainton claims that he produced
this essay in order to display "the way in which it
[Table Talks] may be properly employed."[2] He reveals
in this essay his tedious care in the process of interpreting a primary source of Luther's life.

Bainton often acknowledges ignorance of de-
tails in certain events because the sources do not
allow verification. For example, when discussing Servetus's sudden appearance in Protestant lands in
1530, Bainton states that it is impossible to know
with certainty by what route Servetus traveled. He
points out the silence of primary materials on this
point. The result of Bainton's assessment of this
issue is as follows: "It doesn't matter much except
that we must not indulge in a riot of conjectures."[3]

---

[1]Ibid., p. 115.

[2]Roland H. Bainton, "Luther on Birds, Dogs,
and Babies," in Studies in the Reformation, Collected
Papers in Church History, series 2 (Boston: Beacon
Press, 1963), p. 67.

[3]Bainton, Hunted Heretic, p. 32.

Without empirical verification Bainton refuses to make
unsubstantiated judgments. Bainton's writings display technical accuracy, yet when dealing with interpretations of selected historical issues Bainton's
critical objectivity gives way to personal subjectivity.

A significant aspect of Bainton's use of
primary sources is his marked ability as a linguist.
As a manifestation of both his self-discipline and
his facility in learning, Bainton's skill with languages is clearly evident in his writings. Georgia
Harkness, a former student of Bainton, writes that
"whenever there seemed to be important material to
be delved into in any language not familiar to him,
he proceeded to learn it. I cannot say how many he
now reads and speaks, for he has kept on acquiring
more."[1] Bainton's linguistic ability provides him
with access to an unusually wide range of primary
materials. For example, Bainton freely worked in
several European languages in his research for
Women of the Reformation. This work, done without
the aid of scholarly secondary sources, epitomizes
Bainton's skill in operating with primary documents
alone to produce a major contribution to Reformation
studies. Bainton uses with deftness sources on Luther in German, on Erasmus in Latin, and on Ochino
in Italian. His ability to provide accurate English
translations gives further value to his Reformation

---

[1]Georgia Harkness, "Roland H. Bainton: A
Biographical Appreciation," in Reformation Studies:
Essays in Honor of Roland H. Bainton, ed. Franklin
H. Littell (Richmond, Va.: John Knox Press, 1962),
pp. 14-15.

corpus. Hence Bainton's writings demonstrate technical
accuracy, a heavy dependence on primary documents, and
a prevalent empiricist inclination.

A second area of consideration in Bainton's
historical method is his methodology of writing Church
history. He comments that a volume on Church history
may resemble a "telephone directory" filled with names,
events, and dates or it may resemble an interpretive
essay. Bainton attempts to strike a balance between
these two extremes. To do so, writes Bainton, the
historian must select the most significant men and
movements of a period and enliven the history with
revealing anecdotes.[1]

Bainton frequently develops his writings on
Church history by first presenting the material in
lecture form. Numerous publications originated as
lectures to students. Bainton states that a work
"should be delivered repeatedly in the form of public
lectures. After every such experience there is bound
to be revision."[2] This appears as a standard procedure used by Bainton in the development and writing
of books and monographic works. Bainton reveals in
a telling story that when writing Church of Our Fathers
(a Church history for children) he read the manuscript
to his daughter whose comments were often less than
flattering. Bainton makes use of speaking opportuni-
ties to work through, correct, and polish the manu-
scripts which he prepares for publication.

---

[1]Roland H. Bainton, "Teaching Church History,"
Journal of Bible and Religion 10 (May 1942): 103.

[2]Roland H. Bainton, "Religious Biography," in
Writing for the Religious Market, ed. Robert E. Wolseley (New York: Association Press, 1956), p. 187.

Bainton's literary style is important to his
historical method. The contemporary writer of history
"fights for an audience." For this reason, Bainton
purposely avoids what he calls the verbose and the
parenthetical styles.[1] He writes for laymen as well
as for trained historians. He translates technically
complex scholarship into terms understandable to the
reader who is not a professional historian. Bainton's
style is terse and often journalistic. His writings
are replete with historical anecdotes and frequently
they display touches of humor. Bainton's popular
style does not require him to relinquish his scholarly
precision. On this point Harkness states:

> When others popularize it is often to oversimplify
> and to sacrifice substance if not truth for the
> sake of journalistic clarity and liveliness. This
> Bainton never does. Yet anyone with no previous
> knowledge of Luther can read Here I Stand and come
> away from it with much more knowledge than before,
> not only of Luther but of the crosscurrents of
> the Reformation.[2]

A sensitivity to both scholarship and readability marks
the Bainton corpus.

Perhaps the most obvious characteristic of
Bainton's writing style lies in his unusual skill in
phrasing. He has the facility for finding precise
words which graphically describe a historical episode.
Several examples of this descriptive style follow.

Of selected figures of the Italian Renaissance
Bainton says, "The despots of the Italian Renaissance
were undoubtedly as promiscuous as May flies, as cunning

---

[1] Ibid., p. 188.

[2] Harkness, "Bainton," p. 15.

as spiders, and as remorseless as sharks."[1] Concerning the significance of the Renaissance he writes:
"Those exuberant horsemen of the Renaissance reined
up before the chasms of destiny."[2]

In an evaluation of Erasmus's life Bainton
states, "Erasmus at the end of his life felt that his
lamps had been blown out by the Lutheran gusts."[3]
When Bainton writes of the prodigious work of the
young Luther, he states, "Ideas were so churning
within him that new butter always came out of the
vat."[4] The discussion of the Leipzig Debate brings
out the best in Bainton. Of the debate he writes,
"The Goliath of the Philistines who stepped forth to
taunt Israel was a professor from the University of
Ingolstadt, John Eck by name." Further describing Eck
Bainton comments, "Despite his butcher's face and
bull's voice he was a man of prodigious memory, tor-
rential fluency, and uncanny acumen. . . ."[5]

Occasionally Bainton's zeal for literary eloquence overpowers the average reader. For example,
describing Erasmus's moodiness Bainton writes, "But
he who disported himself with the persiflage of a
Lucian was beset by despondency."[6] Such figures of
speech are rare indeed. Bainton's writing style

---

[1]Roland H. Bainton, The Medieval Church
(Princeton, N.J.: Van Nostrand, 1962), p. 76.

[2]Bainton, Here I Stand, p. 129.

[3]Bainton, Erasmus, p. 277.

[4]Bainton, Here I Stand, p. 88.

[5]Ibid., p. 107.

[6]Bainton, Erasmus, p. 74.

depicts his understanding of the literary task of
the writer of Church history.

Bainton's use of the historical method is
not unique. His work offers no advances in the area
of historical method since he relies on methodology
already developed by the discipline of Church history.
Bainton displays little creativity in his appropriation of the historical method. His expertise is not
in the area of the philosophy of history but in the
area of historical research. Consequently his interests lie more in expanding the field of historical
knowledge than in developing new methods of approaching
history.

As a tool of writing history the biography
strongly appeals to Bainton. He wrote seven full
biographies, his works on women of the Reformation
contain approximately sixty biographical sketches,
and his book Travail of Religious Liberty contains nine
biographical studies.

Bainton contends that the writing of a biography demands that the historian steep himself in the
sources of the subject under consideration, a task
which often requires years of research. He points out
the three major components of his biographical format:
the presentation of the outstanding episodes of a person's life, the essential ideas of the figure studied,
and the significant writings of the individual. In
order for a biography to attract the reader's attention, it must confront the reader with the significance of the subject. Bainton accomplishes this by
choosing a key episode of the subject's life and then
presenting this episode in the opening chapter of the

biography.[1] An example of this procedure is the opening paragraphs of Here I Stand in which Bainton narrates Luther's confrontation with the storm near
Stotternheim.

Paul Crow comments that a theological biography reveals a person's life as a message. The nar-
rative thus presents an interaction among the elements
of personality, the world, and the Gospel. In this
same vein, Leon Edel writes that a biographical portrait seeks to present the life of a person beneath
the surface of historical events, capturing the essential character of the subject.[2] Bainton's biographical
writings contain the interaction of the subject with
his own times and present the essential character of
the person under consideration. The biographies of
Bainton go beyond simple chronological profiles; they
convey the "message" of a subject's life and the importance of this message within the history of the
Church.

The writer of biography must project himself
into the life of the subject so that the historian almost becomes the subject. Bainton writes that he satu-
rates himself in the subject's era in order to identify
closely with the individual studied. A true biography
demands an intimate relationship between historian and
subject. From this historical relationship, explains
Bainton, the biography emerges. "Let this point above

---

[1]Bainton, "Religious Biography," pp. 186, 189.

[2]Paul A. Crow, "Recent Reformation Studies in
Review," Encounter 26 (Winter 1965): 88; Leon Edel,
Literary Biography (Toronto: University of Toronto
Press, 1957), p. 84.

all be remembered: There can be no satisfactory biography without fire, passion, sympathy, pathos, and
affection."[1]

Why does Bainton choose the method of biography as a means of writing history? He finds in the
life of individuals a microcosm of the history of a
certain period. Bainton presents history as seen
through the life of a particular individual. Descriptive of this approach is the following statement of
the significance of Servetus and Calvin.

> His [Servetus's] clash with Calvin was more than
> personal. It was the conflict of the Reforma-
> tion with the Renaissance, and of the right wing
> of the Reformation with the left. Without going
> beyond Servetus and Calvin, one meets most of
> the significant currents of the sixteenth cen-
> tury.[2]

In addition to biography Bainton writes history by presenting the development of men and movements
within the context of the history of ideas. This approach is closely correlated with Bainton's understanding of the rhythms of history. Within the historical
process he sees an oscillation of ideas taking concrete form in the interaction of the Church with culture.

Perhaps Bainton's most distinctive interpretation of the history of ideas is his description of
the tension between the Hebraic and Hellenistic in
western thought. This theme stands out in Bainton's
treatment of the Renaissance and Reformation as well
as in his history of toleration.

---

[1]Bainton, "Religious Biography," p. 191.

[2]Bainton, Hunted Heretic, p. 4.

Many of Bainton's interpretive essays and
biographies stress the significance of the intellectual
background. For example, Bainton states that in order
to understand Servetus "one must first survey briefly
the course of Trinitarian speculation from Augustine
to the Reformation."[1] He places Castellio within the
context of an intellectual tradition germinating in
Cicero and coming to fruition in Thomas Paine. Bainton interprets Ochino as significant in the development of Antitrinitarian thought, with Ochino's ideas
on the atonement providing a continuity from Scotus
and Valdéz to the Racovian Cathechism. Moreover he
interprets Luther's *Anfechtungen* within the larger
context of other figures who, like Luther, struggled
earnestly with their faith.

This approach to history is highly interpretive. Bainton gives great importance to the power of
ideas within history. He attributes more importance
to the factor of ideas in history than he does to the
factors of economics, politics, or environment. Bainton's historiography proposes an organic unity of all
history. The development of ideas becomes the synthesizing element giving continuity to the historical
phenomena.

Concentration on the phenomena of religious
experience within history is another distinctive interpretation in Bainton's writings. Bainton approaches

---

[1]Roland H. Bainton, "Michael Servetus and
the Trinitarian Speculation of the Middle Ages," in
Autour De Michel Servet Et De Sebastien Castellion,
ed. Bruno Becker (Haarlem: H. D. Tjeenk and Zoon N.V.,
1953), p. 31.

the history of the Church as one who stands "within"
the context of the Christian tradition. As such he
sees the dynamic of religious experience as an important influence in the history of Christianity. He
interprets the religious impulse in man as a viable
element in history, an element worthy of notice by
the historian.

Examples of this means of interpretation are
numerous in his works. He contends that the Reformation was basically but not exclusively a religious
encounter. Likewise he interprets Luther as "above
all else" a man of religion. Luther's *Anfechtungen*
arose from his religious sensitivity and not from
psychological dysfunction. Bainton portrays Erasmus
and Servetus from the perspective of their religious
endeavors. Moreover, he interprets Anabaptism as an
attempt to recover primitive patterns of Christianity
rather than as a social or economic movement.

Bainton claims that as a historian he is interested in the religious experience of individuals.
This interest pervades his writings. He contends that
the historian cannot understand the religion of the
past if he himself has no experience with God. Bainton appears to maintain that no true history of Christianity can come from the historian who stands "outside" the Christian tradition. In a discussion of Reformation historiography Bainton laments the fact that
many contemporary writings on the Reformation are
socio-political in nature. For Bainton any interpretation which discounts the dynamic of religious experience is essentially invalid.

Sidney Mead, commenting on the task of the
Church historian, claims that the historian of the

Church is ultimately an evangelist.[1] Bainton fits
the description since he uses history as a tool of
Christian witness. He contends that one cannot confront history itself without the consideration of God
and his providential role within history. He writes,
"The examination of human behavior will carry us soon
beyond the human to inquire about God, providence,
Christ, and Christian ideals."[2]

From a historiographical perspective, the
consideration of the phenomena of religious experience
as an interpretive factor distinguishes Bainton's
writings. His emphasis on the religious element in
history represents a clear interpretive method different in scope from an economic or political historian. Significantly Bainton does not emphasize
the centrality of institutional forms of religion as
interpretive elements. Instead he stresses the religious conscience of individuals, and he sees this
element of history as important for the historian's
understanding of the total historical configuration.

[1]Sidney Mead, "The Task of the Church Historian," The Chronicle 12 (July 1949): 140.

[2]Bainton, Yesterday, pp. 10, 50.

CHAPTER VI

CONCLUSION

As one of the leading Church historians of the
twentieth century, Bainton's contributions to the field
of research are numerous. Six specific contributions
mark his scholarly work. First and perhaps most important Bainton has contributed significant groundbreaking works on figures of history heretofore treated
superficially or not at all. Most notable in this
vein are his biographical works on Joris, Ochino,
Servetus, and Castellio which have advanced the research on these Reformation figures significantly and
have expanded the dimensions of left wing historiography. Also his works on women of the Reformation
comprise a pioneering effort into a largely unexplored
area of Reformation historiography. By virtue of his
three volume work on women Bainton has expanded the
horizons of Reformation research. Likewise his Anabaptist studies emerging in the context of the Bender
generation have provided a positive thrust to left
wing research, contributing to the advance of Anabaptist historiography in the twentieth century.

A second specific contribution lies in the
publication of major biographies on key Reformation
figures. Here I Stand ranks as a standard work on
the life of Luther. Representing years of research,
this biography brings to prominence the importance of
Anfechtungen in Luther interpretation. The biography
of Erasmus is the most thorough work on Erasmus's life

in recent years. This study stands as a classic interpretation on the life of Erasmus, and may rank
with Huizinga's Erasmus and the Age of Reformation
as one of the finest Erasmus biographies of the twentieth
century.

Bainton's general histories constitute a third
contribution to the field of Church history research.
The Reformation of the Sixteenth Century and Christendom
are widely used as textbooks for Church history studies.
These general works contribute to the dissemination of
current historical research among students and laymen
alike.

Fourth, Bainton has made accessible primary
source materials of the Reformation era. His translations of Castellio's Concerning Heretics and several
of the Jorist papers as well as his collection of Servetus documents all advance the effort of historians
working in these areas of research.

Bainton's graceful style of writing is a fifth
contribution to Church history studies. This facet of
Bainton's scholarship is significant because it reflects his philosophy as a teacher. He contends that
Church history is for the Church and not merely for
a select coterie of specialists. Readability is essential for the proliferation of knowledge in the field,
and it is a contribution in that it provides a positive
image to the discipline of Church history.

A final contribution to historical research
centers on Bainton's interpretation of the role of
religious experience in Church history. He emphasizes
the phenemena of religious experience as important in
that it provides a motivating force to men and movements of history. Bainton contends that the key to

understanding Christian history is to understand the
role of faith in individual experience.

Bainton's influence as a Church historian extended beyond the confines of his scholarly discipline.
He contributed much to the life of the Church, expe-
cially in the area of ethical concerns. His writings
on pacifism give a clear statement of the pacifist
position both from the perspective of biblical teaching
and from the perspective of Church history. Likewise
his active involvement in the twentieth century peace
movement contributed to the causes of disarmament
and peace.

Another ethical concern of Bainton is religious
toleration. His extensive writings on toleration,
freedom of conscience, and pluralism have defined
quite clearly the importance of religious toleration.
Bainton's concern for the dignity of the individual
stems from this interest, and consequently he has influenced to varying degrees the manifold expressions
of toleration in modern society.

Likewise Bainton's ecumenical activity was a
contribution to contemporary Christianity. In his
writings and in his life Bainton advocated the unity
of the Christian movement. His scholarly treatments
of the tradition of Christian unity correlated with
his personal activism toward achieving this ideal.
His continued efforts at unity demonstrated his belief
that Congregationalism might serve as a catalyst for
ecumenical developments.

The extensive work done by Bainton provides
marked progress for Reformation historiography in the
twentieth century. His writings have added new
frontiers and broader dimensions to contemporary

Reformation research. Bainton's stature as a leading
Reformation historian shall remain intact for many
years after his death due to the valuable publications
which characterized his career. His influence on both
the discipline of Church history and the contemporary
life of the Church is equal to that of any Church
historian of this century. The extent of the Bainton
corpus itself proves a significant scholarly achievement. As one who stressed the influence of the individual, Bainton's own individual efforts have made
the Church richer indeed.

SELECTED BIBLIOGRAPHY

Primary Sources

Books

Bainton, Roland H. The Age of the Reformation. Princeton, N. J.: Van Nostrand, 1956.

_____. El Alma Hispana y el Alma Sajona. Buenos
Aires: Casa Unida de Publicaciones, 1961.

_____. Behold the Christ. New York: Harper and
Row, 1974.

_____. Bernardino Ochino: Esule E Riformatore
Senese Del Cinquecento, 1487-1563. Translated
by Elio Gianturco. Biblioteca Storica Sansoni,
Nuova Serie IV. Firenze: G. C. Sansoni, 1940.

_____. "Bernardino Ochino of Sienna." New Haven,
Conn.: Yale Divinity Library, 1965. (Typewritten.)

_____. Bibliography of the Continental Reformation.
Monographs in Church History, no. 1. Chicago:
American Society of Church History, 1935; re-
print ed., Hamden, Conn.: Archon Books, 1972.

_____. Christendom: A Short History of Christianity
and Its Impact on Western Civilization. 2 vols.
New York: Harper and Row, 1966.

_____. Christian Attitudes Toward War and Peace:
An Historical Survey and Critical Re-evaluation.
New York: Abingdon Press, 1960.

_____. Christian Unity and Religion in New England.
The Collected Papers in Church History, series
3. Boston: Beacon Press, 1964.

_____. The Church of Our Fathers. New York:
Charles Scribner's Sons, 1941.

_____. The Churches and War: Historic Attitudes
Toward Christian Participation. Reprint from
Social Action (15 January 1945). New York:
Social Action Magazine, 1945.

_____. Comite hollandais pour la commemoration de Servet et de Castellion. Leiden: E. J. Brill, 1951.

_____. The Covenant in the Wilderness. New Haven: Yale University Press, 1954.

_____. David Joris, Wiedertäufer und Kämpfer für Toleranz im 16. Jahrhundert. Leipzig: M. Heinsius Nachfolger, 1937.

_____. Debtors to God. Philadelphia: Westminster Press, 1930.

_____. Early and Medieval Christianity. The Collected Papers in Church History, series 1. Boston: Beacon Press, 1962.

_____. Early Christianity. Princeton, N. J.: Van Nostrand, 1960.

_____. Erasmus of Christendom. New York: Charles Scribner's Sons, 1969.

_____. George Lincoln Burr: His Life. Ithaca, N. Y.: Cornell University Press, 1943.

_____. Here I Stand: A Life of Martin Luther. New York: Abingdon-Cokesburg Press, 1950.

_____. The Horizon History of Christianity. Edited by Marshall B. Davidson. New York: American Heritage Publishing Co., 1964.

_____. Hunted Heretic: The Life and Death of Michael Servetus, 1511-1553. Boston: Beacon Press, 1953; reprint ed., Gloucester, Mass.: Peter Smith, 1978.

_____. The Medieval Church. Princeton, N. J.: Van Nostrand, 1962.

_____. Michel Servet, hérétique et martyr, 1553-1953. Geneva: E. Droz, 1953.

_____. The Office of the Minister's Wife in New England. Boston: Harvard University, 1955.

_____. The Panorama of the Christian Church in
Kodachrome Slides. Boston: Pilgrim Press,
1944.

_____. The Penguin History of Christianity. 2
vols. New York: American Heritage Publishing
Co., 1967.

_____. Pilgrim Parson: The Life of James Herbert
Bainton. New York: Thomas Nelson and Sons,
1958.

_____. The Reformation of the Sixteenth Century.
Boston: Beacon Press, 1952.

_____. Roland Bainton Speaks on the Martin Luther
Motion Picture. New York: Lutheran Church
Productions, 1954.

_____. Studies on the Reformation. Collected
Papers in Church History, series 2. Boston:
Beacon Press, 1963.

_____. The Travail of Religious Liberty: Nine
Biographical Studies. Philadelphia: Westmin-
ster Press, 1951; reprint ed., Hamden, Conn.:
Shoe String Press, 1971.

_____. What Christianity Says About Sex, Love and
Marriage. New York: Association Press, 1957.

_____. Women of the Reformation: From Spain to
Scandinavia. Minneapolis, Minn.: Augsburg
Publishing House, 1977.

_____. Women of the Reformation: In France and
England. Minneapolis, Minn.: Augsburg Publishing House, 1973.

_____. Women of the Reformation: In Germany and
Italy. Minneapolis, Minn.: Augsburg Publishing
House, 1971.

_____. Yale and the Ministry: A History of Educa-
tion for the Christian Ministry at Yale from
the Founding in 1701. New York: Harper and
Brothers, 1957.

_____. Yesterday, Today, and What Next? Minnea-
polis, Minn.: Augsburg Publishing House, 1978.

Articles

Bainton, Roland H. "The Aarhus Conference."   In Luther
Today, pp. 26-33. Martin Luther Lectures,
vol. 1. Decorah, Iowa: Luther College Press,
1957.

_____. "Academic Freedom in the Light of the
Struggles for Religious Liberty." Proceedings
of the Middle States Association of History
Teachers 33 (1935): 37-44.

_____. "Alexander Campbell and Church Unity." In
The Sage of Bethany: A Pioneer in Broadcloth,
pp. 81-94. Edited by Perry E. Gresham. St.
Louis: Bethany Press, 1960.

_____. "Alexander Campbell and the Social Order."
In The Sage of Bethany: A Pioneer in Broadcloth,
pp. 117-29. Edited by Perry E. Gresham. St.
Louis: Bethany Press, 1960.

_____. "The Amistad." Highroad (September 1945):
4-6, 47.

_____. "The Anabaptist Contribution to History."
In The Recovery of the Anabaptist Vision, pp.
317-26. Edited by Guy F. Hershberger. Scottdale, Pa.: Herald Press, 1957.

_____. "The Appeal to Reason and the American Con-
stitution." In The Constitution Reconsidered,
pp. 121-30. Edited by Conyers Read. Rev.
ed. New York: Harper and Row, 1968.

_____. "Basilidian Chronology and New Testament
Interpretation." Journal of Biblical Literature 42 (1923): 81-134.

_____. "The Bible and the Reformation." In Five
Essays on the Bible: Papers Read at the 1960
Annual Meeting of the American Council of
Learned Societies, pp. 20-29. New York:
American Council of Learned Societies, 1960.

_____. "The Bible and the Reformation." In The
Cambridge History of the Bible. 3 vols.,
3:1-37. Edited by S. L. Greenslade. Cambridge: University Press, 1963.

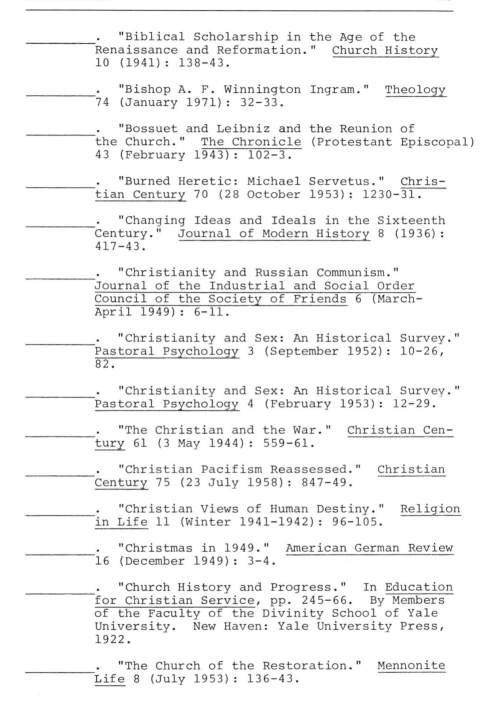

_____. "Biblical Scholarship in the Age of the
Renaissance and Reformation." Church History
10 (1941): 138-43.

_____. "Bishop A. F. Winnington Ingram." Theology
74 (January 1971): 32-33.

_____. "Bossuet and Leibniz and the Reunion of
the Church." The Chronicle (Protestant Episcopal)
43 (February 1943): 102-3.

_____. "Burned Heretic: Michael Servetus." Chris-
tian Century 70 (28 October 1953): 1230-31.

_____. "Changing Ideas and Ideals in the Sixteenth
Century." Journal of Modern History 8 (1936):
417-43.

_____. "Christianity and Russian Communism."
Journal of the Industrial and Social Order
Council of the Society of Friends 6 (March-
April 1949): 6-11.

_____. "Christianity and Sex: An Historical Survey."
Pastoral Psychology 3 (September 1952): 10-26,
82.

_____. "Christianity and Sex: An Historical Survey."
Pastoral Psychology 4 (February 1953): 12-29.

_____. "The Christian and the War." Christian Cen-
tury 61 (3 May 1944): 559-61.

_____. "Christian Pacifism Reassessed." Christian
Century 75 (23 July 1958): 847-49.

_____. "Christian Views of Human Destiny." Religion
in Life 11 (Winter 1941-1942): 96-105.

_____. "Christmas in 1949." American German Review
16 (December 1949): 3-4.

_____. "Church History and Progress." In Education
for Christian Service, pp. 245-66. By Members
of the Faculty of the Divinity School of Yale
University. New Haven: Yale University Press,
1922.

_____. "The Church of the Restoration." Mennonite
Life 8 (July 1953): 136-43.

_____. "The Churches and Alcohol." Quarterly
Journal of Studies on Alcohol 6 (June 1945):
45-58.

_____. "The Churches Shift on War." Religion in
Life 12 (Summer 1943): 323-35.

_____. "Churchmen à la Roland H. Bainton." Journal
of Presbyterian History 51 (Fall 1973): 251-66.

_____. "The Cohesive Power of Protestantism."
The Intercollegian 62 (January 1945):   8-9.

_____. "A Communication for a More Explicit De-
claration of Peace Aims." Christian Century
59 (6 September 1942): 1122-24.

_____. "Congregationalism: From the Just War to
the Crusade in the Puritan Revolution."
Andover Newton Theological School Bulletin 35
(April 1943):   1-20.

_____. "Congregationalism: The Middle Way."
Christendom 5 (Summer 1940): 345-54.

_____. "Continuity of Thought of Erasmus."
American Council of Learned Societies News-
letter 19 (May 1968): 1-7.

_____. "The Development and Consistency of Luther's
Attitude to Religious Liberty." Harvard
Theological Review 22 (1929): 107-49.

_____. "Documenta Servetiana." Archiv für Refor-
mationsgeschichte 44 (1953): 223-34.

_____. "Documenta Servetiana." Archiv für Refor-
mationsgeschichte 45 (1954): 99-108.

_____. "Dürer and Luther as the Man of Sorrows."
The Art Bulletin 29 (December 1947): 269-72.

_____. "Early Christianity as a Youth Movement."
Highroad (February 1946): 35-37.

_____. "The Early Church and War." Harvard
Theological Review 39 (July 1946): 189-212.

_____. "The Enduring Witness: The Mennonites."
Mennonite Life 9 (April 1954): 83-90.

_____. "Erasmo e L' Italia." Revista Storica
Italiana 79 (1967): 944-51.

_____. "Erasmus and Luther and the Dialog Julius
Exclusus." In Vierhundertfünfzig Jahre
lutherische Reformation 1517-1967: Festschrift
für Franz Lau, pp. 17-24. Edited by H. Jung-
hans, I. Ludolphy, and K. Meier. Gottingen:
Vandenhoeck and Ruprecht, 1967.

_____. "Erasmus and the Persecuted." In Scrinium
Erasmianum, 2 vols., 2:197-202. Edited by
J. Coppens. Leiden: E. J. Brill, 1969.

_____. "Erasmus and the Wesen Des Christentums."
In Glaube Geist Geschichte: Festschrift für
Ernst Benz, pp. 200-206. Edited by Gerhard
Muller and Winfried Zeller. Leiden: E. J.
Brill, 1967.

_____. "Ernst Troeltsch--Thirty Years Later."
Theology Today 8 (April 1951): 70-96.

_____. "Eyn Wunderliche Weyssagung, Osiander--
Sachs--Luther." Germanic Review 21 (October
1946): 161-64.

_____. "Feminine Piety in Tudor England."   In
Christian Spirituality: Essays in Honor of
Gordon Rupp, pp. 183-201. Edited by Peter
Brooks. London: S.C.M. Press, 1975.

_____. "Forschungsberichte und Besprechungen."
Archiv für Reformationsgeschichte 43 (1952):
88-106.

_____. "Freedom, Truth, and Unity: Reflections
on the Renaissance." Theology Today 12 (April
1959): 85-96.

_____. "Freedom's Religious Foundations." Chris-
tian Century 76 (26 January 1959): 106-9.

_____. "Friends in Relation to the Churches."
In Christian Unity and Religion in New England.
The Collected Papers in Church History, series
3, pp. 57-70. Boston: Beacon Press, 1964.

_____. "The Frontier Community." Mennonite Life
9 (January 1954): 34-41.

_____. "The Genius of Protestantism." The
Minister's Quarterly 6 (Feburary 1950): 13-18.

_____. "The Great Commission." Mennonite Life
8 (October 1953): 183-89.

_____. "A History of the Ecumenical Movement."
The Ecumenical Review 6 (July 1954): 408-24.

_____. "The Immoralities of the Patriarchs Accord-
ing to the Exegesis of the Late Middle Ages
and of the Reformation." The Harvard Theological
Review 23 (1930): 39-49.

_____. "Individualism, Christian and American."
Vital Speeches of the Day 8 (15 July 1942):
590-92.

_____. "Integrity of Membership." Christian
Century 91 (13 February 1974): 187.

_____. "Interpretations of the Reformation." The
American Historical Review 66 (October 1960):
74-84.

_____. "Is Congregationalism Sectarian?" Chris-
tian Century 71 (24 February 1954): 234-38.

_____. "The Left Wing of the Reformation."
Journal of Religion 21 (April 1941): 124-34.

_____. "Let's Agree on the Reformation." Chris-
tian Century 64 (19 February 1947): 237-39.

_____. "Luther and Spalatin letters recovered in
Boston." Archiv für Reformationsgeschichte
53 (1962): 197.

_____. "Luther and the Via Media at the Marburg
Colloquy." The Lutheran Quarterly 1 (November
1949): 394-98.

_____. "Luther in a Capsule." Bulletin of the
American Congregational Association 3 (May
1952): 1-9.

_____. "Luther on Birds, Dogs, and Babies."
In Luther Today, pp. 3-12. Martin Luther
Lectures, vol. 1. Decorah, Ia.: Luther Col-
lege Press, 1957.

_____. "Luther's Struggle for Faith." Church
History 17 (September 1948): 193-206.

_____. "Luther's Use of Direct Discourse." In
Luther Today, pp. 13-25. Martin Luther Lec-
tures, vol. 1. Decorah, Ia.: Luther College
Press, 1957.

_____. "The Making of a Pluralistic Society--A
Protestant View." In Religion and the State
University, pp. 42-57. Edited by Erich A.
Walter. Ann Arbor, Mich.: University of Michi-
gan Press, 1958.

_____. "Man, God, and the Church in the Age of
the Renaissance." The Journal of Religious
Thought 11 (Autumn-Winter 1953-1954): 119-
33.

_____. "Marriage and Love in Christian History."
Religion in Life 17 (Summer 1948): 391-403.

_____. "Methods of Great Religious Teachers: Cal-
vin and His Circle." International Journal
of Religious Education 9 (November 1932): 6-7.

_____. "Methods of Great Religious Teachers: Mar-
tin Luther." International Journal of Religious Education 9 (October 1932): 6-7.

_____. "Methods of Great Religious Teachers: Saint
Augustine." International Journal of Religious
Education 9 (September 1932): 7-8.

_____. "Methods of Great Religious Teachers: St.
Ignatius Loyola." International Journal of
Religious Education 9 (December 1932): 19-20.

_____. "Michael Servetus and the Pulmonary Transit
of Blood." Bulletin of the History of Medicine
25 (January-February 1951): 1-7.

_____. "Michael Servetus and the Trinitarian Speculation of the Middle Ages." In Autour De Michel Servet Et De Sabastien Castellion, pp. 29-46. Edited by Bruno Becker. Haarlem: H. D. Tjeenk and Zoon N. V., 1953.

_____. "The Ministry in the Middle Ages." In The Ministry in Historical Perspective, pp. 82-109. Edited by H. Richard Niebuhr and Daniel D. Williams. New York: Harper and Brothers, 1956.

_____. "New Documents on Early Protestant Rationalism." Church History 7 (1938): 179-87.

_____. "The Origins of the Epiphany." In Early and Medieval Christianity. The Collected Papers in Church History, series 1. Boston: Beacon Press, 1962.

_____. "Our Debt to Luther." Christian Century 63 (23 October 1946): 1276-78.

_____. "Our Protestant Witness." The Pulpit 19 (December 1948): 272-74.

_____. "The Parable of the Tares as the Proof Text for Religious Liberty to the End of the Sixteenth Century." Church History 1 (1932): 57-89.

_____. "Paraphrases of Erasmus." Archiv für Reformationsgeschichte 57 (1966): 67-76.

_____. "Patristic Christianity." In The Idea of History in the Ancient Near East, pp. 215-36. Edited by R. C. Dentan. New Haven: Yale University Press, 1955.

_____. "Piety and Art." In Traditio, Krisis, Renovatio aus Theologischer Sicht, pp. 609-12. Edited by Bernard Jaspert and Rudolf Mohr. Marburg: Elwert, 1976.

_____. "The Present State of Servetus Studies." Journal of Modern History 4 (1932): 72-92.

_____. "The Problem of Authority in the Age of the Reformation." In Luther, Erasmus and the Reformation: A Catholic-Protestant Reappraisal, pp. 14-25. Edited by John C. Olin, James D. Smart, and Robert E. McNally. New York: Fordham University Press, 1969.

_____. "Probleme der Lutherbiographie." In Lutherforschung Heute, pp. 24-31. Edited by Vilmos Vajta. Berlin: Lutherisches Verlagshaus, 1958.

_____. "Protestant-Catholic Relations in the U.S." Advance 146 (18 October 1954): 13-24.

_____. "Psychiatry and History: An Examination of Erikson's Young Man Luther." In Psychohistory and Religion: The Case of "Young Man Luther," pp. 19-56. Edited by Roger A. Johnson. Philadelphia: Fortress Press, 1977.

_____. "The Puritan Theocracy and the Cambridge Platform." The Ministers Quarterly 5 (November 1949): 16-21.

_____. "The Querela Pacis of Erasmus, Classical and Christian Sources." Archiv für Reformationsgeschichte 42 (1951): 32-48.

_____. "Reassessing Pacifism Reassessed." Christian Century 89 (17 May 1972): 575-77.

_____. "Reconciliation and Reality." Fellowship 9 (December 1943): 208-10.

_____. "Religious Biography." In Writing for the Religious Market, pp. 185-91. Edited by Roland E. Wolseley. New York: Association Press, 1956.

_____. "Religious Liberty and Religious Knowledge: A Commentary on a Sixteenth Century Manuscript of Sebastian Castellio." Article prepared for a festschrift for D. C. Macintosh but not included in the publication, 193-? (Typewritten.)

_____. "The Responsibilities of Power According to Erasmus of Rotterdam." In The Responsibility of Power: Historical Essays in Honor of Hajo Holborn, pp. 54-63. Edited by Leonard Kreiger and Fritz Stern. Garden City, N. Y.: Doubleday and Company, 1967.

_____. "Rhymes and Ripples of Japan." Japanese Christian Quarterly 34 (Spring 1968): 104-11.

_____. "Role of Women in the Reformation." Archiv für Reformationsgeschichte 63 (1972): 141-42.

_____. "Sebastian Castellio and the British American Tradition." Het Boek 30 (1952).

_____. "Sebastian Castellio, Champion of Religious Liberty, 1515-1563." In Castellionicana, Quatre Etudes sur Sebastien Castellion et L'Idee de la Tolerance, pp. 25-79. By Roland Bainton, Bruno Becker, Marius Volkhoff and Sape Van Der Wonde. Leiden: E. J. Brill, 1951.

_____. "Sebastian Castellio and the Toleration Controversey of the Sixteenth Century." In Persecution and Liberty: Essays in Honor of George Lincoln Burr, pp. 183-209. New York: The Century Company, 1931.

_____. "The Sectarian Theory of the Church." Christendom 11 (Summer 1946): 382-87.

_____. "Servet et les Libertins de Genève." Bulletin Sociètè de L'Histoire du Protestantisme Francais 87 (1938): 261-69.

_____. "Servetus and the Genevan Libertines." Church History 5 (1936): 141-49.

_____. "Sex and Religion." Ladies Home Journal 75 (August 1958): 17, 100-1.

_____. "The Smaller Circulation: Servetus and Colombo." Sudhoffs Archiv für Geschichte der Medizin und der Naturwissenschaften 24 (1931): 371-74.

_____. "Die Stellung der Quaker zu Krieg und Frieden." Der Quaeker 23 (January-February 1949): 1-7.

_____. "Straightforward Speech." Yale Divinity
News 34 (May 1938): 1-3.

_____. "The Struggle for Religious Liberty."
Church History 10 (June 1941): 95-124.

Bainton, Roland H., ed. "Survey of Periodical Literature in the United States, 1945-1951." Archiv
für Reformationsgeschichte 43 (1952): 88-106.

Bainton, Roland H. "Teaching Church History." Journal
of Bible and Religion 10 (May 1942): 103-7.

_____. "Technology and Pacifism." Christian Cen-
tury 55 (18 May 1938): 618-19.

_____. "This Grand Errand." Yale Alumni Magazine
(October 1955): 22-23.

_____. "Thomas Hooker and the Puritan Contribution
to Democracy." Bulletin of the Congregational
Library 10 (October 1958).

_____. "Total Abstinence." Christianity Today 2
(7 July 1958): 3-6.

_____. "The Unity of Mankind in the Classical-
Christian Tradition." In The Albert Schwietzer
Jubilee Book, pp. 277-96. Edited by A. A.
Roback. Cambridge, Mass.: Sci-Art Publishers,
1945; reprint ed., Westport, Conn.: Greenwood
Press, 1970.

_____. "Unity, Utrecht and the Unitarians." Chris-
tian Century 55 (5 October 1938): 1189-90.

_____. "The Universal Ministry of All Believers."
Encounter 18 (1957): 131-40.

_____. "War and the Christian Ethic." In The Church
and Social Responsibility, pp. 201-19. Edited
by J. Richard Spann. New York: Abingdon-Cokesbury Press, 1953.

_____. "What About Catholic-Protestant Relations
in the U.S.A.?" Messenger 19 (October 1954):
14-17.

_____. "What Is Calvinism?" Christian Century
42 (12 March 1925): 351-52.

_____. "William Postell and the Netherlands."
Nederlands Archief voor Kerkgeschiedenis 24
(1931): 161-72.

_____. "Without Despairing of the World, The Quaker
Attitude Toward Peace and War." Friends In-
telligencer 106 (Second Month 12, 1949): 87-89.

_____. "Yale and German Theology in the Middle of
the Nineteenth Century." Zeitschrift für
Kirchengeschichte 65 (1956).

Bainton, Roland H., and Calhoun, Robert L. "Christian
Conscience and the State." Social Action 6
(15 October 1940): 4-42.

The Encyclopedia of the Lutheran Church. S.v. "Luther,"
by Roland Bainton.

The Mennonite Encyclopedia. S.v. "Servetus, Michael,"
by Roland Bainton.

Book Reviews

Bainton, Roland H. Review of Action and Person, by
Michael G. Baylor. The American Historical
Review 83 (February 1978): 185-6.

_____. Review of Advocates of Reform, ed. Matthew
Spinka. The American Historical Review 59
(July 1954): 980-1.

_____. Review of Aktensammlung zur Geschichte der
Basler Reformation in den Jahren 1519 bis
Anfang 1534, vol. 3, ed. Paul Roth. The
American Historical Review 44 (April 1939):
706-7.

_____. Review of Aktensammlung zur Geschichte der
Basler Reformation in den Jahren 1519 bis
Anfang 1534, vol. 4, ed. Paul Roth. The
American Historical Review 47 (July 1942):
938.

_____. Review of Aspects De La Propagande Religieuse,
by G. Berthoud. The American Historical Review
63 (April 1958): 654-56.

_____. Review of <u>Authority and Reason in the Early Middle Ages</u>, by A. J. MacDonald. <u>Church History</u> 3 (March 1934): 82.

_____. Review of <u>Christian Hope for World Society</u>, by John T. McNeill. <u>Church History</u> 7 (March 1938): 74-5.

_____. Review of <u>The Christian Scholar in the Age of the Reformation</u>, by E. Harris Harbison. <u>The American Historical Review</u> 62 (April 1957): 612-13.

_____. Review of <u>Christianity and History: Essays</u>, by E. Harris Harbison. <u>The American Historical Review</u> 70 (July 1965): 1148-49.

_____. Review of <u>Christianity on the March</u>, edited by Henry P. Van Dusen. <u>Church History</u> 33 (December 1964): 503.

_____. Review of <u>The Church in the Roman Empire</u>, by Erwin R. Goodenough. <u>Church History</u> 1 (June 1932): 127-8.

_____. Review of <u>Concordia Mundi: The Career and Thought of Guillaume Postel (1510-1581)</u>, by William J. Boccusma. <u>Church History</u> 29 (March 1960): 104-5.

_____. Review of <u>Contributi Alla Storia del Concilio di Trento e Della Controriforma.</u> <u>Church History</u> 18 (September 1949): 189.

_____. Review of <u>Criticism of the Crusades</u>, by Palmer A. Throop. <u>Church History</u> 10 (June 1941): 180-1.

_____. Review of <u>La Decouverte D'un Manuscrit Inconnu De Sébastien Castellion</u>, by Bruno Becker. <u>Church History</u> 9 (September 1940): 270-71.

_____. Review of <u>Le Dottrine Politiche Da Lutero A Suarez</u>, by Giuseppe Santonastaso. <u>Church History</u> 16 (December 1947): 254.

238   ROLAND H. BAINTON

_____ . Review of Die Einziehung Des Geistlichen
Gutes im Albertinischen Sachsen, 1539-1553,
by Helga-Maria Kuhn. The American Historical
Review 73 (December 1967): 510-11.

_____ . Review of The English Presbyterians from
Elizabethan Puritanism to Modern Unitarianism,
by C. Gordon Bolam, Jeremy Goring, H. L.
Short, and Roger Thomas. Church History 38
(March 1969): 123-24.

_____ . Review of Epitres due Coq à L'ane, by
Henri Meylan. Church History 26 (September
1957): 294.

_____ . Review of Eretici Italiani del Cinquecento,
by Delio Cantimori. Church History 9 (September 1940): 269-70.

_____ . Review of European Civilization: Its Origin
and Development, vol. 4, ed. Edward Eyre.
The American Historical Review 42 (January
1937): 295-96.

_____ . Review of Evangelische Evangelienauslegung,
by Gerhard Ebeling. Church History 18 (September 1949): 187.

_____ . Review of Forschungen zur Geschichte und
Lehre des Protesantismus, by Zehnte Reihe.
Church History 24 (March 1955): 75.

_____ . Review of Foundation of American Freedom,
by A. Mervyn Davies. The American Historical
Review 61 (April 1956): 729

_____ . Review of Francis Lamber of Avignon (1487-
1530), by Roy L. Winters. Church History 8
(March 1939): 96-97.

_____ . Review of Francisco de Ossuna Mystik und
Rechtfertigung, by Hans-Jürgen Prien. Church
History 37 (September 1968): 338.

_____ . Review of Franz Lambert Von Avignon und
die Reformation in Hessen, by Gerhard Muller.
The American Historical Review 66 (January
1961): 522.

_____. Review of Ginevra E L'Italia, ed. Delio Cantimori. The American Historical Review 66 (July 1961): 1100-1.

_____. Review of Grundriss Zum Studium Der Kirchengeschichte, by Heinrich Bornkamm. Church History 19 (June 1950): 142.

_____. Review of The Historical Scholarship of Saint Bellarmine, by E. A. Ryan. The American Historical Review 43 (October 1937): 201.

_____. Review of A History of Later Latin Literature from the Middle of the Fourth to the End of the Seventeenth Century, by F. A. Wright and T. A. Sinclair. Church History 1 (September 1932): 182.

_____. Review of Das Hochstift Basel im ausgehenden Mittelalter, by Konrad Hieronimus. The American Historical Review 44 (April 1939): 706.

_____. Review of Hutterite Studies, by Robert Friedmann. Church History 31 (June 1962): 246-47.

_____. Review of The Impact of the Church upon its Culture: Reappraisals of the History of Christianity, by Quirinus Breen. The American Historical Review 74 (December 1968): 540-41.

_____. Review of Inquisition and Liberty, by G. G. Coulton. Church History 8 (March 1939): 92.

_____. Review of An Introduction to Francesco Patrizi's Nova de Universis Philosophia, by Benjamin Brickman. Church History 12 (September 1943): 223-24.

_____. Review of Italy and the Reformation to 1550, by G. K. Brown. The American Historical Review 39 (July 1934): 765-66.

_____. Review of Jacopo Acontio Traduzione di Delio Cantimori Vomini e Dottrine, by Charles D. O'Malley. Church History 25 (March 1956): 87-88.

_____. Review of Jacopo Sadoleto, 1477-1547: Humanist and Reformer, by Richard M. Douglas. The American Historical Review 65 (January 1960): 424-25.

_____. Review of Julius Pflug, Correspondence, edited by J. V. Pollet. Church History 43 (September 1974): 402-3.

_____. Review of L'Angleterre catholique à la veille du schisme, by Pierre Janelle. The American Historical Review 41 (July 1936): 797-98.

_____. Review of Martin Bucers Bedeutung für die europäische Reformationsgeschichte, by Heinrich Bornkamm. Church History 23 (September 1954): 282.

_____. Review of Martin Luther und die Reformation im Urteil des Deutschen Luthertums, by Ernst Zeeden. The American Historical Review 57 (October 1951): 150-51.

_____. Review of Melanchthon, by Franz Hildebrandt. The American Historical Review 52 (July 1947): 773.

_____. Review of Menno Simons, by Cornelius Krahn. Church History 7 (June 1938): 199.

_____. Review of The Mennonite Encyclopedia, Volume I. Church History 26 (June 1957): 187-88.

_____. Review of Millennial Dreams in Action: Essays in Comparative Study, ed. Sylvia L. Thrupp. The American Historical Review 69 (July 1964): 1106-7.

_____. Review of Mistici del Duecento e del Trecento, by Arrigo Levasti. Church History 5 (December 1936): 389-90.

_____. Review of "Mystere" et "Philosphie due Christ" selon Erasme, by Georges Chantraine. The American Historical Review 79 (December 1974): 1536-37.

_____. Review of Naissance et Affirmation de la
Réforme, by Jean Delumeau. The American
Historical Review 71 (January 1966): 511.

_____. Review of New Light on Martin Luther, With
an Authentic Account of the Luther Film of
1953, by Albert Hyma. The American Historical
Review 64 (January 1959): 380-81.

_____. Review of Les Origines de la Réforme à
Genève, by Henri Naef. Church History 5
(December 1936): 388-89.

_____. Review of Pacifism in the United States from
the Colonial Era to the First World War, by
Peter Brock. Church History 39 (March 1970):
127-28.

_____. Review of Il Pensiero di Bernardino Ochino,
by Benedetto Nicholini. Church History 9
(September 1940): 268-69.

_____. Review of Per la Storia Religiosa Dello
Stato di Milano Durante il Dominio di Carlo V,
by Frederico Chabod. Church History 9 (September 1940): 267-68.

_____. Review of Piero Giannone: Riformatore E.
Storico, by Brunello Vigezzi. The American
Historical Review 67 (October 1961): 208-9.

_____. Review of Die Reformation in den italienischen
Talschaften Graubündens nach dem Briefwechsel
Bullingers, by Peter Dalbert. Church History
18 (September 1949): 188-89.

_____. Review of Reginald Pole, by W. Schenk.
The American Historical Review 56 (January
1951): 338-39.

_____. Review of Reich und Reformation, by Stephen
Skalweit. The American Historical Review 73
(June 1968): 1552-53.

_____. Review of The Religious Renaissance of the
German Humanists, by Lewis W. Spitz. The
American Historical Review 69 (October 1963):
127-28.

_____. Review of La Riforma protestante, by Valdo Vinay. Church History 41 (March 1972): 122.

_____. Review of Road to Reformation, by Heinrich Boehmer. Church History 16 (September 1947): 167-76.

_____. Review of St. Philip Neri and the Roman Society of his Times, 1515-1595, by Louis Ponnelle and Louis Bordet. The American Historical Review 38 (October 1932): 98-100.

_____. Review of Schism, Heresy and Religious Protest, edited by Derek Baker. Church History 42 (June 1973): 275-76.

_____. Review of Die Schule bei Martin Bucer in ihrem Verhältnis zu Kirche und Obrigkeit, by Ernst-Wilhelm Kohls. Church History 33 (June 1964): 221-22.

_____. Review of Das Selbastzeugnis Kaiser Konstantins, by Hermann Dorries. Church History 24 (March 1955): 71-72.

_____. Review of De Spiritu Sancto, Der Beitrag des Basilius zum Abschluss des trinitarischen Dogmas, by Hermann Dorries. Church History 26 (December 1957): 384-85.

_____. Review of Die Theologie des Erasmus, by Ernst-Wilhelm Kohls. Church History 36 (June 1967): 222-23.

_____. Review of Toleration and the Reformation, by Joseph Lecler. The American Historical Review 66 (July 1961): 1011-13.

_____. Review of Tracts on Liberty in the Puritan Revolution, edited by William Haller. Church History 4 (March 1935): 69-70.

_____. Review of The Trial of George Buchanan, by James M. Aitken. The American Historical Review 46 (October 1940): 186.

_____. Review of Trumpeter of God, by W. Stanford Reid. The American Historical Review 80 (December 1975): 1340.

_____. Review of The Two Reformations in the Six-
teenth Century, by H. A. Enno van Gelder. The
American Historical Review 68 (October 1962):
81-83.

_____. Review of The Two Treatises of Servetus on
the Trinity, edited by Earl Morse Wilbur.
Church History 2 (March 1933): 60-61.

_____. Review of Wittenberg und Byzanz, by Ernst
Benz. Church History 18 (September 1949):
187-88.

_____. Review of Worship and Theology in England:
From Newman to Martineau, 1850-1900, by
Horton Davies. Church History 33 (March 1964):
107-8.

_____. Review of Yale University Portrait Index,
1701-1951. Church History 21 (June 1952):
171-72.

_____. Review of Young Man Luther, by Erik H.
Erikson. The Yale Review 48 (Spring 1959):
405-10.

_____. Review of Die Zusammenarbeit der Renais-
sancepäpste mit den Turken, Hans Pfeffermann.
The American Historical Review 53 (January
1948): 321-22.

                        Other Works

Bainton, Roland H. "An Interview." A tape-recorded
        interview conducted by Parker Rossman. Waco,
        Tex.: Creative Resources, 197-.

Castellio, Sebastian. Concerning Heretics. Trans-
        lated by Roland Bainton, New York: Columbia
        University Press, 1955; reprint ed., New
        York: Octagon Books, 1965.

Dorries, Hermann. Constantine and Religious Liberty.
        Translated by Roland Bainton. New Haven:
        Yale University Press, 1960.

Gedat, Gustav-Adolf. They Built for Eternity. Trans-
        lated by Roland Bainton. New York: Abingdon-
        Cokesbury Press, 1953.

Holborn, Hajo. Ulrich von Hutten and the German Re-
        formation. Translated by Roland Bainton.
        New Haven: Yale University Press, 1937.

[Luther, Martin.] Luther's Meditations on the Gospels.
        Translated and edited by Roland H. Bainton.
        Philadelphia: Westminster Press, 1962.

[Luther, Martin.] The Martin Luther Christmas Book
        With Celebrated Woodcuts By His Contemporaries.
        Translated and edited by Roland H. Bainton.
        Philadelphia: Fortress Press, 1948.

                    Secondary Sources Cited

                            Books

Althaus, Paul. The Theology of Martin Luther. Trans-
        lated by Robert C. Schultz. Philadelphia:
        Fortress Press, 1963.

Barzun, Jacques, and Graff, Henry F. The Modern Re-
        searcher. 3rd ed. New York: Harcourt,
        Brace and World, 1977.

Benrath, Karl. Bernardino Ochino of Sienna: A Contri-
        bution Towards the History of the Reformation.
        Translated by Helen Zimmern. New York: Robert
        Carter and Brothers, 1877.

Boehmer, Heinrich. Road to Reformation: Martin Luther
        to the Year 1521. Translated by John W.
        Doberstein and Theodore G. Tappert. Phila-
        delphia: Muhlenberg Press, 1946.

Bouyer, Louis. Erasmus and the Humanist Experiment.
        Translated by Francis X. Murphy. London:
        Geoffrey Chapman, 1959.

Buisson, Ferdinand E. Sebastien Castellion. 2 vols.
        Paris. Hachette, 1892.

Chadwick, Owen. The Reformation. Grand Rapids: Wm.
        B. Eerdmans Publishing Co., 1964.

Chatfield, Charles. For Peace and Justice: Pacifism
        in America 1914-1941. Knoxville: University
        of Tennessee Press, 1971.

Clasen, Claus-Peter. Anabaptism: A Social History, 1525-1618. Ithaca, N. Y.: Cornell University Press, 1972.

Cuthbert, Father. The Capuchins: A Contribution to the History of the Counter-Reformation. 2 vols. New York: n.p., 1928; reprint ed., Port Washington, N. Y.: Kennikat Press, 1971.

Davis, Kenneth R. Anabaptism and Asceticism: A Study in Intellectual Origins. Scottdale, Pa.: Herald Press, 1974.

Edel, Leon. Literary Biography. Toronto: University of Toronto Press, 1957.

Erikson, Erik. Young Man Luther: A Study in Psychoanalysis and History. New York: W. W. Norton and Company, 1958.

Faludy, George. Erasmus. New York: Stein and Day, 1970.

Ferguson, Wallace K. The Renaissance in Historical Thought: Five Centuries of Interpretation. New York: Houghton Mifflin Company, 1948.

Friesen, Abraham. Reformation and Utopia: Marxist Interpretation of the Reformation and its Antecedents. Wiesbaden: F. Steiner, 1974.

Fulton, John F. Michael Servetus: Humanist and Martyr. New York: Herbert Reichner, 1953.

Goertz, Hans-Jürgen, ed. Umstrittenes Täufertum 1525-1975: Neue Forschungen. Gottingen: Vandenhoeck and Ruprecht, 1977.

Green, V. H. H. Luther and the Reformation. New York: Capricorn Books, 1964.

Grimm, Harold J. The Reformation Era 1500-1650. 2nd ed. New York: Macmillan Publishing Company, 1973.

Grisar, Hartmann. Martin Luther: His Life and Work. Translated by Frank J. Eble. Edited by Arthur Preuss. 2nd ed. New York: AMS Press, 1971.

Harbison, E. Harris. The Age of Reformation. Ithaca,
     N. Y.: Cornell University Press, 1955.

Harnack, Adolph von. History of Dogma. 7 volumes.
     Translated by Neil Buchanan. New York:
     Russell and Russell, 1958.

Holl, Karl. What Did Luther Understand by Religion?
     Edited by James Luther Adams and Walter F.
     Bense. Translated by Fred W. Meuser and
     Walter R. Wietzke. Philadelphia: Fortress
     Press, 1977.

Huizinga, Johan. Erasmus and the Age of Reformation.
     Translated by F. Hopman. New York: Charles
     Scribner's Sons, 1924; reprint ed., New York:
     Harper and Row, 1957.

Hyma, Albert. The Youth of Erasmus. University of
     Michigan Publications in History and Political
     Science, volume 10. Ann Arbor: University of
     Michigan Press, 1930.

Klaassen, Walter. Anabaptism: Neither Catholic nor
     Protestant. Waterloo, Ont.: Conrad Press,
     1973.

Lau, Franz. Luther. Translated by Robert H. Fisher.
     Philadelphia: Westminster Press, 1963.

Lienhard, Marc, ed. The Origins and Characteristics
     of Anabaptism. The Hague: Martinus Nijhoff,
     1977.

Littell, Franklin H. The Anabaptist View of the Church:
     A Study in the Origins of Sectarian Protestant-
     ism. Studies in Church History, vol. 8.
     Chicago: American Society of Church History,
     1952; 2d ed., Boston: Star King Press, 1958.

Littell, Franklin H., ed. Reformation Studies: Essays
     in Honor of Roland H. Bainton. Richmond, Va.:
     John Knox Press, 1963.

Lortz, Joseph. The Reformation in Germany. 2 vols.
     Translated by Ronald Walls. New York:
     Herder and Herder, 1968.

Mandelbaum, Maurice. The Anatomy of Historical Knowl-
     edge. Baltimore: Johns Hopkins University
     Press, 1977.

Ritter, Gerhard. Luther: His Life and Work. Trans-
    lated by John Riches. New York: Harper
    and Row, 1959.

Rupp, Gordon. Luther's Progress to the Diet of Worms.
    London: S.C.M. Press, 1951; reprint ed., New
    York: Harper and Row Publishers, 1964.

Schwiebert, E. G. Luther and His Times. St. Louis:
    Concordia Publishing House, 1950.

Smith, Preserved. Erasmus: A Study of His Life, Ideals
    and Place in History. New York: Harper and
    Brothers, 1923.

Stauffer, Richard. Luther as Seen by Catholics.
    Ecumenical Studies in History, vol. 7.
    Richmond: John Knox Press, 1967.

Stayer, James M. Anabaptists and the Sword. Lawrence,
    Kan.: Coronado Press, 1972.

Todd, John M. Martin Luther: A Biographical Study.
    Westminster, Md.: Newman Press, 1965.

Vajta, Vilmos, ed. Lutherforschung Heute: Referate
    und Berichte des 1. Internationalen Luther-
    forschungskongresses. Berlin: Lutherisches
    Verlagshaus, 1958.

Voise, Waldermar. Sebastian Castellio, 1515-1563.
    Warsaw: Ksiaska and Wiedza, 1963.

Wilbur, Earl Morse. A History of Unitarianism. 2
    vols. Boston: Beacon Press, 1945.

Williams, George Huntston. The Radical Reformation.
    Philadelphia: Westminster Press, 1962.

Zweig, Stefan. Erasmus of Rotterdam. Translated by
    Eden and Cedar Paul. New York: Viking Press,
    1934.

                        Articles

Archiv für Reformationsgeschichte 64 (1973): 5-12.

"Bainton, Roland H(erbert)." Current Biography Year-
    book. New York: H. W. Wilson Company, 1963.

Bender, Harold S. "The Anabaptist Vision." In The
    Recovery of the Anabaptist Vision, pp. 29-54.
    Edited by Guy F. Hershberger. Scottdale, Pa.:
    Herald Press, 1957.

Bornkamm, Heinrich. "Luther und sein Vater." Zeitschrift
    für Theologie und Kirche 66 (1969): 38-61.

Burckhardt, Paul. "David Joris und seine Gemeinde in
    Basel." Basler Zeitschrift für Geschichte und
    Altertumskunde 48 (1949): 5-106.

Crow, Paul A. "Recent Reformation Studies in Review."
    Encounter 26 (Winter 1965): 87-96.

David, Kenneth R. "The Origins of Anabaptism: Ascetic
    and Charismatic Elements Exemplifying Con-
    tinuity and Discontinuity." In The Origins
    and Characteristics of Anabaptism, pp. 27-41.
    Edited by Marc Lienhard. The Hague: Martinus
    Nijhoff, 1977.

The Encyclopedia of the Lutheran Church. S.v. "Luther
    Research," by Harold J. Grimm.

Ferguson, Wallace K. "The Church in a Changing World:
    a Contribution to the Interpretation of the
    Renaissance." The American Historical Re-
    view 59 (October 1953): 1-18.

_____. "The Interpretation of the Renaissance: Sug-
    gestions for a Synthesis." Journal of the
    History of Ideas 12 (October 1951): 483-95.

_____. "Renaissance Tendencies in the Religious
    Thought of Erasmus." Journal of the History
    of Ideas 15 (October 1954): 499-508.

Friedman, Jerome. "Michael Servetus: The Case for
    Jewish Christianity." Sixteenth Century
    Journal 4 (April 1973): 87-110.

_____. "Michael Servetus: Exegete of Divine His-
    tory." Church History 43 (December 1974):
    460-69.

_____. "The Reformation Merry-Go-Round: The Ser-
    vetian Glossary of Heresy." Sixteenth Cen-
    tury Journal 7 (April 1976): 73-80.

Friedmann, Robert. "Recent Interpretations of Ana-
    baptism" Church History 24 (June 1955): 132-
    51.

Friesen, Abraham. "The Marxist Interpretation of Ana-
    baptism." Sixteenth Century Essays and Studies
    1 (June 1970): 17-34.

Gray, Hanna H. "Renaissance Humanism: The Pursuit of
    Eloquence." Journal of the History of Ideas
    24 (October-December 1963): 497-514.

Grimm, Harold J. "Luther's Inner Conflict: A Psychological
    Interpretation." Church History 4 (September
    1935): 173-86.

Guggisberg, Hans R. "Sebastian Castellio on the Power
    of the Christian Prince." In The Responsibility
    of Power: Historical Essays in Honor of Hajo
    Holborn, pp. 63-84. Edited by Leonard Krieger
    and Fritz Stern. Garden City, N. Y.: Doubleday
    and Company, 1967.

Hagen, Kenneth G. "Changes in the Understanding of
    Luther: The Development of the Young Luther."
    Theological Studies 29 (September 1968): 472-96.

Harkness, Georgia. "Roland H. Bainton: A Biographical
    Appreciation." In Reformation Studies: Essays
    in Honor of Roland H. Bainton, pp. 11-18.
    Edited by Franklin H. Littell. Richmond, Va.:
    John Knox Press, 1962.

Hillerbrand, Hans J. "Anabaptism and the Reformation:
    Another Look." Church History 29 (December
    1960): 404-23.

_____. "Origins of Sixteenth Century Anabaptism:
    Another Look." Archiv für Reformationsgeschichte
    53 (1962): 152-80.

Hovland, C. Warren. "Anfechtung in Luther's Biblical
    Exegesis." In Reformation Studies: Essays
    in Honor of Roland H. Bainton, pp. 46-60.
    Edited by Franklin H. Littell. Richmond, Va.:
    John Knox Press, 1962.

Jones, Rufus M. "A Forgotten Hero of the Reformation."
    The Constructive Quarterly 1 (June 1913):
    412-23.

Kaegi, Werner. "Hutten und Erasmus." Historische
    Vierteljahrschrift 22 (1924-25): 200-78,
    461-514.

Klaassen, Walter. "Anabaptist Understanding of the
    Separation of the Church." Church History
    46 (December 1977): 421-36.

_____. "The Nature of the Anabaptist Protest."
    The Mennonite Quarterly Review 45 (October
    1971): 291-311.

_____. "Spiritualization in the Reformation."
    Mennonite Quarterly Review 37 (April 1963):
    67-77.

Kleinhans, R. G. "Luther and Erasmus, Another Per-
    spective." Church History 39 (December 1970):
    459-69.

Kristeller, Paul Oskar. "Paganism and Christianity."
    In The Classics and Renaissance Thought,
    pp. 70-91. Cambridge, Mass.: Harvard Univer-
    sity Press, 1955.

Lortz, Joseph. "The Basic Elements of Luther's In-
    tellectual Style." In Catholic Scholars
    Dialogue with Luther, pp. 3-33. Edited by
    Jared Wicks. Chicago: Loyola University
    Press, 1970.

_____. "Reformatorisch und Katholisch beim jungen
    Luther (1518-1519)." In Humanitas-Christianitas:
    Walter V. Loewenisch zum 65. Geburtstag, pp.
    47-62. Edited by K. Beyschlag, G. Maron, and
    E. Wolfel. Wittenberg, 1968.

McNair, Philip. "Ochino's Apology: Three Gods or Three
    Wives?" History 60 (October 1975): 353-73.

McSorley, Harry J. "Erasmus and the Primacy of the
    Roman Pontiff: Between Conciliarism and
    Papalism." Archiv für Reformationsgeschichte
    65 (1974): 37-54.

Manschreck, C. L. "Erasmus: Recent Studies--A Review
    Article." Church History 41 (December 1972):
    524-27.

Mead, Sidney E. "The Task of the Church Historian."
    The Chronicle 12 (July 1949): 127-43.

Nürnberger, Richard. "Calvin und Servet: Eine Begegnung
    Zwischen reformatorischem Glauben und modernem
    Unglauben im 16. Jahrhundert." Archiv für
    Reformationsgeschichte 49 (1958): 196-204.

O'Malley, J. W. "Erasmus and Luther" Continuity and
    Discontinuity as Key to Their Conflict." Six-
    teenth Century Journal 5 (October 1974): 47-65.

Oberman, Heiko A. "Simil gemitus et raptus: Luther
    und die Mystik." In The Church, Mysticism,
    Sanctification, and the Natural in Luther's
    Thought: Lectures Presented to the Third
    International Congress on Luther Research, pp.
    20-59. Edited by I. Asheim. Philadelphia:
    Fortress Press, 1967.

Ozment, Steven E. "Homo Viator: Luther and Late Medi-
    eval Theology." In The Reformation in Medi-
    eval Perspective, pp. 142-54. Edited by
    Steven E. Ozment. Chicago: Quadrangle Books,
    1971.

_____. "Luther and the Late Middle Ages: The
    Formation of Reformation Thought." In Transi-
    tion and Revolution: Problems and Issues of
    European Renaissance and Reformation History,
    pp. 109-52. Edited by Robert Kingdon. Minnea-
    polis: Burgess Publishing, 1974.

Packull, Werner O. "Some Reflections on the State of
    Anabaptist History: The Demise of a Normative
    Vision." Studies in Religion 8 (1979): 313-23.

Peachey, Paul. "Marxist Historiography of the Radical
    Reformation: Causality or Covariation?" Six-
    teenth Century Essays and Studies 1 (June
    1970): 1-16.

Die Religion in Geschichte und Gegenwart. S.v. "Cas-
    tellio (Castalio, Chatillon), Sebastian," by
    H. Liebing.

Stayer, James M.; Packull, Werner O.; and Depperman,
    Klaus. "From Monogenesis to Polygenesis:
    The Historical Discussion of Anabaptist Ori-
    gins." The Mennonite Quarterly Review 49
    (April 1975): 83-121.

Williams, George H. "Introduction." In Spiritual and
    Anabaptist Writers. The Library of Christian
    Classics, vol. 25, pp. 19-40. Philadelphia:
    Westminister Press, 1957.

Yoder, John H. "'Anabaptists and the Sword' Revisited:
    Systematic Historiography and Undogmatic Non-
    resistants." Zeitschrift für Kirchengeschichte
    85 (1974): 126-39.

                        Book Reviews

Douglas, Elizabeth A. Review of Behold the Christ, by
    Roland H. Bainton. Christian Scholar's Re-
    view 7 (November 1977): 260-62.

Erling, Bernhard. Review of Studies on the Reformation:
    Collected Papers in Church History, series 2,
    by Roland Bainton. The Lutheran Quarterly
    16 (Fall 1964): 83-84.

Foster, Virgil E. Review of The Horizon History of
    Christianity, by Roland H. Bainton. Inter-
    national Journal of Religious Education
    41 (April 1965): 4.

Garrison, W. E. Review of Hunted Heretic, The Life and
    Death of Michael Servetus, 1511-1553, by
    Roland H. Bainton. Christian Century 70
    (18 November 1953): 1326-27.

Grimm, Harold J. Review of Early and Medieval Chris-
    tianity: The Collected Papers in Church
    History, series 1, by Roland H. Bainton. The
    American Historical Review 68 (October 1962):
    180-81.

Manschreck, Clyde L. Review of Erasmus of Christendom,
    by Roland Bainton. Church History 41 (Decem-
    ber 1972): 524-27.

McNally, Virginia. Review of Behold the Christ, by
    Roland H. Bainton. America 131 (2 November
    1974): 262-63.

Norwood, F. A. Review of Early and Medieval Chris-
    tianity: The Collected Papers in Church His-
    tory, series 1, by Roland H. Bainton. Church
    History 31 (December 1962): 457-58.

Outler, Albert C. Review of Yale and the Ministry:
    A History of Education for the Christian
    Ministry at Yale from the Founding in 1701,
    by Roland H. Bainton. Christian Century
    74 (6 November 1957): 1319-22.

Pauck, Wilhelm. Review of Bibliography of the Con-
    tinental Reformation: Materials Available
    in English, by Roland H. Bainton. Church
    History 4 (September 1935): 243.

Snyder, Ross. Review of The Church of Our Fathers,
    by Roland H. Bainton. Church History 10
    (December 1941): 378-79.

Tracy, James D. Review of Erasmus of Christendom, by
    Roland H. Bainton. The American Historical
    Review 77 (February 1972): 128-29.

Watson, Philip S. Review of Erasmus of Christendom,
    by Roland H. Bainton. Christian Century
    86 (23 July 1969): 996.

Ziegler, Edward Krusen. Review of Christian Attitudes
    Toward War and Peace, by Roland H. Bainton.
    Brethren Life and Thought 6 (Autumn 1961): 60.

TEXTS AND STUDIES IN RELIGION